COMPUTER VIRUSES
AND ANTI-VIRUS WARFARE
Second Revised Edition

COMPUTER VIRUSES AND ANTI-VIRUS WARFARE
Second Revised Edition

JAN HRUSKA
Technical Director, SOPHOS Limited,
Abingdon, Oxfordshire

ELLIS HORWOOD
NEW YORK   LONDON   TORONTO   SYDNEY   TOKYO   SINGAPORE

First published in 1992 by
ELLIS HORWOOD LIMITED
Market Cross House, Cooper Street,
Chichester, West Sussex, PO19 1EB, England

A division of
Simon & Schuster International Group
A Paramount Communications Company

Printed and bound in Great Britain
by Hartnolls, Bodmin

British Library Cataloguing in Publication Data

A catalogue record for this book is available from the British Library

ISBN 0–13–036377–4 Pbk

Library of Congress Cataloging-in-Publication Data

Available from the publisher

TABLE OF CONTENTS

To Bozena Bozicek-Ferrari

PREFACE AND ACKNOWLEDGEMENTS

Good God! What a genius I had when I wrote that book!

Jonathan Swift, Of The Tale of A Tub

PREFACE TO THE FIRST EDITION

This book is about computer viruses which occur on IBM-PC/XT/AT/PS2 and compatible machines running PC-DOS. It does not attempt to deal in any depth with viruses on other machines or operating systems, like the Apple Macintosh or Xenix, although most of the defences and investigative techniques are similar.

The subject of computer viruses is treated from scratch, but basic familiarity with the structure of the 8086 family of microprocessors and their assembly language is assumed. The book provides a framework for discussing a wide variety of virus-related issues:

· How can a virus penetrate a computer ?

· What does a virus consist of ?

· How complicated is it to write a virus ?

· Who writes viruses ?

· How does one protect against viruses ?

· How effective is anti-virus software ?

Apart from procedural advice on how to fight the virus problem, the book also contains the source code of two anti-virus programs: a pattern checker (*SEARCH*) and a fingerprinting program (*FINGER*). Both are written in 'C' (with a few lines of assembly language) and can be used as practical anti-virus tools. For those readers who prefer to buy software, rather than write it, there is also a list of manufacturers of anti-virus software.

A glossary of computer security-related terms is included.

Names such as *IBM*, *Microsoft* and *PC-DOS*, are trademarks, and any name should be assumed to be a trademark unless stated otherwise. Throughout the book, references are made to DOS. Unless stated otherwise, this means Microsoft's MS-DOS (PC-DOS) running on the IBM-PC and compatible personal computers.

The book was created using the *Runoff* text processing package, typeset by *Aldus Pagemaker* on a *Compaq 386/20* and printed on a *Hewlett-Packard LaserJet-IID*.

I am grateful to several people for their help. In alphabetical order **Sophie Cannin**, for her continuing support and stoic patience; **Petra Duffield**, who proof-read the text; **David Ferbrache,** who supplied reference material from Virus-L bulletin board; **Joe Hirst**, whose painstaking disassemblies of PC viruses have revealed so much; **Keith Jackson**, who made several suggestions; **Richard Jacobs**, who wrote the majority of the software featured in the book; **Peter Lammer**, who wrote parts of the text; **Karen Richardson**, who wrote the section 'Creating User Awareness'; **Alan Wear**, who gave advice on the psychiatric aspects of virus writing; **Edward Wilding**, who made several suggestions; and all the others who have attended my talks and seminars over the past two years, asked questions and taught me so much.

J. H.

Oxford, Christmas 1989

PREFACE TO THE SECOND EDITION

The unexpectedly favourable reception enjoyed by the first edition of this book took me by surprise. As the field of computer viruses is evolving at an extremely rapid pace, the second edition will be out of date almost as soon as it is published. However, certain basic principles of anti-virus warfare remain valid regardless of the technical developments of virus code, and it is those that I hope will be of most value to the reader. Nevertheless, in order to try and keep the book as technically up to date as is humanely possible, I have gone through the whole manuscript and made a large number of refinements, corrections and additions.

A whole new chapter on viruses on networks has been added, in order to reflect the rapid increase in the use of networks, the increased sophistication of new viruses which are network-aware and the increase in the corresponding need for security measures.

All appendices have been updated: this includes the rapidly varying list of anti-virus software manufacturers as well as the expanding bibliography. Some terminology has also been updated to reflect de-facto usage amongst the virus experts and PC users.

The book is now maintained in *Aldus Pagemaker 4* format on a *Compaq 386/33L* and printed on a *Hewlett-Packard LaserJet-IIISi*.

I wish to thank the many readers who have sent me comments and helpful criticisms. In addition, this book would not have been possible without the continuing anti-virus research efforts at *Sophos* and the *Virus Bulletin*. In particular, I am grateful to **Richard Jacobs** and **James Beckett** for the technical intelligence, **Petra Duffield** for keeping various lists up to date and **Fridrik Skulason** and **Jim Bates** for their technical analyses. Special mention is due of **Joe Hirst**, who has been a source of unfailing encouragement as well as introducing me to the mysteries of EBCDIC, and **Keith Jackson** for his input to the glossary of terms as well as his helpful comments. **Peter Lammer** and **Julie Hollins** proofread the manuscript and made a number of suggestions. My gratitude also goes to **Sophie** and **Zulu Cannin** who could not care less about computer viruses, as well as to all the virus researchers with whom I have exchanged ideas and virus collections over the last few years.

J. H.

Oxford, July 1992

1

AN OVERVIEW OF THREATS TO COMPUTER SYSTEMS

'You threaten us, fellow? Do your worst,
Blow your pipe there till you burst!'

Robert Browning, 'The Pied Piper of Hamelin'

When the possibility of computer viruses was first mentioned in the scientific papers published in 1984, nobody took it seriously. It did not take long before the first wide-scale computer virus infection swept the United States in 1986. This virus infection (by the *Brain* virus) caused a media sensation, but not an outrage. People were genuinely fascinated by the novel concept of a computer virus but few saw its full dangerous potential. To some people it was not even clear whether computer viruses occurred accidentally or whether they were deliberately written.

One or two reputable computer experts went as far as stating publicly that the existence of a computer virus was completely impossible, and even if it was possible, it would not last very long.

Little did they know! To date thousands of businesses have suffered from virus contamination. Unlike older viruses (1986/87 vintage) which would place a silly message or a bouncing ball on the screen, many new viruses are highly destructive, programmed to corrupt and destroy data. As viral infections become more and more widespread, the damage to data is increasing at an alarming pace.

The virus danger is here to stay. In most of the world it has reached epidemic proportions and the number of viruses seems to continue doubling approximately every 9 months, reaching about 1500 in June 1992.

Computer viruses are only one of the many possible forms of attack on computer systems; other common forms are **Trojan horses** and **logic bombs**, but since they often occur together, their analysis is important in the context of this book. For example, a virus will almost certainly be introduced into a computer system without the explicit consent of the system owner. It will be hidden in the boot sector of a floppy disk or attached to a legitimate program. The infected disk and the infected program are Trojan horses used to introduce virus code surreptitiously into a computer system. Likewise, most viruses incorporate side-effects which trigger only when certain conditions are fulfilled. The mechanism which does the triggerring is a logic bomb.

1.1 TROJAN HORSES

A Trojan horse is a program which performs services beyond those stated in its specifications. These effects can be (and often are) malicious. An example of a Trojan horse is the program *ARC513* found on some bulletin boards which pretends to be an improved version of the legitimate data compression utility *ARC*. In reality, it deletes the file specified for compression.

A list containing the names of known Trojan horses was started some time ago and was called 'The Dirty Dozen'. Unfortunately, as it is easy to rename a program, or to write a new Trojan, the list grew rapidly and now contains hundreds of names. It is available on some bulletin boards, but no such list can ever be complete.

Apart from the fact that Trojan horses can be stand-alone programs, the term is also used to describe any item which surreptitiously introduces malicious code into a computer system. This can be a floppy disk with virus code hidden in a bootstrap sector or a program with a virus attached to it.

1.1.1 TROJAN EXAMPLE 1: BATCH FILES

The following short batch file, called 'SEX.BAT' is an example of a very simple Trojan horse. **DO NOT try this out, as it deletes all files in the hard disk root directory**. It is however worth understanding how it works:

```
DEL  <SEX.BAT C:\*.*
Y
```

This sequence redirects the input to the DEL command from the console to the file SEX.BAT which also contains the answer 'Y' to DOS's question 'Are you sure?'.

If somebody notices this interesting file 'SEX.BAT' on a floppy disk, and simply types 'SEX' to see what the command does, all the files in the root directory of his drive C (usually the hard disk) will be deleted.

This is an example of a very simple Trojan horse; much greater damage can be caused by skilled, malicious programmers.

1.1.2 TROJAN EXAMPLE 2: ANSI.SYS

The traditional Trojan horse is a program which needs to be **executed intentionally** in order to cause damage. However, it is possible to activate a Trojan horse unwittingly simply by using the DOS command 'TYPE' to display the contents of a text file which contains embedded escape sequences. These escape sequences are intercepted by the ANSI.SYS driver, which is loaded by a command in the CONFIG.SYS file on many PCs, and used by some legitimate software. The Trojan horse writer will often redefine one or more keys on the keyboard. Redefining 'A' as 'S' and 'Q' as 'W' may cause some confusion, but redefining 'd' as 'DEL *.DAT' could have more serious consequences.

This is very easily done. If the following sequence

```
ESC[100;"DEL  *.DAT";13p
```

(where ESC is the Escape character, hexadecimal 1B) is incorporated in the file README which an unsuspecting user is invited to TYPE, every time that he presses 'd', the keystroke will be expanded by ANSI.SYS to 'DEL *.DAT' followed by a carriage return. Much more devious schemes can be devised, for example substituting 'd' with 'FORMAT C:' and 'n' as 'y' followed by 'Enter'. If the user types 'd' at the command line, this will be expanded into 'FORMAT C:'. The FORMAT program will prompt the user with

```
Warning! All data on drive C: will be lost.
Proceed (Y/N)?
```

When the poor user sees that, the instinctive reaction will be to type 'n' as quickly as possible; ANSI.SYS will substitute this with 'y' and the data on the hard disk stands a good chance of being lost (nevertheless, utilities exist which allow 'unformatting' of hard disks which have been formatted accidentally).

Bulletin board operators normally scan all messages for escape sequences, in order to prevent unsuspecting readers of messages from picking up this type of Trojan, while VAX/VMS MAIL converts escape characters to printable characters in order to prevent this type of attack.

The easiest way to combat this type of Trojan attack on PCs is to eliminate the statement

```
DEVICE=ANSI.SYS
```

from the CONFIG.SYS file. Many applications today do not use ANSI.SYS escape sequences to output to the screen but call the BIOS routines directly. There are also ANSI.SYS drivers available which do not allow the redefinition of keyboard codes.

1.1.3 TROJAN EXAMPLE 3: THE AIDS DISK THROUGH THE POST

On 11th December 1989 some twenty thousand envelopes were posted in London, containing a 5 1/4" floppy disk marked "AIDS Information Version 2.00" (Fig. 1.1) and an instruction leaflet (Fig. 1.2). The recipient was encouraged to insert the disk and install the package. On the reverse of the leaflet (Fig. 1.3), in very small print, was the 'License Agreement' which requested the user to send US$189 or US$378 for using the software (two types of 'license'). The Agreement threatened unspecified action if that fee was not paid (*'Most serious consequences of your failure to abide by the terms of this license agreement: your conscience may haunt you for the rest of your life; you will owe compensation ...'*).

Once an unsuspecting user installed the package, the program printed an 'invoice' giving the address in Panama to which payment should be sent: "PC Cyborg Corporation, P.O. Box 87-17-44, Panama 7, Panama". The AIDS package poses as a legitimate program giving information on AIDS and assessing the user's risk group after asking him/her to fill in a questionnaire.

However, the installation procedure makes modifications to the AUTOEXEC.BAT file, with the effect that every time AUTOEXEC.BAT is executed, a counter in a hidden file is incremented. When this has happened a random number of times (around 90) the damage sequence is activated. The user is instructed to wait, while most of the names of the files

Fig. 1.1 - The AIDS information disk

AIDS Information - Introductory Diskette

Please find enclosed a computer diskette containing health information on the disease AIDS. The information is provided in the form of an interactive computer program. It is easy to use. Here is how it works:

- The program provides you with information about AIDS and asks you questions
- You reply by choosing the most appropriate answer shown on the screen
- The program then provides you with a confidential report on your risk of exposure to AIDS
- The program provides recommendations to you, based on the life history information that you have provided, about practical steps that you can take to reduce your risk of getting AIDS
- The program gives you the opportunity to make comments and ask questions that you may have about AIDS
- This program is designed specially to help: members of the public who are concerned about AIDS and medical professionals.

Instructions

This software is designed for use with IBM® PC/XT™ microcomputers and with all other truly compatible microcomputers. Your computer must have a hard disk drive C, MS-DOS® version 2.0 or higher, and a minimum of 256K RAM. First read and assent to the limited warranty and to the license agreement on the reverse. [If you use this diskette, you will have to pay the mandatory software leasing fee(s).] Then do the following:

Step 1: Start your computer (with diskette drive A empty).

Step 2: Once the computer is running, insert the Introductory Diskette into drive A.

Step 3: At the C> prompt of your root directory type: A:INSTALL and then press ENTER. Installation proceeds automatically from that point. It takes only a few minutes.

Step 4: When the installation is completed, you will be given easy-to-follow messages by the computer. Respond accordingly.

Step 5: When you want to use the program, type the word AIDS at the C> prompt in the root directory and press ENTER.

Fig. 1.2 - The AIDS information disk instruction leaflet (reproducing the original poor print quality)

on the hard disk are encrypted (scrambled) and marked 'Hidden'. The only non-hidden file contains the following message:

```
If you are reading this message, then your software lease
from PC Cyborg Corporation has expired. Renew the software
lease before using this computer again. Warning: do not
attempt to use this computer until you have renewed your
software lease. Use the information below for renewal.


Dear Customer:


It is time to pay for your software lease from PC Cyborg Corporation.
Complete the INVOICE and attach payment for the lease option of your choice.
If you don't use the printed INVOICE, then be sure to refer to the important
reference numbers below in all correspondence. In return you will receive:
- a renewal software package with easy-to-follow, complete instructions;
- an automatic, self-installing diskette that anyone can apply in minutes.
```

Limited Warranty

If the diskette containing the programs is defective, PC Cyborg Corporation will replace it at no charge. This remedy is your sole remedy. These programs and documentation are provided "as is" without warranty of any kind, either express or implied, including but not limited to the implied warranties of merchantability and fitness for a particular purpose. The entire risk as to the quality and performance of the programs is with you. Should the programs prove defective, you (and not PC Cyborg Corporation or its dealers) assume the entire cost of all necessary servicing, repair or correction. In no event will PC Cyborg Corporation be liable to you for any damages, including any loss of profits, loss of savings, business interruption, loss of business information or other incidental, consequential, or special damages arising out of the use of or inability to use these programs, even if PC Cyborg Corporation has been advised of the possibility of such damages, or for any claim by any other party.

License Agreement

Read this license agreement carefully. If you do not agree with the terms and conditions stated below, do not use this software, and do not break the seal (if any) on the software diskette. PC Cyborg Corporation retains the title and ownership of these programs and documentation but grants a license to you under the following conditions: You may use the programs on microcomputers, and you may copy the programs for archival purposes and for purposes specified in the programs themselves. However, you may not decompile, disassemble, or reverse-engineer these programs or modify them in any way without consent from PC Cyborg Corporation. These programs are provided for your use as described above on a leased basis to you; they are not sold. You may choose one of the following types of lease: (a) a lease for 365 user applications or (b) a lease for the lifetime of your hard disk drive or 60 years, whichever is the lesser. PC Cyborg Corporation may include mechanisms in the programs to limit or inhibit copying and to ensure that you abide by the terms of the license agreement and to the terms of the lease duration. There is a mandatory leasing fee for the use of these programs; they are not provided to you free of charge. The prices for "lease a" and "lease b" mentioned above are US$189 and US$378, respectively (subject to change without notice). If you install these programs on a microcomputer (by the install program or by the share program option or by any other means), then under the terms of this license you thereby agree to pay PC Cyborg Corporation in full for the cost of leasing these programs. In the case of your breach of this license agreement, PC Cyborg Corporation reserves the right to take any legal action necessary to recover any outstanding debts payable to PC Cyborg Corporation and to use program mechanisms to ensure termination of your use of the programs. These program mechanisms will adversely affect other program applications on microcomputers. You are hereby advised of the most serious consequences of your failure to abide by the terms of this license agreement: your conscience may haunt you for the rest of your life; you will owe compensation and possible damages to PC Cyborg Corporation; and your microcomputer will stop functioning normally. Warning: Do not use these programs unless you are prepared to pay for them. You are strictly prohibited from sharing these programs with others, unless the programs are accompanied by all program documentation including this license agreement; you fully inform the recipient of the terms of this agreement; and the recipient assents to the terms of the agreement, including the mandatory payments to PC Cyborg Corporation. PC Cyborg Corporation does not authorize you to distribute or use these programs in the United States of America. If you have any doubt about your willingness or ability to meet the terms of this license agreement or if you are not prepared to pay all amounts due to PC Cyborg Corporation, then do not use these programs. No modification to this agreement shall be binding unless specifically agreed upon in writing by PC Cyborg Corporation.

Fig. 1.3 - The AIDS information disk 'license' agreement (reproducing the original poor print quality)

```
Important reference numbers: A302980-1887436-
```

```
The price of 365 user applications is US$189. The price of a lease for the
lifetime of your hard disk is US$378. You must enclose a bankers draft,
cashier's check or international money order payable to PC CYBORG CORPORATION
for the full amount of $189 or $378 with your order. Include your name,
company, address, city, state, country, zip or postal code. Mail your order
to PC Cyborg Corporation, P.O. Box 87-17-44, Panama 7, Panama.
```

The author and perpetrator of this scam was eventually established to be Dr. Joseph Lewis Popp, 41, from Willowick, Cleveland, US. After a lengthy legal battle he was extradited to the UK on 22nd February 1991, but at his trial at Southwark Crown Court in London his case was suspended after psychiatrical testimony that he was unfit to stand trial. He was legally classified as a 'public disgrace' and returned to the US.

This is a typical example of attempted extortion through the use of a Trojan horse. The user is first invited to install the package (which cannot be easily deinstalled) and then blackmailed into paying money in return for safe passage.

1.2 LOGIC BOMBS

A logic bomb is a programming IF statement which causes the execution of some program code when a certain condition is fulfilled (Fig. 1.4). The condition can be time, the presence or absence of data such as a name etc. A hypothetical example of a logic bomb would be a maliciously modified copy of a spreadsheet which zeroed a particular cell every Tuesday between 10 and 11 a.m., but otherwise did not reveal its presence. The results would be very confusing and difficult to trace.

Logic bombs are frequently found in the more sophisticated cases of computer crime. A recent case involved a systems programmer who was maintaining a payroll package. He decided to 'ensure' his continuing employment by introducing a short sequence of instructions which checked whether his name was in the payroll file. If it was, nothing would happen. But if it was not (as a result of him being fired), files would be deleted and other damage would occur. He was fired, and the logic bomb triggered the destruction. Only after having been promised reinstatement by the employer did he agree to point out the logic bomb in the code. He was not prosecuted.

Another example of a logic bomb happened at IBM. At 7:30 a.m. on 11th April 1980 all IBM 4341s ceased to operate. The problem was eventually traced to a logic bomb triggered on that date, which was placed in software by a disgruntled employee.

Logic bombs are often found in viruses, where the payload (which produces the side-effects) is triggered when a certain condition is met. For example, the *Cascade* virus produces its side-effects only between 1st October 1988 and 31st December 1988. The *Michelangelo* virus trashes disks on 6th March of any year. The *Italian* virus puts the bouncing ball on the screen only if a disk access is made during a 1-second interval every 30 minutes. The delay due to the logic bomb allows the virus to spread unnoticed, and show its side-effects after it has reproduced extensively.

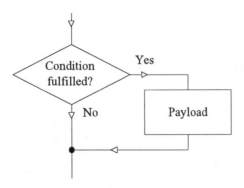

Fig. 1.4 - Logic bomb program flow

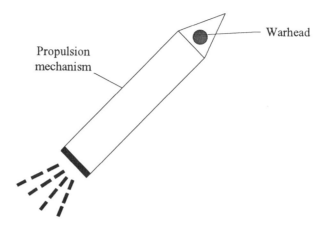

Fig. 1.5 - Missile delivering a warhead

1.3 VIRUSES

A computer virus is best defined as computer code which has four characteristics:

1. Self-replication: Viruses make copies of themselves, spreading across floppy disks, computer systems and networks. This similarity with their biological counterparts has given viruses their name. Self-replication is a unique virus characteristic which distinguishes viruses from other computer programs.

2. Executable path: **For a virus to do anything, it must be executed.** Viruses are designed in such a way that this can occur without any user intervention whatsoever: for example, the user accidentally bootstraps the PC while an infected floppy disk is in drive A or he executes an infected program. This characteristic is very important to bear in mind in a number of circumstances:

   · When dealing with a virus attack

   · When formulating anti-virus strategy

   · When studying virus behaviour

3. Side-effects: Viruses do not normally consist only of self-replicating code; they also contain code which produces side-effects or a 'payload' which is released when a predetermined set of conditions is fulfilled. It is easy to program the payload side-effects to be malicious. Some viruses do not contain any side-effects.

4. Disguise: The successful spread of a virus depends on how long it can replicate unnoticed before its presence is made known by the activation of side-effects. Replicating longevity is achieved through two methods of disguise - encryption

(scrambling) and interrupt interception. These are described in Section 3.3: Virus Hiding Mechanisms.

This tactic is probably the most fascinating virus characteristic since it is remarkably similar to the way that biological viruses (and bacteria) operate. If a human gets infected with a virus, there will be a time delay called incubation during which he will not exhibit any symptoms of the disease, but will nevertheless be infectious to other humans. Since there are no recognisable outside indicators of his impending disease, other human beings will not have any reason to avoid contact, thereby facilitating the transmission of the virus and its long term spread. It is remarkable that computer viruses and biological viruses, despite having so distinctly different structure, employ very similar techniques in order to ensure survival.

The analogy between virus characteristics and those of a missile have been pointed out by Fred Cohen. A missile (Fig. 1.5) contains a warhead (conventional, chemical, nuclear etc.) and the means of delivering that warhead over a distance. The warhead is the equivalent of a virus payload, while the propulsion mechanism is the equivalent of the virus self-replicating code.

The above characteristics are discussed in greater detail in later chapters. For examples of viruses see Chapter 4: Common IBM PC viruses.

1.4 WORMS

Worms are similar to viruses, but replicate in their entirety, creating exact copies of themselves, without needing a 'carrier' program. Worms are normally found on computer networks and multi-user computers, and use inter-computer or inter-user communications as the transmission medium.

Fig. 1.6 - Christmas tree worm output

1.4.1 WORM EXAMPLE 1: CHRISTMAS TREE ON IBM VM

Probably the best known mainframe worm was the *Christmas Tree worm* which spread widely on BITNET, the European Academic Research Network (EARN) and IBM's internal network. It was launched on 9th December 1987 and, amongst other effects, paralysed the IBM worldwide network on 11th December 1987.

The *Christmas Tree worm* is written in REXX and can spread on VM/CMS installations. The program is a combination of a Trojan horse and a chain letter. When run, it draws a Christmas tree on screen (Fig. 1.6), sends itself to all the user's correspondents in the user files NAMES and NETLOG and then deletes itself.

The source code of this worm was published in R. Burger's book *Computer Viruses: A High Tech disease* as well as being available from a number of sources. The worm has since then reappeared several times in both its original form and modified versions.

1.4.2 WORM EXAMPLE 2: INTERNET WORM ON UNIX

A number of widely publicised worm attacks have occurred on Unix systems. The most widely reported attack was the Internet worm which struck the US DARPA Internet computer network on 2nd November 1988. The worm was released by Robert T. Morris, a Cornell University student, on a public access machine at MIT (**prep.ai.mit.edu**). The worm replicated by exploiting a number of bugs in the Unix operating system running on VAX and Sun Microsystems hardware, including a bug in *sendmail* (an electronic mail program) and in *fingerd* (a program for getting details of who is logged in). Stanford University, Massachusetts Institute of Technology, the University of Maryland and Berkeley University were infected within 5 hours of the worm being released. The NASA Research Institute at Ames and the Lawrence Livermore National Laboratory were also infected, as well as some 6000 other computer systems. The UK was unaffected.

The worm consisted of some 4000 lines of 'C' code and once it was analysed, the specialists distributed bug fixes to *sendmail* and *fingerd*, which prevented further spreading. From the decompilation, it appears that the worm was not malicious. It did, however, cause the overloading of infected systems.

1.4.3 WORM EXAMPLE 3: SPAN WORM ON VAX/VMS

On 16th October 1989 VAX/VMS computers on the SPAN network were attacked by a worm. The worm propagated via DECnet protocols and if it discovered that it was running with system privileges, it changed the system announcement message to that shown in Fig. 1.7.

The worm also changed the DECNET account password to a random string and mailed the information on the password to the user GEMPAK on SPAN node 6.59. If the worm had system privileges, it disabled mail to the SYSTEM account and modified the system login command procedure to *appear* to delete all files (it didn't actually do it). The worm then proceeded to access other systems by picking node numbers at random and used the

W O R M S   A G A I N S T   N U C L E A R   K I L L E R S

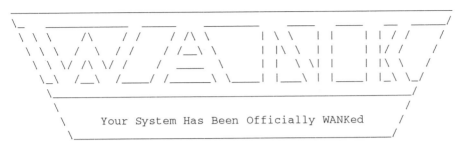

You talk of times of peace for all, and then prepare for war.

Fig. 1.7 - WANK worm logon message

PHONE command to get a list of active users on the remote system. After accessing the RIGHTSLIST file, it attempted to access the remote system using the list of users found, to which it added a list of 81 standard users coded into the worm. It penetrated accounts where passwords were the same as the name of the account or were null.

The worm then looked for an account which had access to SYSUAF.DAT. If such an account was found, the worm copied itself to that account and started executing. Within a very short time, the Computer Emergency Response Team (CERT) in the USA (telephone 412-268-7090) issued a warning and a corrective response.

This was the second well-known virus attack on DECNET: the first (HI.COM) was released on 22nd December 1988 from a European HEPNET node, probably originating at the Institute of Physics at the University of Neuchatel in Switzerland.

2

HOW CAN A VIRUS PENETRATE A COMPUTER?

He has the gift of quiet.

John Le Carré

There is nothing magic about the way a virus penetrates a computer. The methods of entry are well understood and taking them into account when using a PC is the first step towards combating the virus threat.

By far the most important point to realise is that the only way that a virus can infect a computer is as a result of **the virus code being executed**. Viruses are designed in such a way that the act of executing them is surreptitious and occurs without the knowledge (or consent) of the user. In practice this may mean accidentally bootstrapping a PC from an infected floppy disk (thereby executing the contents of the boot sector) or executing a program which has a virus attached to it.

Any medium which can be used for storing or transmitting data is potentially a virus carrier. It is entirely dependent on the media characteristics as to what type of virus it will be able to carry. This is analysed in detail in Section 2.3: Virus Carrier Media, while virus types are discussed in Section 3.1: Virus Types. Certain user actions have been shown to carry a high risk of infection: this is discussed in Section 2.4: Virus Infiltration Routes and Methods.

2.1 HOW DOES AN INFECTION HAPPEN?

It is very important to distinguish between *a virus being active in RAM* (Random Access Memory) and *an infected medium.*

The virus becomes active in RAM when virus code is executed. This active state is cleared by switching off the PC. On the other hand most media infected with a virus will carry the virus even after power failure. This is illustrated in the first four blocks of Fig. 2.1.

For example, if a PC becomes infected with the *Italian* virus by bootstrapping from an infected floppy disk, the virus will a) become active in RAM and b) infect the hard disk. If the power is switched off, the virus will disappear from RAM, but **not** from the hard disk. When the power is switched on and the PC bootstrapped (started) from the hard disk, the virus will become active in RAM.

Blocks 5 and 6 of Fig. 2.1 demonstrate how the infection spreads onto further floppy disks, while blocks 7 and 8 show that correct bootstrapping can ensure that the virus is not active in memory while anti-virus actions (such as scanning for viruses) are performed.

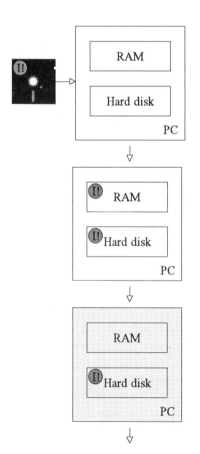

1. In an uninfected PC both the RAM and the hard disk are free from infection. An infected floppy disk is introduced into the floppy disk drive.

⑴ shows infected items

2. When an infected program from the floppy disk is run, the hard disk becomes infected and the virus becomes active in RAM.

3. If power is now switched off, the hard disk remains infected while the contents of RAM (including the virus) are lost.

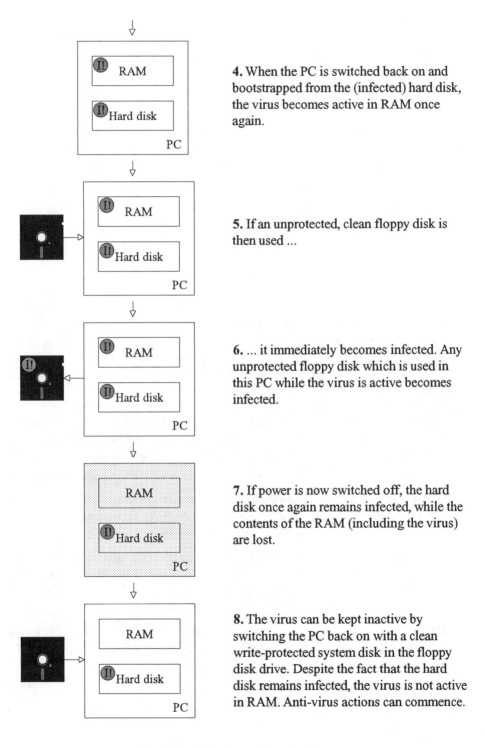

4. When the PC is switched back on and bootstrapped from the (infected) hard disk, the virus becomes active in RAM once again.

5. If an unprotected, clean floppy disk is then used ...

6. ... it immediately becomes infected. Any unprotected floppy disk which is used in this PC while the virus is active becomes infected.

7. If power is now switched off, the hard disk once again remains infected, while the contents of the RAM (including the virus) are lost.

8. The virus can be kept inactive by switching the PC back on with a clean write-protected system disk in the floppy disk drive. Despite the fact that the hard disk remains infected, the virus is not active in RAM. Anti-virus actions can commence.

Fig. 2.1 - Infecting a PC and disks

2.2 EXECUTABLE PATH

In order to penetrate a computer, a virus must be given a chance to execute. Since executable objects on a PC are known, **all possible virus attack points can be listed.** By making sure that only legitimate, virus-free code is executed, one can protect the system from infection.

In addition to the obvious executable files such as COM and EXE programs, **any file which contains executable code** should be treated as a potential virus carrier. This includes files with interpreted BASIC commands, spreadsheet macros etc.

On a PC, the attack points are most easily listed by analysing the steps which are performed when the PC is bootstrapped, either by switching it on, or by performing a so-called 'warm boot' (pressing the Ctrl, Alt and Del keys simultaneously).

The normal PC bootstrapping sequence is shown in Fig. 2.2 and consists of the following steps:

1. When the computer is switched on, or a warm boot is performed (Ctrl-Alt-Del), a PC first executes the program held in its ROM (Read Only Memory). The ROM program usually tests whether the first floppy drive (A:) contains a disk. If it does, the PC loads into memory a short program stored in the first sector on the disk (the Bootstrap Sector), and starts executing it. If the disk is not a 'system' disk, this program displays the message 'Non-system disk', or similar, and waits for the user to insert a 'system' disk. If the first floppy drive does not contain a disk, the PC will bootstrap from the first hard disk by loading the first physical sector (sector 1, head 0, track 0) into memory and executing it. This is the master boot sector, which in turn loads and executes the first sector of the 'active partition'. This is the DOS boot sector which is similar in function to the bootstrap sector on a floppy disk. The bootstrap process then proceeds in a similar way to bootstrapping from a floppy disk.

    On IBM-AT computers, the system will also access the CMOS memory prior to performing this step. Various system parameters in CMOS memory can be set up (usually using the SETUP utility supplied with the PC).

2. The program in the DOS boot sector reads the operating system (DOS) from disk into memory and transfers control to it. DOS is contained in the first two files found in the root directory, which are usually called IO.SYS and MSDOS.SYS, although different names such as IBMBIO.SYS and IBMDOS.SYS are also used.

3. The file CONFIG.SYS is then consulted. This is a text file which describes the desired configuration of the system (file buffer allocation, device drivers etc.). Device drivers like ANSI.SYS are loaded into memory at this stage.

4. DOS then loads COMMAND.COM and executes it. COMMAND.COM is a COM file which processes commands such as DIR, TYPE etc. Note that COMMAND.COM is a default command line processor supplied by Microsoft, but DOS allows other command line processors such as 4DOS.COM to be used.

5. A special batch file (AUTOEXEC.BAT) is then executed, thus completing the bootstrapping procedure. If no AUTOEXEC.BAT file is found, the system prompts the user for date and time.

6. The user is then presented with the system prompt and the system awaits user commands. Any command is either an internal DOS command, the name of a COM file, the name of an EXE file, or the name of a BAT file. The system will search for these files in the current subdirectory as well as all subdirectories specified in the PATH command and execute the first one it finds. The order of precedence is shown in Fig. 2.3. Programs can also load executable overlay files (OVL) as and when needed. Overlay files usually have extensions such as OVL, OV1, OV2 etc.

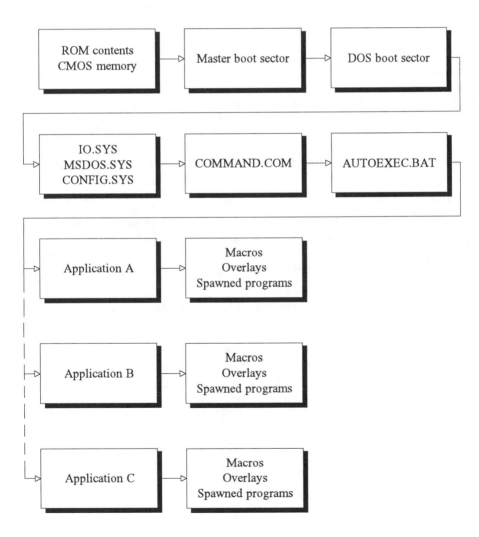

Fig. 2.2 - Bootstrapping sequence

Precedence of command execution:

1. Internal commands (DIR, TYPE)
2. COM file
3. EXE file
4. BAT file

For example, if a directory contains files DIR.COM and DIR.EXE and the user enters DIR, COMMAND.COM will execute the internal DIR command. If the directory contains files ABC.COM, ABC.EXE and ABC.BAT and the user enters ABC, COMMAND.COM will execute ABC.COM in preference to ABC.EXE and ABC.BAT.

Fig. 2.3 - The order of precedence of commands entered at the command line

7. Applications often use macros which are, in effect, executable code. This can take the form of interpreted BASIC commands, spreadsheet macros, word-processing macros and so on.

In order for an item to be susceptible to infection, it must be both executable and modifiable. The following items satisfy these two conditions:

1. **Master boot sector** - viruses such as *New Zealand* and *Joshi* attack the master boot sector.

2. **DOS boot sector** - viruses such as the *Italian* and *Mistake* attack the DOS boot sector.

3. **DOS files IO.SYS and MSDOS.SYS** - possible attack points, although to date no viruses infect either file. CONFIG.SYS is a text file, and cannot contain a virus, but it could easily load and execute any virus written as a device driver.

4. **Device drivers**, SYS files such as ANSI.SYS, RAMDRIVE.SYS - possible attack points, although to date no known viruses infect them.

5. **COMMAND.COM** - at least one virus (*Lehigh*) targets this file specifically.

6. **AUTOEXEC.BAT** - a possible attack point, though normally affected by Trojan horses rather than viruses.

7. **Applications - EXE and COM files** - many viruses attack these files. Overlay files (normally OVL, OVR, OV1 etc) can also become infected.

8. **Files with macros** - no viruses, other than experimental ones, have been shown to attack these files.

In practice, the two requirements for an item to be susceptible to infection (i.e. that it is executable and modifiable) are supplemented by another *de facto* condition: the item must also be exchanged often enough between PCs. This reduces the above list of items at risk to master boot sectors, DOS boot sectors and COM and EXE executable files. Viruses which infect master or DOS boot sectors are known as **boot sector viruses**, viruses which infect COM and EXE files are known as **parasitic viruses**, while viruses which infect both master or DOS boot sectors as well as COM and EXE files are known as **multi-partite viruses**. The other two types of viruses (**companion viruses** and **link viruses**) use different techniques which is discussed in greater detail in Section 3.1: Virus Types.

To keep the system free from viruses the user must make sure that the code contained within the items at risk remains virus-free and uncorrupted. Unfortunately, this is harder than it seems.

2.3 VIRUS CARRIER MEDIA

Any medium which can be used for the transmission or storage of executable code is a potential carrier of **parasitic** and **multi-partite viruses**, while any medium which can be used to bootstrap the PC is a potential carrier of **boot sector** and **multi-partite viruses**.

The PC becomes infected with a parasitic or a multi-partite virus when the user executes an infected program. The PC becomes infected with a boot sector or a multi-partite virus when the user bootstraps the PC from an infected medium.

2.3.1 FLOPPY DISKS

Floppy disks are the most common medium for information exchange. They are used for distributing programs or exchanging information between PCs. They can act as carriers of parasitic viruses which hide in any executable on the disk, of bootstrap sector viruses, which hide in the bootstrap sector of the disk or of multi-partite viruses which can hide both in the bootstrap sector and any executable.

Executing an infected program or bootstrapping from an infected disk need not be a conscious action on the part of the user. For example, a PC will become infected automatically if it is bootstrapped from a disk infected with a boot sector virus. **Note that the floppy disk need not be a system disk!** This can happen quite easily if a floppy is left overnight in a PC which is then switched on in the morning. The PC can also become infected if a short power failure occurs while the machine is unattended with floppy disk in the drive. When the user returns to the PC he will probably not notice that the PC has been bootstrapped in his absence.

2.3.2 REMOVABLE HARD DISKS

Removable hard disks are becoming more popular in secure systems where the mass storage device has to be locked away physically when the PC is not attended. However, as they can be moved from one PC to another, they can act as carriers of both parasitic viruses, boot sector viruses and multi-partite viruses.

2.3.3 MAGNETIC TAPE CARTRIDGES

Magnetic tape cartridges are normally used for storing PC backups. The PC cannot be booted from them, and as such they can only carry parasitic or multi-partite viruses.

2.3.4 OTHER STORAGE MEDIA

There are several other storage media used with PCs (Bernoulli drives, optical disks, 1/2" magnetic tapes etc.). **As a rule, if the medium can be used to bootstrap the PC, it should be considered capable of carrying bootstrap sector viruses, multi-partite viruses, as well as parasitic viruses. If the medium cannot be used to bootstrap the PC, it can only carry parasitic and multi-partite viruses.**

2.3.5 NETWORKS

PC networks provide a means for rapid exchange of information. They are also an excellent propagation medium for viruses and as such present a major security risk. They are treated in detail in Chapter 8: Viruses and Networks.

2.3.6 MODEMS

Modems offer the PC a means of communicating with other PCs, normally via an intermediate storage facility such as bulletin board or electronic mail servers. If these offer the facility to upload and download executable images, they can act as carriers of parasitic and multi-partite viruses. Bootstrap sector viruses cannot be transmitted unwittingly via modems.

2.4 VIRUS INFILTRATION ROUTES AND METHODS

Some user actions have been shown to carry a high risk of leading to infection. The following list of routes and methods of virus infiltration has been assembled by analysing real-life cases in which organisations and individuals became infected. The results of the Dataquest survey of 602 North American companies with 300 or more PCs in Fig. 2.4 shows the sources of infections in large organisations; the proportions are probably not true for all PC users.

2.4.1 PIRATED SOFTWARE

It is easy to copy software and in most countries it is illegal to do so. But unless it is done on a large scale, the risk of prosecution at the moment is much smaller than the risk of

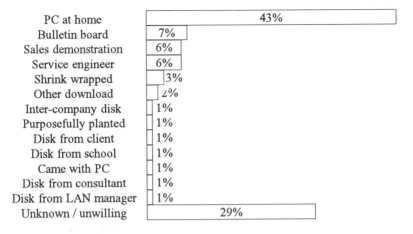

PC at home	43%
Bulletin board	7%
Sales demonstration	6%
Service engineer	6%
Shrink wrapped	3%
Other download	2%
Inter-company disk	1%
Purposefully planted	1%
Disk from client	1%
Disk from school	1%
Came with PC	1%
Disk from consultant	1%
Disk from LAN manager	1%
Unknown / unwilling	29%

Fig. 2.4 - Sources of infection; from Dataquest survey, October 1991

contracting a virus infection. Games are probably the most commonly pirated software and they tend to move between PC users at a far greater speed than 'serious' pirated software. For this reason, they are also most prone to picking up a parasitic virus on the way.

2.4.2 BULLETIN BOARDS (BBS)

Bulletin boards normally provide a means of downloading and uploading software which is classified either as 'public domain' (free for all) or 'shareware' (copy freely, but pay if you use it). Most reputable boards are run under the close supervision of the SYSOP, the SYStem OPerator, who is at great pains to ensure the integrity of the software available from the bulletin board as well as the absence of Trojan horses (see Section 1.1.2: Trojan Example 2: ANSI.SYS).

Unfortunately, it is almost impossible to analyse all traffic on a bulletin board manually and many SYSOPs resort to automatic virus scanning of any uploaded executables. This is certainly better than nothing, but becomes ineffective if the software is distributed 'packed' using some non-standard dynamic packing utility (see also Section 7.1.2: Scanning software).

Bulletin boards are very useful for exchanging information and opinions. Their use should be confined to that and they should not be used for downloading software which was uploaded by other users.

There have been a significant number of cases of virus-infected software being uploaded onto public bulletin boards, including a bulletin board used to distribute market-leading anti-virus software.

2.4.3 SHAREWARE

Shareware is an attractive concept developed in the USA. The software carries the traditional copyright, but all users are encouraged to copy it and pass it on to others. If

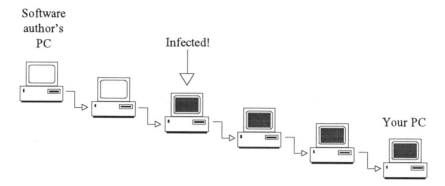

Fig. 2.5 - Unsafe software distribution. An infected user's PC will propagate the infection to all downstream recipients of the software.

anybody ends up using it, he is under moral obligation to send a small sum (usually US$20 to US$50) to the author. The attraction lies in the fact that one ends up trying the software before paying for it. Market forces help to ensure the distribution and survival of good software and the eventual demise of rubbish. Unfortunately, shareware distribution is not without problems. Although most authors send 'the latest version' once payment has been received, users often end up trying (and using) the original version obtained from a friend of a friend of a friend. By the time one receives 'the latest version', the computer may be infected many times over with any viruses the original software picked up on the way (Fig. 2.5).

Some companies distribute shareware through catalogues, guaranteeing 'the latest version' when shareware is purchased. Obviously, this is better than the 'friend of a friend of a friend' method, and the company has a vested interest in distributing uncontaminated software. Many shareware packages now include a checksum program and a list of correct checksums for all files supplied with the package. As long as the checksum program is not infected and the checksumming algorithm is cryptographically strong, this provides an assurance of file integrity (see Section 7.1.2: Checksumming Software).

Shareware is nevertheless a cheap way of obtaining software, some of which is of excellent quality.

2.4.4 PUBLIC DOMAIN SOFTWARE

Unlike shareware, public domain software is completely free for anybody to use. Unfortunately, it suffers from the same distribution risks as shareware, with the added disadvantage that there is often nobody to supply 'the latest version'.

There are a number of notable exceptions to the above, such as the *Kermit* communications package, which is fully supported by Columbia University in New York, USA. Anybody can obtain the latest version in return for a fee to cover administration costs.

2.4.5 SHARED PCS (PC AT HOME)

A surprisingly large number of infections in business PCs occur through the use of home computers for company work. The companies concerned usually have sound anti-virus security measures in place, but still suffer virus attacks by overlooking this loophole.

In one case known to the author an executive's 14-year old son used his father's home PC to play games obtained from the school playground (unbeknown to his father). The executive, having brought home a report to finish, unwittingly took an infected disk back to work the next morning and in turn, infected his office PCs with the *New Zealand* virus. His son was out of favour for some time, but the company learned a valuable lesson.

2.4.6 FLOPPY DISKS SUPPLIED BY COMPUTER MAGAZINES

Some computer magazines supply floppy disks containing free software. On a number of occasions such disks have been found to carry virus code, for example:

· PC Today Vol 4 No 4, Database Publications, August 1990, *Disk Killer* (only the boot sector contained the virus code while the rest of the virus was overwritten and ineffective), 40,000 copies

· PC-WORLD Benelux, 9th November 1990, IDG Communications, *Cascade*, 16,000 copies

· Archimedes World, February 1992, Argus Specialist Publications, *Module* (Archimedes virus), 15,000 copies

· PC Fun, January 1992, MC Publications, *New Zealand*, 20,000 copies

The major problem with such events is the number of infected disks involved and the resulting wide spread of the virus. Any software and disks obtained from magazines should be used with utmost care and any 'Virus Checked' labels found on such disks treated with scepticism.

2.4.7 SERVICE ENGINEERS

Service engineers are often a great source of the latest games, diagnostics and similar software. Seeing five or ten customers a day, they are an effective propagation medium for any copyable software.

In one case in 1988 a service engineer on a visit to a government organisation in England demonstrated an entertaining program called 'MUSHROOM'. Everyone wanted to run MUSHROOM. Unfortunately, that copy of MUSHROOM.COM had been infected with the *Cascade* virus, which in turn spread to many PCs in the organisation and triggerred on 1st October of that year. The engineer eventually examined the original source of the program and discovered that it was not infected. The infection was picked up along the way, probably on one of the customers' computers.

Much can be done to prevent viruses from infiltrating organisations through this route. All diagnostic disks used by service engineers should be write-protected, or, alternatively, the customer should have a set of his own write-protected disks. Service engineers should resist the temptation to distribute software, which is not only dangerous, but also often illegal.

At least one large computer company has expressly prohibited its service engineers from carrying any floppy disks. All disks used on the customers' PCs, including diagnostics, must either already be in the possession of the user or come shrink-wrapped from the factory. More and more computer maintenance companies are equipping their engineers with virus-scanning software, which allows them to determine quickly whether a problem is due to a virus or something else.

2.4.8 SHRINK-WRAPPED SOFTWARE

Shrink-wrapped software normally refers to commercial software packages which come in a shrink-wrapped sealed container - usually for legislative purposes rather than anti-virus measures. Many manufacturers state that by breaking the seal, the user implicitly agrees to abide by the licencing terms and conditions. There is also a good chance that the software has not been tampered with from the time it left the manufacturing plant.

There have however been several cases of viruses distributed on shrink-wrapped disks, for example:

· Zinc Software's *Interface Library*, 20th November 1991, *Form*

· Focus *2the*^{MAX}VGA card software, December 1991, *Michelangelo*, 1,000 copies

· Novell's *NetWare Encyclopedia*, 11th December 1991, *NoInt*, 3,800 copies

· Intel's Version 3.01 of *LANSpool 286 and 386*, 6th March 1992, *Michelangelo*, 830 copies

Apart from disks being infected at source, there have been a number of cases where dealers opened shrink-wrapped software, loaded it onto their (already infected) machines for demonstration purposes and resealed the package before offering it for sale. The virus was thus found on seemingly shrink-wrapped disks and the real reason for infection did not emerge until after an investigation by the software manufacturer. **Many such incidents could be prevented if all manufacturers delivered software on permanently write-protected floppy disks.**

Although there is always a chance that shrink-wrapped software will contain a virus, the probability, in practice, is still small. The reasons for this are twofold: Companies marketing shrink-wrapped software have a large investment in their products and a lot to lose from bad publicity should the products prove to be virus carriers. They also provide stringent QA procedures, which aim to ensure the integrity of the software leaving the factory. The result is a traceable step-by-step software development process in a controlled environment, which is a basis for efficient anti-virus measures.

3

VIRUS STRUCTURE

Now, what I want is Facts...Facts alone are wanted in life.

Charles Dickens, 'Hard Times'

A virus is a purposefully written computer program which consists of two parts: **Self-replicating code** and the **'payload'**, which produces side-effects (Fig. 3.1). In a typical PC virus, the replicating code may be between 400 and 2000 bytes long, while the size of the payload will depend on the side-effects. Typically this is a few hundred bytes.

Before infecting an executable, most viruses try to determine whether they have already infected it, by testing for some infection **signature**. If the signature (sometimes also referred to as "virus marker") is there, the executable is already infected and it will not be reinfected. The signature can have various forms. Some viruses use a sequence of characters such as 'sURIV' (VIRUs spelt backwards) in a fixed position, some test the file size for divisibility by a number, others test whether the number of seconds in the file datestamp is set to 62. At least one virus (*Jerusalem*) does not test correctly for its own signature, which results in reinfections and thus unlimited growth of executable images.

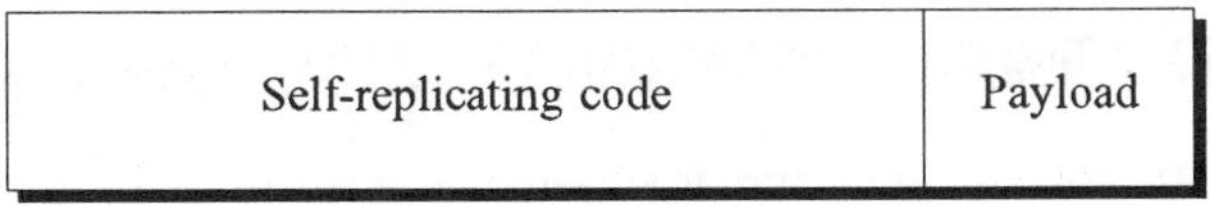

Self-replicating code	Payload

Fig. 3.1 Virus structure

The side-effects of a virus are limited only by the imagination of the virus author and can range from annoyance to serious vandalism.

3.1 VIRUS TYPES

Viruses can be divided into five categories: **Bootstrap sector viruses, Parasitic viruses, Multi-partite viruses, Companion viruses** and **Link viruses**. The distinction between these categories is somewhat blurred; for example, companion and link viruses could be assumed to be special cases of parasitic viruses.

3.1.1 BOOTSTRAP SECTOR VIRUSES

Bootstrap sector viruses modify the contents of either the master bootstrap sector or the DOS bootstrap sector, depending on the virus and type of disk, usually replacing the legitimate contents with their own version. The original version of the modified sector is normally stored somewhere else on the disk, so that on bootstrapping, the virus version will be executed first. This normally loads the remainder of the virus code into memory, followed by the execution of the original version of the bootstrap sector (Fig. 3.2). From then on, the virus generally remains memory-resident until the computer is switched off.

Bootstrap sector viruses are spread through **physical exchange of any media which can be used for bootstrapping** (in most cases by physical exchange of floppy disks). As a consequence, they spread comparatively slowly. Nevertheless, one often finds Trojan horse programs whose only function is to infect the boot sector of the PC and start the infection. Known as 'droppers' they allow the spread of boot sector viruses via bulletin boards, thereby vastly increasing the spreading potential and the speed with which the virus can spread over large distances.

A PC becomes infected with a boot sector virus only if the user (accidentally) bootstraps from an infected disk. It is completely safe to insert an infected disk into the drive and copy data from it (using the COPY command). The PC will not become infected unless it is booted while an infected disk is in drive A. However, the DISKCOPY command should not be used as this is an image copier which will copy the virus code as well.

Examples of bootstrap sector viruses include *Brain* (floppy disk bootstrap sector only), *Italian* (DOS bootstrap sector) and *New Zealand* (master bootstrap sector).

The mechanism of a bootstrap sector virus normally uses three distinct components:

1. **the bootstrap sector** - replaced with an infected version; this is where the virus gains access.

2. **one previously unused sector** - for storing the original bootstrap sector.

3. **a number of previously unused sectors** - where the bulk of the virus code is stored.

There are a number of bootstrap sector viruses which do not store the original bootstrap sector anywhere else (e.g. *SVC 6.0*).

The mechanism for acquiring unused sectors varies from virus to virus. Some viruses such as *Form* and *Disk Killer* look for unused clusters in the disk's File Allocation Table (FAT) and when found, label them as 'bad'. This prevents the operating system from allocating these clusters to files and possibly overwriting the virus code. Other viruses such as *New Zealand* use part of the hard disk which is not normally used by the operating system (Sector 2, Head 0, Track 0 onwards). *New Zealand* stores the original boot sector into Sector 7, Head 0, Track 0 on hard disks. On floppy disks, the virus adopts a different strategy and stores the original boot sector into Sector 3, Head 1, Track 0, both of which can cause serious loss of data on some disks.

Other examples of requisitioning space include using track 40 on 360K floppy disks (*Den Zuk*) and decreasing the size of the first partition on the hard disk (*Tequila*).

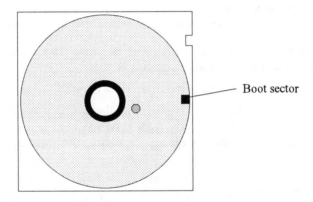

Fig. 3.2a Uninfected disk

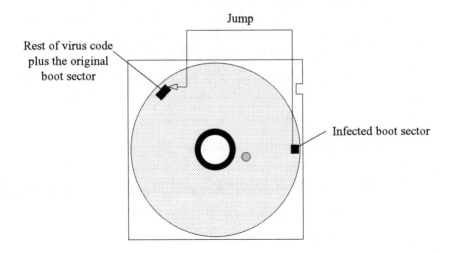

Fig. 3.2b Infected disk

It is important to realise that all boot sector viruses modify the bootstrap sector in some way, and it is the only item one needs to examine for signs of infection. The place where the rest of the virus code is stored is not of much practical interest, except, perhaps, when trying to find the original bootstrap sector in order to copy it back and 'disinfect' the disk.

3.1.2 PARASITIC VIRUSES

Parasitic viruses modify the contents of COM and/or EXE files. They append themselves to the file, leaving the bulk of the program intact (Fig. 3.3). The execution flow is hence diverted in such a way that virus code executes first. Once the virus code has executed, the execution flow passes to the original program which, in most cases, executes normally. The extra execution time due to the virus is usually not perceptible to the user. Some viruses append themselves to the end of the original file, some prepend themselves in front of the file, some do both and some insert themselves in the middle of the file.

Parasitic viruses spread through **any medium which can be used for storage or transmission of executable code** such as floppy disks, tapes, networks etc. The infection will generally spread if an infected program is executed.

It is of crucial importance to the virus that its code is executed before the infected program. The virus runs at the same privilege level as the original program and once running, can do anything: replicate, install itself into memory, release the side effects etc.

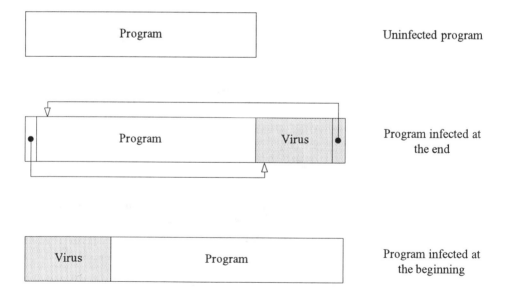

Fig. 3.3 Program infection with a parasitic virus

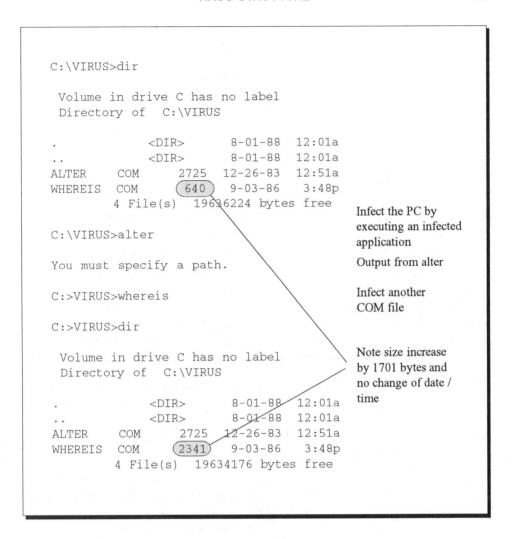

```
C:\VIRUS>dir

 Volume in drive C has no label
 Directory of  C:\VIRUS

        .              <DIR>        8-01-88   12:01a
        ..             <DIR>        8-01-88   12:01a
 ALTER      COM        2725    12-26-83   12:51a
 WHEREIS    COM         640     9-03-86    3:48p
        4 File(s)   19636224 bytes free

C:\VIRUS>alter

You must specify a path.

C:>VIRUS>whereis

C:>VIRUS>dir

 Volume in drive C has no label
 Directory of  C:\VIRUS

        .              <DIR>        8-01-88   12:01a
        ..             <DIR>        8-01-88   12:01a
 ALTER      COM        2725    12-26-83   12:51a
 WHEREIS    COM        2341     9-03-86    3:48p
        4 File(s)   19634176 bytes free
```

Infect the PC by executing an infected application

Output from alter

Infect another COM file

Note size increase by 1701 bytes and no change of date / time

Fig. 3.4 Infecting an application with *Cascade*

Most parasitic viruses, like *Cascade*, spread when another (uninfected) program is loaded and executed. Such a virus, being memory-resident, first inspects the program for infection already in place. If it is not infected, the virus will infect it. If it is already infected, further infection is not necessary (although some parasitic viruses like *Jerusalem* do reinfect ad infinitum). Infection by the *Cascade* virus is shown in Fig. 3.4.

Parasitic viruses which are not memory-resident do not install themselves in memory, but spread by finding the first uninfected program on disk and infecting it. One such example is the *Vienna* virus.

3.1.3 MULTI-PARTITE VIRUSES

A comparatively recent development has been the emergence of viruses which exhibit the characteristics of both bootstrap sector and parasitic viruses. Viruses such as *Flip* infect COM and EXE files (like parasitic viruses) as well as the master boot sector (like boot sector viruses). By exploiting 'the best of both worlds' their chances of replication are much higher than if they were to use only one method (Fig. 3.5). It is not surprising that comparatively few multi-partite viruses in existence today account for a disproportionately large number of infections.

Multi-partite viruses are spread through **physical exchange of any media which can be used for bootstrapping** (in most cases physical exchange of floppy disks) as well as through **any medium which can be used for storage or transmission of executable code** such as disks, tapes and networks. The virus will become active if the PC is bootstrapped from an infected disk or if an infected program is executed.

Most multi-partite viruses such as *Flip* are fully multi-partite, which means that a PC infected by bootstrapping from an infected disk will infect other disks as well as executables, while a PC infected by executing an infected file will infect other executables as well as disks. Some multi-partite viruses are only partially multi-partite; for example, *Spanish Telecom* in EXE and COM files will infect other EXE and COM files as well as the boot sectors, while the same virus in a boot sector will only infect other boot sectors.

The speed of propagation of multi-partite viruses is similar to that of parasitic viruses as they can be uploaded easily onto bulletin boards and thus spread over great distances very quickly.

3.1.4 COMPANION VIRUSES

Companion viruses exploit the MS-DOS property that if two programs with the same name exist in a directory, the operating system will execute a COM file in preference to an EXE file.

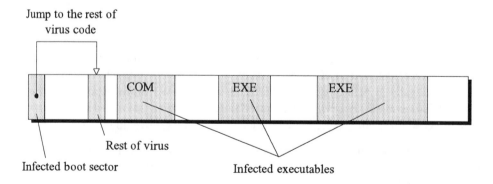

Fig. 3.5 - Disk infected with a multi-partite virus

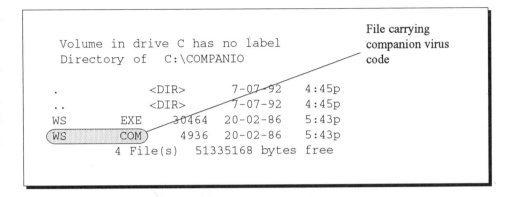

Fig. 3.6 - Companion virus infection

A companion virus creates a COM file with the same name as the EXE file it 'infects', storing its own virus code in the COM file. When a user types in the program name, the operating system executes the COM file, which executes the virus code and, in turn, loads and executes the EXE file. The virus makes **no change at all** to the contents of the 'infected' EXE file.

The directory listing in Fig. 3.6 shows an unsophisticated companion virus which has infected WS.EXE by creating WS.COM. More sophisticated companion viruses label the companion COM file with the DOS 'hidden' attribute, which means that they will not be shown in directory listings. This, however, is also a nail in the coffin of such viruses, since the DOS COPY command does not copy hidden files and the virus is thus denying itself the prime means of propagation: copying of executable files by users.

Companion viruses are spread through **any medium which can be used for storage or transmission of executable code** (but see above comment on hidden files). The virus will become active if one of its COM programs is executed.

It is unlikely that companion viruses will form a major threat in the future.

3.1.5 LINK VIRUSES

Link viruses work by linking the first cluster pointer of the directory entry of every executable file to a single cluster containing the virus code. The original number of the first cluster is saved in the unused part of the directory entry (Fig. 3.7).

Link viruses are spread through **any medium which can be used for storage or transmission of executable code**. A PC will become infected if an infected program is executed.

As of August 1992, the only link virus in the wild was *DIR II*, which first appeared in mid 1991 and has since become remarkably widespread.

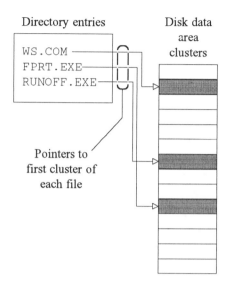

Fig. 3.7a - Directory entries in an uninfected system

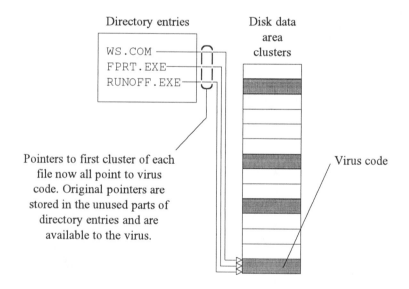

Fig. 3.7b - Directory entries in a system infected with a link virus

3.2 VIRUS BEHAVIOUR AFTER GAINING CONTROL

3.2.1 MEMORY-RESIDENT VIRUSES

Memory-resident viruses install themselves into memory as Terminate and Stay Resident (TSR) processes when they gain control. They will normally intercept one or more interrupts and infect other objects when certain conditions are fulfilled (e.g. when the user attempts to execute an application (*Cascade*) or when the user accesses a drive (*Brain*)). Switching the PC off will clear the virus from memory; warm bootstrapping with Ctrl-Alt-Del may not, as some viruses such as *Yale* intercept the Ctrl-Alt-Del interrupt and survive the warm boot.

3.2.2 NON-MEMORY-RESIDENT VIRUSES

Non-memory-resident viruses are active only when an infected application is executed. They execute their code completely at that stage and do not remain in memory. Other executables are generally infected only when an infected program is executed (e.g. *Vienna* or *Datacrime*).

Although this approach may seem less infectious than one used by memory-resident viruses, the infectiousness of these viruses is in practice just as high, if not higher, than that of the memory-resident viruses. They are also more difficult to spot, since they do not change the interrupt table or the amount of available memory, and their infectious behaviour can be more unpredictable.

3.2.3 HYBRIDS

Some viruses use a combination of these two methods. The *Typo* virus, for example, infects executables on invocation of an infected program, but also leaves a small TSR element in memory after infection. The TSR section contains the payload, while the non-resident portion of the virus contains the replication code. In other hybrid viruses these functions might be allocated differently.

3.3 VIRUS HIDING MECHANISMS

Viruses often place obstacles in the path of anyone trying to find or eradicate them. Two mechanisms are commonly used: encryption and interrupt interception.

3.3.1 ENCRYPTION

Encryption or scrambling of the virus code is used by some viruses in order to make them appear different in each infected application. This is designed to make the extraction of a fixed search pattern more difficult, since the majority of the virus code changes on every infection (Fig. 3.8). Before the virus code can be executed, it must be decrypted in order to become a meaningful sequence of instructions. The decryption routine **must be in**

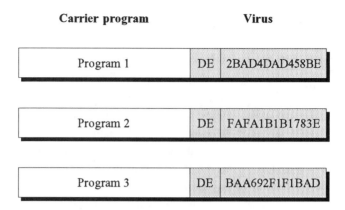

Fig. 3.8 Three programs infected with an identical encrypted virus

plaintext (unencrypted) form and it usually contains about ten or twenty bytes which are identical and common to every infected executable (Shown as 'DE' in Fig. 3.8). An encrypted virus will look identical only when it uses the same encryption key to encrypt its code.

Although encryption algorithms in current viruses are simple and the keys are straight-forward (*Cascade's* decryption routine is shown in Fig. 3.9), the possibilities for introducing complications are practically endless. For example, a virus can use two stages of encryption, where the key for encrypting the second stage is stored in an encrypted form in the first stage. Such 'refinements' make disassembly of the virus more difficult and even viruses encrypted using simple techniques can be tricky to disassemble.

One of the techniques increasingly commonly used by virus writers is to make the virus vary the decryption routine between infections. These viruses are known as polymorphic. Since there is no code which remains the same between infections, it is impossible to extract a fixed hexadecimal pattern. This somewhat complicates the search and an algorithmic approach has to be used; the virus scanner is told about a number of virus

```
          lea     si,[bx+start_of_virus]
          mov     sp,virus_length
again:    xor     [si],si          ; first xor
          xor     [si],sp          ; second xor
          inc     si
          dec     sp
          jnz     again            ; loop until finished
```

Fig. 3.9 - *Cascade* decryption routine

characteristics such as infective length, bytes which do not change between infections and so on, which are used to recognise virus-infected code.

The trend of writing polymorphic viruses seems to have been started by one Mark Washburn in the US with his 'experimental' virus *1260*. This was followed by a number of creations in the *V2Pn* series (*V2P2*, *V2P6* etc.), all of which were written as a direct challenge to anti-virus software manufacturers. It is interesting that Mark Washburn views himself as a 'good guy' who is helping anti-virus research.

A recent development in polymorphic viruses is the development of the *Mutation Engine* by a virus-writer (or possibly a group) calling him/itself Dark Avenger. This 'toolkit' allows a quick transformation of any normal virus into a polymorphic one, saving programming effort. Dark Avenger and his associates posted the object code of the *Mutation Engine* on a number of bulletin boards with detailed instruction on how it should be used. They even valiantly offer technical support to budding virus writers via a virus-exchange bulletin board in Sofia, Bulgaria. The document accompaning the toolkit states that it is copyright ©1991 CrazySoft, Inc and is written by Mad Maniac.

3.3.2 INTERRUPT INTERCEPTION: STEALTH VIRUSES

Interrupt interception can be used very successfully to hide the presence of a virus actively once it has gained control of the PC.

DOS applications use software interrupts to communicate with the operating system in a portable way. The jump addresses are stored in the interrupt table located at the beginning of memory (Fig. 3.10). This is set up by the operating system to point to the correct addresses depending of the version of DOS. When an application issues an interrupt, a jump occurs to a predetermined address. If a virus changes one or more of these addresses, any jumps to the operating system can be routed via the virus, which can then decide what to do with a particular request (Fig. 3.11). The fact that such modification of

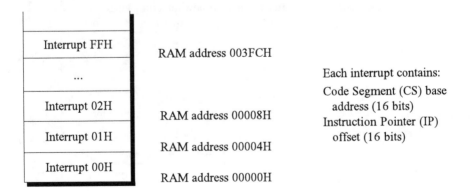

Fig. 3.10 Interrupt table

the interrupt table is possible has led to the emergence of 'stealth' viruses, which are characterised by a highly effective ability to hide themselves.

For example, if the *Brain* virus is active in memory and an application requests the operating system to read from disk the contents of the boot sector (the hiding place of *Brain*), the virus will return the contents of what the legitimate boot sector would contain, instead of the actual contents. *Brain* achieves this by modifying ('hooking itself into') the interrupt table.

Several other viruses use this stealth technique. For example, *4K* intercepts some 18 functions of the DOS interrupt 21H, including Find First Matching File (11H), Find Next Matching File (12H), Open File (3DH) and Close File (3EH). Amongst other things, the virus will subtract 4096 from any infected file length displayed by the DIR command. It goes much further: it will 'disinfect' any infected file if an application tries to read from it, only to reinfect it on closing the file. A virus scanner or a checksummer will therefore not discover *4K* in infected files if the virus is active in memory.

Joshi is another stealth virus which hides the contents of an infected boot sector by intercepting ROM BIOS disk services interrupt 13H and returning the contents of the original boot sector if a disk read is attempted. The virus also intercepts the keyboard interrupt 9H, traps Ctrl-Alt-Del (warm boot) and survives it. Correct anti-virus bootstrapping, which includes switching the power off and booting from a clean, write-protected floppy, has never been more important than today.

3.3.3 BINARY VIRUSES

Binary viruses are a special case of encrypted viruses. A virus carries the replicating code in full, but only half of the payload. Only when the 'other half' virus is encountered

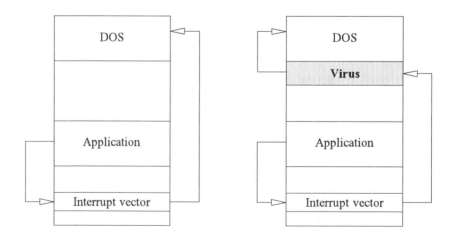

Fig. 3.11 Interrupt routing before and after the virus gains control

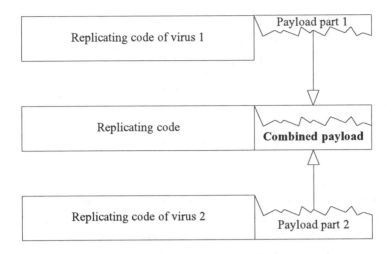

Fig. 3.12 Binary virus - two parts combining to get a meaningful payload

(which carries the other half of the payload), the combination of the two payloads produces meaningful code which can be executed (Fig. 3.12). The combining could be done by performing an exclusive-or (XOR) operation on the two halves. In a binary virus, the payload cannot be analysed unless the researcher has access to both halves of the virus.

Although the concept of binary viruses has been discussed by researchers, it has not been seen in any viruses to date. The only case in which this concept *may* have been incorporated is the *dBASE* virus. As part of the payload, the original virus contains the following sequence:

```
        CLI
        MOV     AX,3            ; Set count
LABEL:  MOV     CX,100H
        MOV     DX,0            ; Page 0 RAM
        MOV     DS,DX           ; Segment 0
        XOR     BX,BX           ; Offset 0
        PUSH    AX              ; Save the count
        INT     3H              ; ?
        INT     3H              ; ?
        POP     AX              ; Restore count
        INC     AX              ; Next
        CMP     AL,1AH          ; Reached 26 ?
        JL      LABEL           ; Go again
        ...                     ; Continue
```

This sequence does not do much *unless* either of the following happens:

1. An 'other half' virus changes the two INT 3H instructions (which assemble as 1 byte each = 2 bytes) into one INT 26H instruction (which assembles as 2 bytes)

2. An 'other half' virus changes the interrupt table so that interrupt 3H points to interrupt 26H

If either of the above happens, the payload becomes destructive. On triggering, the (modified) virus will overwrite the first 256 sectors of each drive from D to Z, using the Absolute Disk Write interrupt 26H.

The virus patterns for *dBASE* shown in Appendix G reflect the above possibility. The standard *dBASE* pattern is the one found in the seen and disassembled virus, while the *dBASE destroy* pattern is the pattern in the so far unseen (destructive) virus. Although this is one explanation for the *dBASE* mystery, other possibilities are that the seen version is the pre-release, non-destructive version, which could easily be modified into a destructive one, or alternatively that someone has 'disarmed' a copy of the destructive virus.

3.3.4 VIRUSES WHICH INFECT THE FIRST CLUSTER OF THE DATA AREA

This hiding technique has been discussed on a number of bulletin boards in Bulgaria. As of June 1992 no such viruses have appeared, but this technique could be used by virus writers in the future. It is based on copying the first cluster of the data area (which is the first cluster of the first file in the root directory) into an unused cluster, modifying the first root directory file entry to point to that cluster, and then copying the virus code into the first cluster of the data area. The hiding mechanism of such a virus is based on the fact that in older versions of DOS the system files are assumed by the bootstrap code to be stored in this location, and are loaded without reference to the normal directory/FAT mechanism, whereas most scanners will examine that file as a file, relying on DOS to open it and read it. Since DOS relies on information in the root directory, a scanner is not going to see the data loaded during bootstrapping.

This technique does not work under DOS 5 as the bootstrapping is performed differently.

3.3.5 SPARSE INFECTION: THE UNSCANNABLE VIRUS

There has been much speculation as to whether it is possible to write a virus which would not be detectable by scanners (see Chapter 7: Anti-virus software). A completely polymorphic virus which infects sparsely, seems to fit the bill.

Such a virus would assume that a common characteristic, such as the number of minutes in the file's time stamp being greater than 30, signifies that the file is infected. It would therefore only infect 50% of all files, leaving the other 50% untouched (the ones with minute stamp greater than 30). After infection it would set the time stamp value of the infected files to a value greater than 30. A scanner would not be able to discover its presence in infected files, other than labelling vast numbers of files as potentially infected (the ones with the minute stamp less than or equal to 30). And then somebody will write a virus which infects only if the number of minutes in the time stamp is *greater* than 30 ...

3.3.6 HIGH LEVEL LANGUAGE VIRUSES

Most viruses are written in assembly language. The main advantage for the virus author is that he can 'reach into the machine' to a much greater extent than is possible when using a high-level language. Furthermore, the code is smaller and more efficient, both of which contribute to increased difficulty in discovering the virus. However, high level languages do offer a number of advantages which favour virus spread.

Burger's *Computer Viruses - a High Tech Disease* contains a number of viruses written in Compiled Basic and Pascal. Recently a number of viruses have been discovered in the wild which were originally written in Turbo-Pascal and C. For example: *Jocker*, an overwriting virus from Poland, probably written in Pascal; *Kamikaze*, an overwriting virus from Bulgaria written in Turbo-Pascal; *Sentinel*, written in Turbo-Pascal; *TPworm*, a 'companion' virus written in C.

All of these viruses are large (between 4000 and 12000 bytes) and comparatively slow when executed. Their binary image depends not only on the compiler used to create them, but also on the state of various optimisation levels used during compilation. Supposing that there are some 20 C compilers for DOS in existence, and each offers 6 possible optimisations and/or memory models, a single piece of virus source code in a high level language could quite easily be transformed into 1280 different binary images. If only ten such viruses are written using polymorphic techniques (self-modifying and encrypting), virus scanners would soon start creaking under the strain.

Furthermore, the extraction of a reliable pattern is difficult in compiled viruses, since similar segments of code appear in other legitimate programs compiled with the same compiler. Excessive false positives invariably result if the pattern is not chosen extremely carefully.

3.4 VIRUS SIDE-EFFECTS

Virus side-effects (or the virus 'payload') are normally the first indication to the user that his PC is infected. Not surprisingly, they are also the part which is most interesting to the majority of users.

They are normally the easiest part of the virus to program. They are also the easiest part to **change** (see Section 5.4: Virus Mutations). There have been several examples of mutated viruses having had their side-effects completely changed from the original (e.g. *Cascade-format* and *Cascade*).

Virus side-effects range from annoyance (such as the bouncing ball in *Italian*) and data modification (like the *Dark Avenger* virus) to data destruction (*Michelangelo*). The side-effects are completely open to the imagination of the programmer. With the current practice to rely on backups against virus-caused damage to data, the most serious threat are viruses which cause gradual and random data corruption. By the time that a user realises that corruption has been taking place, all his backups could already be corrupted.

When the first viruses appeared, their side-effects were on the whole confined to annoyance, which prompted several people to treat **all** viruses as innocuous, and as dangerous as a pet cat. Unfortunately, recent viruses are more like hungry tigers; fine behind bars in a zoo, but rather less so in the wild.

4

VIRUS FACTS AND FICTION

But are they all horrid, are you sure they are all horrid?

Jane Austen, 'Northanger Abbey'

4.1 THE NUMBERS GAME

In August 1992 there were between 1500 and 2000 viruses known to the research community, of which only about 50 were causing real problems in the wild. Just like biological viruses, some computer viruses are more common than others. Their spread will depend on factors such as their type, the length of time in the wild, method of replication, amount of stealth employed etc.

Figs. 4.1 to 4.3 show the worldwide attack statistics reported to *Sophos* over three 6-month periods. Two virus characteristics seem to determine the spread of any particular virus: its capability to infect the boot sector and the age of the virus. For example, in the first 6 months of 1992, over 80% of virus infections were due to viruses which infect boot sectors (pure boot sector viruses and multi-partite viruses), while *Cascade* (a comparatively old parasitic virus) accounted for almost 7% of the infections. The older the virus, the more chance it has to spread. The wide spread of boot sector viruses is probably due to the fact that floppy disks are exchanged on a large scale, with PC users being unaware that non-system disks can carry a virus.

The increase in stealth, multi-partite viruses *Tequila* and *Spanish Telecom* from the second half of 1991 to the first half of 1992 should also be noted.

It is also interesting that in the first half of 1992 only 36 viruses were responsible for all the attacks reported to *Sophos*, despite the fact that there were some 1700 viruses known to the research community (see also Appendix G: Known IBM-PC viruses). Almost all of the reported cases involved a few PCs, but a number of large-scale attacks (100+ PCs) were also reported. These usually involved file servers and were in a majority of cases attributable to poor use of network security features (see Chapter 8: Viruses and Networks).

19 other viruses	28.2%
Joshi	4.2%
Yankee	5.1%
4K	5.1%
Jerusalem	5.1%
Vacsina	6.0%
Dark Avenger	8.6%
Cascade	8.6%
New Zealand	29.1%

Fig. 4.1 - Virus reports from 1st January 1991 to 30th June 1991 (117 reports)

19 other viruses	26.6%
Jerusalem	3.9%
Michelangelo	4.4%
Spanish Telecom	4.4%
Joshi	5.5%
Cascade	5.5%
Tequila	8.8%
Form	16.6%
New Zealand	24.3%

Fig. 4.2 - Virus reports from 1st July 1991 to 31st December 1991 (181 reports)

28 other viruses	25.8%
Joshi	2.4%
1575	2.6%
Michelangelo	4.1%
Spanish Telecom	5.6%
Cascade	6.8%
Tequila	10.0%
New Zealand	20.9%
Form	21.8%

Fig. 4.3 - Virus reports from 1st January 1992 to 30th June 1992 (340 reports)

4.1 HOW ARE VIRUS ATTACKS DISCOVERED

In the overwhelming majority of reported cases, users discover a virus when they first use anti-virus software.

Nevertheless, in a surprisingly large number of cases users discover a virus by observing something unusual. In one case the user was running a very large application which could just fit into the available memory. The alarm bells were triggered when that application failed to load (due to an infection by *4K*). In another instance, the user suspected a virus when a poem was displayed on his screen and subsequent attempts to access the hard disk proved futile. *Maltese Amoeba* was the culprit.

Security experts often find themselves in a situation when they have to distinguish between hardware malfunction and a real virus attack. As this more often than not happens over the telephone, the diagnosis is not easy. Depending on the user's 'virus-literacy', common PC problems may regularly be attributed to viruses. Indeed, some of the side-effects exhibited by viruses such as *Nomenklatura* closely resemble hardware failure and are very difficult to distinguish.

Most virus help-desk personnel develop a 'nose' as to what problems are likely to be due to hardware or software and to distinguish them from virus symptoms. One of the best indicators of a virus attack is the repetition of the same symptoms across several PCs of several makes and configurations, e.g. when every PC which is switched on fails (this actually happened on 6th March 1992 when about 100 PCs were switched on before a mass infection by *Michelangelo* was suspected).

Not all mass-reproduced symptoms are necessarily due to a virus. In one particular case a disk drive connector suffered from an intermittent fault, which caused intermittent data corruption. As a result, some programs on that PC became corrupted and stopped working. When copied to other PCs, exactly the same symptoms were observed, and a virus infections was suspected. It took a while to establish positively that no virus was involved.

4.2 VIRUSES AND THE CALENDAR

It is frequently the case that PC users become 'virus-aware' when a well-known date approaches, e.g. 6th March (*Michelangelo*) or any Friday which is also the 13th day of the month (*Jerusalem*). As more and more viruses appear, the 'virus calendar' gets fuller and fuller. Frequent 'advice' which is available in those circumstances is to advance the system clock by one day. One of the most ironic cases when such advice proved fatal, involved a PC user who advanced his clock on Thursday, 12th December 1991 in order to avoid Friday, 13th. He then forgot to set the clock back and switched on his PC on 5th March 1992, intending to set the date forward in order to avoid *Michelangelo*. This triggered the virus and he lost his hard disk.

Fig. 4.4 shows some of the viruses which trigger on particular dates and their side effects and further emphasizes the point that calendar watching is inadvisable. Combatting viruses is a day-in day-out job.

Virus name	Activation date	Side effect
5120	after 1 Jun 92	terminates infected programs
4K	22 Sept	hangs PC
Cascade	1 Oct-31 Dec 88	displays falling characters
Cascade Format	1 Oct-31 Dec not '93	formats disk
Casino	15 Jan, Apr, Aug	destroys FAT if game lost
Christmas Japan	25 Dec	displays message
ChristmasTree	19 Dec	displays message
Datacrime	13 Oct	formats disk/displays message
Dec24th	24 Dec	displays message
Durban	Sat 14	overwrites first 100 sectors
Faust	13th day of month	displays message, hangs PC
Form	18th day of month	produces key clicks
Frogs Alley	5th day of month	overwrites FAT and root directory
Hybrid	Fri 13 after '91	formats disk
Jerusalem	Fri 13	deletes programs when run
Joshi	5 Jan	displays message
July 13th	13 Jul	unknown
Kennedy	6Jun, 18Nov, 22Nov	displays message
Maltese Amoeba	1 Nov, 15 Mar	overwrites 120 sectors
Michelangelo	Mar 6	formats disk
Monxla	13th day of month	damages programs
PcVrsDs	Mon 23rd not '90	formats disk
Pretoria	Jun16	damages root directory
South African	Fri 13	deletes programs when run
Suriv	Apr 1	displays message
Taiwan	8th day of month	overwrites FAT
Tenbyte	1 Sep	corrupts data written to disk
Thursday 12	Thu 12	displays message
Traceback	28 Dec	displays falling characters
Violator	15 Aug	unknown
XA1	1 Apr	overwrites boot sector

Fig. 4.4 - Activation dates of some viruses

4.3 CAN VIRUSES CAUSE HARDWARE DAMAGE

This is a perennial question asked by PC users. The answer is yes, but it depends on the type and configuration of the hardware. For example, some graphics boards are prone to damage if programmed incorrectly, while setting the right byte in the bootstrap sector to the value 0 makes the hard disk drive unusable and moderately difficult for a layman to repair. On the other hand, the hardware design of standard PCs is such that it is impossible to damage individual components through software (unlike one of the early home PCs which could burn an on-board chip through bad programming).

One of the recent childish attempts to cause damage was found in a virus which stops memory refresh, which causes the loss of data in RAM, but no lasting damage.

4.4 MODEM VIRUS, CMOS VIRUS AND OTHER NONSENSE

From time to time (usually near 1st April of any year) news appear about one or other improbable form of virus structure and behaviour. Examples abound:

· Modem virus hoax which began in 1988 with a message from one 'Mike RoChenle' on a bulletin board which warned about a 'virus which distributes itself on the modem sub-carrier present in all modems operating at 2400 baud or more'.

· Mains virus hoax 1988, probably a parody of the modem virus, started by 'Robert Morris III' (Robert Morris was the author of the Internet worm, See Section 1.4.2: Internet Worm on Unix). This virus was supposed to ride on the 'powerline 60Hz subcarrier and attack virtually any computer system'.

· CMOS virus, the sighting of which is claimed from time to time by 'experts' who ought to know better. CMOS contains information on the configuration of a PC (usually about 40 bytes), but **no executable code**. As such, it can be affected by a virus, but not infected. Some confusion may arise from the fact that some portable PCs have the whole of RAM implemented in non-volatile CMOS technology which can, of course, become infected in the same way as the standard volatile RAM.

· Viruses invading washing machine controllers, nuclear missile controllers etc. There have been several reports of such 'viruses'. By definition, a closed environment such as the one present in almost all microcontrollers where there is no exchange of executable code, is not at risk from virus infections.

· A printer virus which is supposed to reside in the printer memory and jump back into the PC at the first opportune moment. A few reports referred to viruses residing in inkjet printer heads.

· Other barely believable cases, for example a report by ABC News in January 1992 that NSA laboratories at Fort George Meade in Maryland managed to implant a 'virus' into Iraqi mainframe computer which subsequently wreaked havoc on the Irai air defence network (*Virus Bulletin*, February 1992).

5

WHO WRITES VIRUSES?

Only the insane take themselves quite seriously.

Sir Thomas Beecham

5.1 VIRUS WRITERS' PROFILE

It is not easy to establish the origins of a virus, and it is rare to find any firm clues in the virus code. One notable exception is the *Brain* virus which has a name, address and telephone number embedded in the bootstrap sector (Fig. 5.1). *Brain* was written by the owners of the computer shop 'Brain Computer Services' in Lahore, Pakistan. Similarly, the *Tequila* virus contains the address of the authors (two teenage Swiss brothers).

It is very common for virus writers to hide their true identity under a pseudonym (*Dark Avenger, Betaboys, Rock Steady, Bad Guy* etc). Nevertheless, there are individuals who have publicly stated their involvement in virus writing, for example Mark Washburn, Patrick Toulme and Mark Ludwig, who quite openly participate in anti-virus conferences discuss virus-related subjects on commercial bulletin boards etc. Almost invariably they plead the right of free speech and seem convinced that their virus-writing efforts contribute to general anti-virus research.

The few such cases of known virus writers do not provide sufficient statistical evidence from which to draw a firm profile of a virus writer. It is nevertheless possible to identify a number of groups as potential (high likelihood) originators of viruses. It is also interesting to analyse their motivation from the psychiatric point of view.

```
000000   fa e9 4a 01 34 12 00 05    08 00 01 00 00 00 00 20    ..J.4... .......
000010   20 20 20 20 20 20 57 65    6c 63 6f 6d 65 20 74 6f          We lcome to
000020   20 74 68 65 20 44 75 6e    67 65 6f 6e 20 20 20 20    the Dun geon
000030   20 20 20 20 20 20 20 20    20 20 20 20 20 20 20 20
000040   20 20 20 20 20 20 20 20    20 20 20 20 20 20 20 20
000050   20 28 63 29 20 31 39 38    36 20 42 61 73 69 74 20     (c) 198 6 Basit
000060   26 20 41 6d 6a 61 64 20    28 70 76 74 29 20 4c 74    & Amjad  (pvt) Lt
000070   64 2e 20 20 20 20 20 20    20 20 20 20 20 20 20 20    d.
000080   20 42 52 41 49 4e 20 43    4f 4d 50 55 54 45 52 20     BRAIN C OMPUTER
000090   53 45 52 56 49 43 45 53    2e 2e 37 33 30 20 4e 49    SERVICES ..730 NI
0000a0   5a 41 4d 20 42 4c 4f 43    4b 20 41 4c 4c 41 4d 41    ZAM BLOC K ALLAMA
0000b0   20 49 51 42 41 4c 20 54    4f 57 4e 20 20 20 20 20    IQBAL T OWN
0000c0   20 20 20 20 20 20 20 20    20 20 20 4c 41 48 4f 52             LAHOR
0000d0   45 2d 50 41 4b 49 53 54    41 4e 2e 2e 50 48 4f 4e    E-PAKIST AN..PHON
0000e0   45 20 3a 34 33 30 37 39    31 2c 34 34 33 32 34 38    E :43079 1,443248
0000f0   2c 32 38 30 35 33 30 2e    20 20 20 20 20 20 20 20    ,280530.
000100   20 20 42 65 77 61 72 65    20 6f 66 20 74 68 69 73      Beware  of this
000110   20 56 49 52 55 53 2e 2e    2e 2e 2e 43 6f 6e 74 61     VIRUS.. ...Conta
000120   63 74 20 75 73 20 66 6f    72 20 76 61 63 63 69 6e    ct us fo r vaccin
000130   61 74 69 6f 6e 2e 2e 2e    2e 2e 2e 2e 2e 2e 2e 2e    ation... ........
000140   2e 2e 2e 2e 20 20 24 23    40 25 24 40 21 21 20 8c    .... $#@ %$@!! ..
000150   8e d8 8e d0 bc 00 f0 fb    a0 06 7c a2 09 7c 8b 0e    ........ .|..|..
000160   07 7c 89 0e 0a 7c e8 57    00 b9 05 00 bb 00 7e e8    .|...|.W ......~.
000170   2a 00 e8 4b 00 81 c3 00    02 e2 f4 a1 13 04 2d 07    *..K.... ......-.
000180   00 a3 13 04 b1 06 d3 e0    8e c0 be 00 7c bf 00 00    ........ ....|...
000190   b9 04 10 fc f3 a4 06 b8    00 02 50 cb 51 53 b9 04    ........ ..P.QS..
0001a0   00 51 8a 36 09 7c b2 00    8b 0e 0a 7c b8 01 02 cd    .Q.6.|.. ...|....
0001b0   13 73 09 b4 00 cd 13 59    e2 e7 cd 18 59 5b 59 c3    .s.....Y ....Y[Y.
0001c0   a0 0a 7c fe c0 a2 0a 7c    3c 0a 75 1a c6 06 0a 7c    ..|....| <.u....|
0001d0   01 a0 09 7c fe c0 a2 09    7c 3c 02 75 09 c6 06 09    ...|.... |<.u....
0001e0   7c 00 fe 06 0b 7c c3 00    00 00 00 32 e3 23 4d 59    |....|.. ...2.#MY
0001f0   f4 a1 82 bc c3 12 00 7e    12 cd 21 a2 3c 5f 0c 05    .......~ ..!.<_..
```

Fig. 5.1 - *Brain* virus bootstrap sector

5.1.1 HACKERS

Hackers are people analogous to drug addicts. They need their 'fix' and cannot leave the machine alone. Like addicts they seek novelty and new experiences. Writing a virus gives them this, but unlike addicts who get immediate relief after a fix, they are not usually present when the virus triggers and releases the payload.

5.1.2 FREAKS

This is an irresponsible subgroup of hackers, in the same way that while some drug addicts remain reasonably responsible (and use sterile needles), others (psychopaths) become irresponsible (and share needles). Freaks have serious social adjustment problems and often bear general, unspecified grudges against society. They have no sense of responsibility or remorse about what they do, and are prepared to exploit others in order to achieve their aims.

There are several reasons why freaks write viruses: Some do it for 'fun', others for money. Some of them may be mentally distressed, sick of their life or family and want to 'hit out'. The mentality of the freak virus writer is not unlike that of a person who leaves a poisoned jar of baby-food on a supermarket shelf. He delivers his potion, leaves and is untraced, and in his absence the victim falls.

Freaks may sometimes include a message in the virus e.g. 'Your PC is now Stoned!' and 'LEGALISE MARIJUANA' in the *New Zealand* virus, and 'Bloody! Jun. 4, 1989' in *Beijing*, which is probably a reference to the Tianamen Square massacre. There may be some overlap between freaks and politically motivated terrorists.

5.1.3 UNIVERSITY STUDENTS

Most universities offer free, often uncontrolled, computer facilities to students. Illegal software copying is widespread, and it is no coincidence that most campuses have had problems with large-scale virus outbreaks. These are not necessarily caused by locally developed viruses. The technical ability necessary to write a virus is however within the reach of a first-year computer science student, who may see such a project as an intellectual challenge.

Students are not only a potential source of PC viruses, but also a potential source of malicious code for minicomputers and mainframes. Whereas average members of the public can buy a cheap PC comparatively easily, they cannot (yet) buy an IBM System 370 or a DEC VAX. Most students have access to minis and mainframes, and experience so far has shown that a large proportion of malicious code written for those computers (mainly worms) has its origins in academia.

5.1.4 EMPLOYEES

Companies normally perceive disgruntled employees as a major security risk. Although a computer-literate employee could write a virus from scratch, it is more likely that he would either implant an existing virus into his organisation's PCs or modify a virus, perhaps to target his organisation in a specific way.

Readiness to cause damage by programming has already been shown by numerous cases of logic bombs placed by disgruntled employees into computer systems.

The motive for an employee writing and/or implanting a virus is often vindictiveness. There is, however, not a great deal of difference between revenge and extortion. The disgruntled employee may harbour a genuine grievance. The extortionist's desire for revenge is deeper (possibly subconscious) and he himself may not understand it. Vindictiveness may accompany a strong sense of morality or moral duty making a disgruntled employee, in some peoples' eyes (above all his own), a freedom fighter (cf. 'Terrorist Organisations').

5.1.5 COMPUTER CLUBS

Some computer clubs have been very active in providing their members with information on how to write viruses. For example the *Chaos Computer Club* (CCC) in Hamburg, West Germany, has produced a 'Virus Construction Set' for the Atari ST, which allows the construction of customised viruses and the selection of virus effects from a menu. A much less sophisticated tool has appeared for IBM PCs (*VCS*) and was probably written by the members of the same organisation.

Other clubs have a history of creating viruses. The *Swiss Crackers Association* (SCA), for example, released a virus for the Amiga which displays

```
Something wonderful has happened. Your Amiga is alive...
```

Members of clubs usually have shared values and ideals. It is quite possible that *real* troublemakers will not join computer clubs; clubs are for the insecure, who gain a sense of security through sharing.

5.1.6 TERRORIST ORGANISATIONS

Evidence that terrorist organisations are involved in virus-writing is scarce. Nevertheless, organisations such as the Italian Red Brigades specifically include destruction of computer systems as an objective in their manifestos. This could be done by means other than the traditional use of explosives.

It has been asserted that the *Jerusalem* virus was written by sympathisers of the PLO, but several authoritative researchers dispute this. The only evidence linking the virus with the PLO is the trigger date (Friday 13th), which coincided with the last day of the existence of the Palestinian state. *Jerusalem-IRA* is a mutation which contains a long list of encrypted names, together with texts such as '.. died for Ireland' and '.. is still a political hostage'.

Terrorists are fanatics, for whom nothing else matters. They may have been indoctrinated from an early age and are loyal to a group which holds them (in return) in very high regard. They are, in their own eyes, modern-day martyrs.

5.2 DISSECTION OF A CAPTURED VIRUS

Once a virus has been discovered, a user's first instinct is often to eradicate all occurrences of it. However, one should always endeavour to 'capture' a virus sample for analysis, as this can be helpful to other sites infected with the same virus.

Even if the virus is not completely analysed immediately, a hexadecimal pattern can often be extracted in a comparatively short time, which helps to detect occurrences of the same virus elsewhere. Full analysis of a virus will invariably involve its full disassembly, i.e. reverse engineering its binary code into commented and understood source code.

5.2.1 VIRUS DISASSEMBLY

Sometimes virus disassembly can be simplified by commercially available disassemblers such as SOURCER (V Communications), but in many cases the very best tool is DEBUG, a powerful utility supplied as a part of DOS. DEBUG is comparatively simple to use and has a number of functions which make it suitable for the job. It can read disk sectors and files, disassemble areas of memory and single-step through a program.

Disassembling a virus is an iterative process which includes discovering first which parts of the virus are data areas (and thus not to be disassembled) and which are instructions. Once that has been done, the output of DEBUG can be redirected to a file which will contain the disassembled virus. Take as an example a hypothetical simple virus in the file VIR.COM, which has been analysed with DEBUG and which has a JMP 110H instruction as the first 3 bytes, followed by 13 bytes of data, followed by code from 110H to 432H. It is useful to build up the sequence of DEBUG commands in a file, to avoid re-typing them continuously. The file INSTR could contain the following DEBUG instructions:

```
U 100 102 ; Disassemble locations 100 to 102
D 103 10F ; Dump locations 103 10F
U 110 432 ; Disassemble locations 110 to 432
Q         ; Quit
```

DEBUG would then be invoked with the command

```
DEBUG VIR.COM <INSTR >VIR.ASM
```

which instructs it to read input from the file INSTR and output to file VIR.ASM which will contain the disassembly of VIR.COM.

U 100 102 will disassemble the first 3 bytes, D 103 10F will 'dump' 13 bytes of data in hexadecimal, while U 110 432 will disassemble instructions between addresses 110 and 432 Hex.

Disassembly of boot sector viruses can be slightly more complicated, as they normally occupy more sectors than just the boot sector. The boot sector has to be analysed first in order to discover which other sectors the virus uses. The principle of redirecting DEBUG input and output can be used in the same way as for parasitic viruses.

For example, to load the boot sector of drive A (drive 0) into memory, use the DEBUG instruction

```
L CS:100 0 0 1
```

This will load the contents of the boot sector into memory starting at location 100 relative to the code segment (CS).

If a virus uses disk areas not accessible by DEBUG (for example the master boot sector in *New Zealand*), the best approach is to write a small assembly language program (using DEBUG) to issue the appropriate BIOS interrupt(s) and read in the disk area in question. This can be written out to a file (using DEBUG again), or analysed directly. The program shown in Fig. 5.2 entered into DEBUG with the A (Assemble) command starting at location 100 will read the hard disk master boot sector into memory by using the BIOS interrupt 13H, service 02. This service requires that ES:BX points to the memory location where the contents of the sector will be stored (in this example ES is set to the same value as DS) and BX is set to 800H in the current data segment.

```
MOV     AX,DS
MOV     ES,AX    ; Set ES
MOV     AX,0201  ; Service 02H, 1 sector
MOV     CX,0001  ; Track 0, sector 1
MOV     DX,0080  ; Head 0, drive 80
MOV     BX,0800  ; Set in combination with ES
INT     13       ; BIOS
JMP     10E      ; Halt here
```

Fig. 5.2 - Assembly program which reads the master boot sector of the first hard disk

Typing G 10E will execute the program, placing the breakpoint at location 10E (JMP 10E). Location DS:0800 can now be either Dumped or Unassembled (D 0800 or U 0800).

An alternative method of reading in boot sector viruses for disassembly is to use a disk editing tool such as the *Norton Utilities* or *PC Tools* and copy the contents of the required object into a DOS file. The contents of the file can then be loaded into DEBUG for analysis.

Encrypted viruses present a slightly greater challenge to the researcher, as they have to be decrypted before being disassembled. This is sometimes quite tricky, since the virus writer may have used anti-DEBUG measures. Taking *Cascade* as an example, the decryption routine makes use of the Stack Pointer (SP). If the DEBUG breakpoint facility is used, the stack pointer must be valid and have at least 6 bytes available. Likewise, the target address will be modified by DEBUG to cause an INT 3H (one byte CC Hex instruction will be inserted there). *Cascade* uses SP, making it more difficult to use the breakpoint facility. Placing a breakpoint in the first encrypted instruction does not work, since the decryption routine in *Cascade* will decrypt the INT 3H instruction, producing a garbage byte. Analysing an encrypted virus is guaranteed to make one familiar with DEBUG.

Once the disassembled virus has been written out to a file (like VIR.ASM in the above example) the real fun begins. Analysis of the assembly code will reveal how the virus works, what it does and how it propagates. One should normally have available good PC documentation, which includes lists of interrupts (the *New Peter Norton Programmer's Guide to the IBM PC & PS/2* or *The MS-DOS Encyclopedia* are suitable). One then works one's way painstakingly through the disassembly, documenting instructions, interrupts and memory locations. The picture will soon start to emerge. The replicating part of the virus will be isolated as well as its payload. Any payload trigger conditions should be analysed very carefully, as these are easy to misinterpret (Does it trigger on 12th or 13th day of the month? Is it 12 decimal or 12 hexadecimal i.e. the 18th day?).

Once the disassembly has been finished (or even before doing it) one can usually extract a hexadecimal pattern which can be used to search for the virus. 16 bytes are normally sufficient, provided that the pattern is chosen carefully so that it represents a fairly unique set of instructions, unlikely to be found in other executables. Treat the disassembly as a confidential document and do not distribute it carelessly.

5.3 FORENSIC EVIDENCE

Every virus contains forensic evidence which can be used to trace its origin. Is it a derivative of another virus? Does it contain any interesting messages? Does it use a new replicating technique? Which software tools were used to write it?

5.3.1 WHICH ASSEMBLER?

There are different ways of assembling 8086 family instructions, which produce identical results when executed. For example

```
XCHG  BX,AX
```

could be assembled as 93 Hex, 87D8 Hex or 87C3 Hex. The result of the execution would be the same.

For example, when the *Yale* virus was analysed, it was discovered that it had been assembled with the A86 assembler and not Microsoft's MASM.

5.3.2 ILLEGAL INSTRUCTIONS

Some viruses contain instructions which are either not documented or not allowed by the target processor. Such instructions may execute correctly on the 8086 family processors, but will be trapped as illegal by the 80286 or 80386 processors.

There are several examples of this. The *Italian* virus uses the instruction

```
MOV CS,AX
```

(8EC8 Hex), which is executed properly by the 8086 processor, but trapped as an illegal instruction on 80286 and 80386 processors. Similarly, *Yale* uses the instruction

```
POP CS
```

(0F Hex), which executes correctly on an 8086, but is trapped as illegal on 80286 and 80386 processors.

5.3.3 PROGRAMMING STYLE

Faced with the same programming task, ten programmers will program it in ten different ways. This is especially true in assembly language, in which most PC viruses are written. PUSHing registers in a particular order onto the stack, using SHORT in JMP forward instructions, and other such constructs can all form a distinctive 'handwriting' of a programmer. Although this is difficult to quantify, looking at several programs written by the same person will give the researcher a feeling of *deja vu.*

Some time ago there was a debate on one of the bulletin boards as to whether the *dBASE* and *Typo* viruses were written by the same person. The programming style is certainly very similar; for example both viruses use an identical but unusual method to transfer control to the original program:

```
MOV AX,100H
JMP AX
```

There are also notable differences, such as the code used to modify interrupt 21H. The *dBASE* virus is 'well behaved' and uses DOS INT 21H functions 35H and 25H, whereas *Typo* writes directly to memory.

Making judgements about programming style requires experience in the programming language concerned.

5.3.4 LANGUAGE AND SPELLING

Viruses often have messages incorporated in the code and one can get strong clues to the country of origin of a virus by looking at the language (English, French, Icelandic), spelling (American-British), dates (Month-Day-Year or Day-Month-Year), ways of expressing oneself and so on.

For example, *Datacrime* virus contains the statement

```
RELEASED 1 MARCH 1989
```

This was almost certainly not written by an American (who would have put 'MARCH 1, 1989') and quite probably not by a Briton either (who would have most likely written it as '1ST MARCH 1989'). An English-speaking European is a likely culprit. As another example, the *Fu Manchu* virus insults four politicians (Thatcher, Reagan, Botha and Waldheim). Calling someone 'a c***' is typically British and not used often in the USA. Another clue is offered by the positioning of the relevant strings within the virus. The Thatcher insult comes first, before Reagan, Botha or Waldheim. Would an American do that? Probably not.

5.3.5 PLACE AND TIME OF FIRST DETECTION

Place and time of first detection of a virus can offer powerful clues as to its origins. This was how the *Italian* virus was tracked to the Polytechnic of Turin and *Jerusalem* to the Hebrew University in Jerusalem.

The speed of virus spread is usually much slower than most people expect. This means that the logging of occurrences is important, even with a significant margin of error in reporting the time of discovery. The place of discovery is more difficult to get wrong and can also be used in plotting the progress of a virus.

Electronic communications are making the plotting of the virus spread more difficult, since a user can contract a virus from a program downloaded from bulletin boards one mile away or 10,000 miles away equally easily. This is more common in the case of parasitic viruses than boot sector viruses, but the emergence of 'droppers' and multi-partite viruses (see Section 3.1: Virus Types) has made the spread of boot sector infections much faster.

5.3.6 ANCESTORS

Sometimes it is possible to determine the predecessors of a virus, since the authors have copied the majority of the code to produce a new virus (as was the case with *Fu Manchu*, which is a derivative of *Jerusalem*, or *Jerusalem* itself, which is a final version of a succession of viruses starting with *Suriv 1.01* and continuing with *Suriv 2.01* and *Suriv 3.00*). The author(s) of the series even preserved 'backward compatibility', so that *Jerusalem* does not infect files already infected with *Suriv 1.01, Suriv 2.01* or *Suriv 3.00*. The author of *Fu Manchu* (almost certainly a different person) did not have to (or want to) support previous virus releases and this backward compatibility is absent from the *Fu Manchu*.

5.4 VIRUS MUTATIONS

Virus mutations occur when a captured virus is modified in some way. This is done by intentional assembly programming and is quite distinct from mutations of biological viruses, which occur by chance. Virus mutations are a major problem for anybody involved in anti-virus research since a complete virus analysis has to be performed on every mutation, multiplying the efforts many-fold.

Mutating existing viruses seems to have become a favourite pastime for the would-be virus writers not blessed with sufficient intellect to write a virus from scratch. They realise that their activities put anti-virus software producers to immense research and sample-gathering effort, and they seem to revel in this. Comments found on various bulletin boards testify to that (see Fig. 5.3).

5.4.1 CHANGING VIRUS SIDE-EFFECTS

A typical virus has some 500 to 1000 instructions, most of which form the self-replicating mechanism. Virus side-effects normally occupy only a small part of a virus, and are quite easy to change. It is relatively easy even for a mediocre programmer to modify an existing virus. The *New Zealand* virus has some 50 mutations, most of which involve simple changes to the original 'Your PC is now Stoned!' message.

It is worth noting that **the complete destruction of data on the hard disk can be programmed in only 5 assembler instructions** and that modifying a known virus to do this can be done in a few minutes using DEBUG.

5.4.2 VIRUS 'IMPROVEMENTS'

There are several examples of improvements and corrections made to viruses. The *Cascade* virus in its original form has an infective length of 1701 bytes. It also exists in a version which has an infective length of 1704 bytes, which is a consequence of removing some superfluous branch instructions and introducing segment overrides. Whether that was done by the person who wrote the original is not known. The *New Zealand* virus exists in two main versions, where the second is a reorganised and tidied-up version of the first.

5.4.3 MUTATIONS TO FOOL PATTERN-CHECKING PROGRAMS

Virus scanning software usually relies on searching for a pattern known to exist within a virus. If a maliciously inclined person wanted to release a version of the virus which would not be recognised by the pattern checker, he could either change the order of instructions which are not order-dependent or implement the same effect using different instructions.

For example

```
MOV  AX,7F00H
MOV  BX,0
```

within a virus could be switched around to read

```
MOV  BX,0
MOV  AX,7F00H
```

Any pattern checker relying on the pattern produced by the first sequence of instructions (B800 7FBB 0000) would not recognise the mutated sequence (BB00 00B8 007F).

```
; -*-*-*-*-*-*-*-*-*-*-*-*-*-*-*-*-*-*-*-*-*-*-*-*-*-*-*-*-*-*-*-*-*-*-
;                   Parasite Virus Version 1.0
; October 1991
;                       Written by --*> Rock Steady <*--
;                      [NukE] Head Programmer
;     Copy-ya-right (c) 1991 [NukE] InterNat'nl Software Development
;
; Virus NOTES: It's here `Parasite` Virus. And UNDETECTABLE as of the
; October 1991 from McAfee ScanV82  This virus is a Branch from the
;  Sicilain Mob Ia I made! However this baby is fucken DANGEROUS!!!
; -*-*-*-*-*-*-*-*-*-*-*-*-*-*-*-*-*-*-*-*-*-*-*-*-*-*-*-*-*-*-*-*-*-*-
; VIRUS: Well this Virus InFects Only *.COM and the COMMAND.COM. One thing
;        about this Virus is that On MONDAYS it wipes out the BOOT,FAT,DIR
;        sectors from you C: Drive! What I like to call "Bloody Mondays"
;        So it Wipes Drive C: and then Displays a Message!
;        Other than Mondays the virus copies itself to as Many files it
;        can find thru the PATH from DOS and searching for Sub-Directories
;        With-in those Dos PATHs... Or if it can't find a PATH well then it
;        Starts at the ROOT dir and works thru the drive... 70% of the time
;        the virus will just spread and copy itself. 20% of the time the
;        virus will Make "Machine Gun Noices" in the PC speaker then
;        displaying my message and then continues to infect files...
;        FINALLY the last 10% of the time the virus will Re-Boot the system!
```

```
;          Aarrggghh..So the "Average" Lamo user will know FAST something is
;          fucking his system... and the BEST part is that SCAN can't find this
;          virus!!! So the user better "TRY" to get rid of it before Monday!!!
;          hehe...Anyways I put a "NICE" message in he virus CODES!!! READ IT!!!
;       Take Pctools or Norton Utilities and VIEW the Virus and read my
;          handy message at the end of the virus!!!
;_-*-*-*-*-*-*-*-*-*-*-*-*-*-*-*-*-*-*-*-*-*-*-*-*-*-*-*-*-*-*-*-*-*-*-*-*-*-
;                          Rock Steady's Notes
; Contact me if you can...Thru any of the [NukE] Site All over the WorlD!
; Basically in MonTreal (World Head Base) , other Montreal SiTes, Texas,
; California, Britsh Columbia!
; Tell me your views on the virus... and help spread my Latest Viruses!!!
;_-*-*-*-*-*-*-*-*-*-*-*-*-*-*-*-*-*-*-*-*-*-*-*-*-*-*-*-*-*-*-*-*-*-*-*-*-
; BTW: I'm not responsible for the Damage my virus "May" create! Because I
; DON'T SPREAD THEM!!! ALL YOU LAMERS DO!!! I just create them!
; ~~~~~                          - PeAcE -
;                          Rock Steady
;_-*-*-*-*-*-*-*-*-*-*-*-*-*-*-*-*-*-*-*-*-*-*-*-*-*-*-*-*-*-*-*-*-*-*-*-*-
  -*-*-*-*-*-*-*-*-*-*-*-*-*-*-*-*-*-*-*-*-*-*-*-*-*-*-*-*-*-*-*-*-*-*-
*-              - ParaSite Virus IIB  -                          -*
-*            - Programmed by: Rock Steady  -                    *-
*-              - Completed December 8th  -                      -*
-*-*-*-*-*-*-*-*-*-*-*-*-*-*-*-*-*-*-*-*-*-*-*-*-*-*-*-*-*-*-*-
*-    Length 909 Bytes          Undetectable from SCANV85-       -*
-*                                                               *-
*- FEATURES: It's SMALL!!! It lost about 300 Bytes from the orignal  -*
-*    ParaSite. All Text were removed, but I did leave a header on the  *-
*-    Virus. Anyhow it works about the same as the first! Meaning it   -*
-*    will infect all COMs 70% and 20% play machine gun noices and then *-
*-    10% will reboot the system! And on MONDAYS BOOM! You get your FAT -*
-*    Get formated on your hard Dirve C:! ooops!                    *-
*-                                                                  -*
-*  IMPROVEMENTS: I scambled several lines that would of made it a    *-
*-    clone to the FIRST ParaSite! Meaning if SCAN detect ParaSite    -*
-*    I it will NOT Detect ParaSite II! Because on the Bytes which    *-
*-    were scrambled all over the virus! And I improved a FAST and    -*
-*    BETTER way of infection. The Virus will NOW ALWAYS TRY TO INFECT*-
*-    COMMAND.COM! Anytime it is activated it will infect a COM and   -*
-*    THEN CHECK TO SEE that COMMAND.COM is infected! if not it will  *-
*-    be infected! So even after being cleaned out, if the user forgets*
-*    JUST ONE FILE it will infect COMMAND.COM and boom the whole     *-
*-    procedure starts AGAIN! even if files are HIDDEN or READ ONLY   -*
-*    they will be infected!!! And dates are not changed! And NO      *-
*-    MEMORY is taken up! the file will just increase by a mere 907   -*
-*    Bytes... Anyhow enjoy!                                         *-
*-*-*-*-*-*-*-*-*-*-*-*-*-*-*-*-*-*-*-*-*-*-*-*-*-*-*-*-*-*-*-*-*-*-
-*              Comming Soon in a PC near you...                  *-
*-         ~~~~~~~~~~~~~~~~~~~~~~~~~~~~~~~~~~~~                    -*
*- AMILIA Virus (A .COM & .EXE & COMMAND.COM infector, Will)      -*
-*  ~~~~~~         (be a TSR Virus! Deticated to no other but)    *-
*-              (my Girl... She will hurt you so don't fuck)      -*
-*              (with her... Yeah it will format the FAT or)      *-
*-              (and create LOTS of bad shit...)                  -*
-*              (Expected Release Decemeber 24th, 1991)           *-
*-*-*-*-*-*-*-*-*-*-*-*-*-*-*-*-*-*-*-*-*-*-*-*-*-*-*-*-*-*-*-*-*-*-
-*              Hope you enjoy all my Viriis New & Old...         *-
*-         Contact me in any NuKE Site BBS for any comments       -*
-*              Or just to chat...                                *-
*-                                                                -*
-*                    Rock Steady                                 *-
*-                    -PeAcE-                                     -*
-*-*-*-*-*-*-*-*-*-*-*-*-*-*-*-*-*-*-*-*-*-*-*-*-*-*-*-*-*-*-*-*-*-
```

Fig. 5.3 - Sample text pulled down from a hackers' bulletin board

A significantly large number of individuals seem to be engaged in doing exactly that. Reverse-engineering a virus scanning program reveals the patterns for which the scanner is looking. Once that is known, it is easy to modify the virus so that the scanner does not detect it and release it into the wild.

5.4.4 NEW VIRUSES

Sometimes the mutations of an existing virus will be so extensive that the new virus bears little resemblance to the original. Hex patterns extracted from the original are unlikely to be present in the new virus. *Fu Manchu* is, for example, such an extensive mutation of *Jerusalem*, that it is classed as a new virus. *Vienna*, which is probably the most extensively mutated virus of all, has several 'sons' which are known under different names.

5.5 VIRUS EXCHANGE BULLETIN BOARDS

Many hackers, freaks and other individuals engaged in computer-related misdeeds (such as virus writing), share and exchange information via bulletin boards. This has been a contributory factor for many PC users to regard **all** bulletin boards with great suspicion, which in most cases is not justified.

Virus writing and virus spread is certainly greatly helped by the wide availability of certain bulletin boards operated by individuals or small groups, which often carry discussions on virus techniques and provide virus samples. Furthermore, specialised 'virus exchange' bulletin boards exist which either support a particular virus product (e.g. *Dark Avenger's* bulletin board in Sofia supporting the *Mutation Engine*, or the *Hell Pit* board in California supporting the *Virus Creation Laboratory*) or which operate on the principle that one must *upload* a new virus in order to be allowed to *download* the whole collection.

Although the police in several countries have tried to close down virus exchange bulletin boards, this has so far been unsuccessful for a variety of reasons, which range from ineffective or non-existent legislation to the difficulty in obtaining intelligence on the exact bulletin board activity.

6

ANTI-VIRUS PROCEDURES - FIVE COUNTERMEASURES

Put your trust in God, my boys, and keep your powder dry.

Valentine Blacker (1778-1823)

The fight against viruses involves the application of five countermeasures: **Preparation**, **Prevention**, **Detection**, **Containment** and **Recovery**. This 5-step approach can be applied to most security problems; for example, when trying to protect against fire, one should:

- **Prepare** for the possibility by purchasing and maintaining fire extinguishers, training the staff etc.

- **Prevent** the fire from breaking out by minimising the use of naked flames, using non-flammable materials etc.

- **Detect** the fire as early as possible by installing fire detectors, fire alarms etc.

- **Contain** any outbreak by making sure that fire doors are closed, using fire extinguishers etc.

- **Recover** from the effects of the fire by restoring the functioning of the affected part of the organisation

6.1 PREPARATION

The following subsections outline what should be done **before** a virus attack occurs.

6.1.1 REGULAR AND SOUND BACKUPS

It is important that backups of storage media are available. This is not only important in case of an attack by a destructive virus, but also in the case of any other failure of a storage device. In case of data loss, the system can be restored as efficiently as possible. As part of the backup procedure, the master disks for all software (including the operating system) should be write-protected and stored in a place such as a fireproof safe. This will enable a speedy restoration of any infected executables.

The backups should be **sound**, which means that there is little point in doing them **unless the integrity of data is known to be intact at the time of doing the backup.** They should also be tested at regular intervals by performing complete restorations of the system to ensure that the data *can* actually be restored.

It should be borne in mind that some viruses such as *Dark Avenger* and *Nomenklatura* gradually corrupt data stored on disks. If an infection is not noticed for an extended period of time and backup media are reused, a situation can occur in which all copies of one or more files become corrupt and not restorable. The common strategy of reusing 3 sets of media cyclically is **not** an ideal backup strategy. Media should be regularly archived, i.e. stored in a safe place and not reused. The frequency of archiving will depend on the type of data held on the PC; obviously, higher frequency requires more media storage.

6.1.2 WRITE-PROTECTED SYSTEM FLOPPY DISK

A write-protected system floppy disk should be prepared in advance and contain all system files plus AUTOEXEC.BAT, CONFIG.SYS and any other system files or device drivers such as ANSI.SYS. Note that CONFIG.SYS normally refers to other files which are loaded into memory before the system is started, using statements such as 'DEVICE=filename'. **All these files should be copied onto the floppy disk**, and CONFIG.SYS on the floppy should be modified, if necessary, to ensure that it refers to the files on the floppy disk, rather than the original copies on the hard disk.

If a computer becomes infected, this disk can be used to bootstrap the computer cleanly. This will ensure that the computer can be examined through a 'clean' operating system, not giving the virus the chance to gain control and employ hiding techniques such as interrupt interception (see Section 3.3: Virus Hiding Mechanisms).

This system disk **must be write-protected;** this is a hardware protection against the modification of any information on the disk (see Section 6.4.3: Write-protect Tabs). No virus, or for that matter, any software, can write to a write-protected floppy disk on IBM-PCs and compatibles.

6.1.3 CONTINGENCY PLAN

This plan, which will be put into action in case of a virus attack, is usually part of the overall organisational security contingency plan and should include information on the following topics:

· People within the organisation responsible for dealing with the attack and their deputies

· Consultant(s) outside the organisation who can be called in to help deal with the attack

· Exact procedures for isolating infected disks, PCs and networks

· Public Relations procedures to prevent unauthorised leaks about the attack spreading outside the organisation

6.2 PREVENTION

The need to communicate introduces a potential virus entry path into any secure environment. Application software has to be purchased or updated, new operating systems installed, disks interchanged. The higher the volume of inbound traffic, the more opportunity a virus has of entering the environment.

The suppliers of executable code are potentially the most prolific distributors of a virus. Most users assume that software received from reputable companies is virus-free and any anti-virus barriers will promptly be raised when such an executable arrives on the doorstep. Fortunately, most software companies do realise their potential as sources of virus infection and take appropriate countermeasures.

Practical techniques to prevent virus entry into an organisation include: **creating user awareness**, implementing **hygiene rules**, using **access control**, providing a **'dirty' PC** and providing a **quarantine PC**.

6.2.1 CREATING USER AWARENESS

Creating user awareness is one of the most important factors within an effective virus prevention policy. Users must be made aware that execution of unauthorised software (such as demonstration disks and games) can lead to virus penetration and consequent losses to the organisation.

The problems are similar to those faced by the Government in persuading drug addicts not to share needles. While most computer users **do** behave sensibly and obey the rules, there will always be some who go on playing illegally-copied games and other software on company computers and exposing the whole organisation to risk. As the AIDS disk scare showed, a number of people are happy to install **anything** on their PC, showing a blind trust in the creators of any software (see Section 1.1.3: The AIDS Disk Through the Post).

Strengthening awareness is a matter of commonsense: measures include the use of leaflets, posters, virus demonstrations, presentations, showing educational virus videos and so on.

6.2.2 HYGIENE RULES

The observance of **hygiene** rules is by far the most effective way of preventing a virus attack.

Every executable item which is to run on a computer should be treated with suspicion. A set of rules should be designed to counteract the virus infiltration routes and methods outlined in Section 2.4 and could include the following:

· Do not use pirated software. The practice is not only illegal in most countries but also carries a high risk of virus infection.

· Do not use software 'pulled down' from bulletin boards. A plethora of bulletin boards offer free software for downloading, but in most cases little checking is done on these programs and their origins. Their potential for carrying a virus is high.

· Do not use shareware. A copy of the shareware program you get may be the 10th or the 50th copy and the risk of the program picking up a virus before it has reached you is significant.

· Do not use public domain software. Problems due to its distribution and the subsequent risk from viruses are similar to shareware.

· Be careful when bringing in disks from home to your place of work. Does anybody else use your home PC when you are not there? This is currently a major cause of virus infections in a commercial environment.

· Do not use programs supplied by computer magazines. They are not only potential virus carriers, but due to their often poor quality, can also cause unexplained crashes, conflicts and other problems.

· Beware of diagnostic software used by service engineers. Ask them if they use anti-virus software. Scan their disks for known viruses before allowing them to be used.

· Use only programs from reputable manufacturers. A reputable manufacturer will implement anti-virus security procedures in order to ensure that its software is shipped virus-free. **Software should be supplied on permanently write-protected disks**, which greatly decreases the chances of a disk becoming infected after it has left the manufacturer's premises. Shrink-wrapping the software or placing the software in a sealed envelope should ensure that the purchaser is the first person to use that copy of the original disk. There have, nevertheless, been cases of dealers tampering with shrink-wrapped software.

6.2.3 ACCESS CONTROL

Access control products can be deployed very effectively to prevent unauthorised use of computer resources, thereby decreasing the likelihood of virus infection. There is a wide variety of access control products available, ranging from the very secure to the completely useless. Complex products are not necessarily the most secure: used judiciously, good virus protection can be obtained even from the simplest products.

Note that it is **not** possible to guarantee the prevention of master boot sector viruses by using an access control product implemented purely in software, since the virus gains control **before** the access control package.

6.2.4 DIRTY PC

A dirty PC is a physically isolated machine, not connected to networks, which can be used for trying out new software, playing games and essentially doing anything which would be dangerous to do on a machine used for day-to-day work.

Employees should be encouraged to use a dirty PC to try out any 'non-work' software coming from outside, including demonstration disks and games. No company work should ever be done on that machine, and no disks used on the dirty PC should be used in any other computer. Anti-virus software should be run as often as possible to check this machine.

This concept is a powerful tool against viruses, although it can be difficult to 'sell' to management if budgets and resources are strained. Furthermore, in some instances the provision of a dirty PC may be seen as a direct invitation and encouragement to PC users to bring doubtful disks into the organisation. The decision whether or not to use a dirty PC will depend on a number of factors.

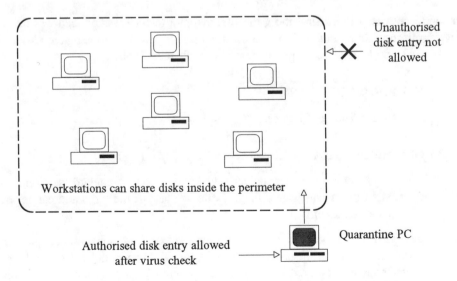

Fig. 6.1 - Quarantine PC used for checking all incoming disks

6.2.5 QUARANTINE PC

A quarantine PC is a stand-alone machine, not connected to networks and under careful configuration control. It is used only for running virus-scanning software (see Section 7.1.3) to check all floppy disks coming into the organisation. It is similar in function to the barrier guard in military barracks. Only disks which have been cleared are allowed through (Fig. 6.1).

Once the disks have been cleared, they can circulate freely within the organisation.

Use of quarantine PCs is the backbone of the anti-virus strategy in many large organisations today. Its success depends largely on whether the organisation can enforce the checking of **all** incoming disks. Disk authorisation products exist which do not allow the use of floppy disks on company PCs until they have been checked and electronically labelled.

6.3 DETECTION

Should a virus nevertheless bypass the preventative measures and penetrate the organisation, there should exist a reliable way of detecting its presence before its side-effects are triggered.

6.3.1 'STRANGE' OCCURRENCES

Sometimes users will notice 'strange' things happening, such as the executable file sizes changing (Fig. 3.4) or the amount of available memory decreasing (Fig. 6.2). Programs may take longer to load than usual or a disk light might flash when it should not. All these occurrences could point to a virus attack, but they should not be relied upon for detecting virus presence. They depend too much on the subjective powers of observation of an individual to be usable in a reliable way.

In one recent case of virus infection, the first symptom which was noticed was that a large application would not load any more. After investigating the problem, the *4K* virus was discovered (*4K* decreases the size of the available memory by 6K).

6.3.2 ANTI-VIRUS SOFTWARE

This is discussed in detail in Chapter 7.

6.3.3 CONFIRMING THAT THE VIRUS IS NOT A MUTATION

If a virus has been detected, it must be verified whether it is a 'standard' version or a mutation. Most anti-virus software will only check a part of the virus and cannot be relied upon for spot-on identification.

The final confirmation is best left to one of the companies or individuals specialising in virus research. In most cases the process is straight-forward: two identical executables or disks are infected with a captured virus and with a previously analysed sample. A simple comparison will reveal any differences. The process is somewhat more complicated when analysing an encrypting virus, in which case a full disassembly is normally required.

6.4 CONTAINMENT

Once a virus is detected, infected PCs and disks have to be identified and isolated. A contingency plan prepared in advance will be extremely valuable at the moment of virus discovery. A point-by-point checklist makes it more difficult to forget an important item in the general panic which sometimes follows a virus attack.

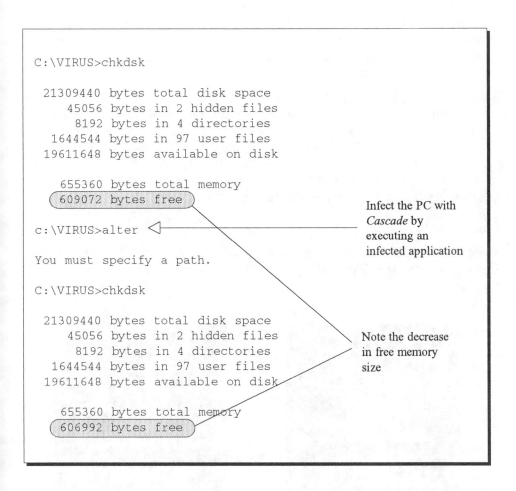

Fig. 6.2 Free memory decreases when the PC is infected with *Cascade*

6.4.1 NETWORK ACCESS

Depending on where on the network the virus has been discovered, the type of the network and the type of the virus, one may take the decision to disconnect the PCs physically from the network (see Chapter 8: Viruses and Networks).

6.4.2 DISK INTERCHANGE

Any unauthorised disk interchange between PCs should be temporarily suspended. Masking tape placed over floppy disk drive slots is a good physical indicator that disk drives should not be used.

6.4.3 WRITE-PROTECT TABS

All floppy disks which are not purposefully intended to be infected should be write-protected. On $5^1/_4$" disks (Fig. 6.3) the application of the write-protect tab prevents writing to the disk. On $3^1/_2$" disks (Fig. 6.4) the appearance of a window on the sliding shutter signifies that the disk is write-protected.

Write-protection on disks is a hardware function and no amount of software manipulation can persuade the hardware to change its mind and write to a write-protected disk. The signal from the write-protect sensor (which can be mechanical or optical) is linked to the floppy disk controller chip and used as an input to a logical gate which blocks the WRITE signal. For example, on the TEAC FD-55 1.2M drive, the signal from the File Protect Sensor (FPT) is processed by the WRITE/ERASE logic in the control circuit LSI forming the WG signal as follows:

```
WG=DSEL & IWG & FPT
```

where DSEL is the Drive Select signal and IWG is the Write Gate input. WG is further processed by the Read/Write LSI which supplies the current to the Read/Write and Erase coils.

Fig. 6.3a Write-unprotected $5^1/_4$" disk   **Fig. 6.3b Write-protected $5^1/_4$" disk**

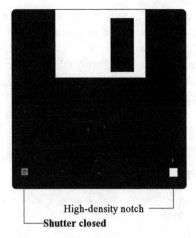

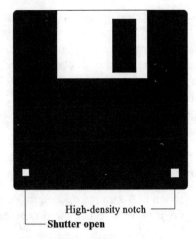

High-density notch ——┐   High-density notch ——┐
└—Shutter closed   └— Shutter open

Fig. 6.4a Write-unprotected 3¹/₂" disk   **Fig. 6.4b Write-protected 3¹/₂" disk**

A word of caution: A number of (conflicting) reports have been published regarding the effectiveness or otherwise of silver (or black) write-protect tabs on $5^1/_4$" disks. On some older drives, which used a mirror under the floppy disk notch to reflect the light back to the photo-sensitive element next to the light source, placing a silver (or a shiny black) write-protect tab was the same as bringing the mirror closer to the light source, which made the drive believe that the disk was not write-protected. Unfortunately, some reports have wrongly indicated that **matt** tabs were the culprits, resulting in spectacular confusion.

If in doubt, try copying a file onto a disk write-protected using a tab of your favourite colour. Matt black tabs are generally reliable.

6.5 RECOVERY

Recovery from a virus attack involves **two main stages**:

1. Elimination of the virus from the infected hard and floppy disks, and

2. Recovery from any virus side-effects

6.5.1 CLEANING HARD DISKS

To eliminate the virus from an infected hard disk, the PC should be switched off and then bootstrapped from a **write-protected system floppy disk** (see Section 6.1: Preparation). Infected objects (bootstrap sectors, executables) should be identified and replaced with clean copies.

Replacing **infected executables** is easy: delete the old copy using the DOS command 'DEL' and 'COPY' the originals from the manufacturers' delivery disks. Using 'DEL' first is not really necessary, but it helps to avoid mistakes.

Replacing **infected bootstrap sectors** can be done with disk-editing tools such as *Norton Utilities, PC Tools or Sophos Utilities,* but if you are not absolutely certain what you are doing, the 'brute force' approach is preferable. All files on the hard disk should be backed up first and the disk reformatted. For hard disks infected with DOS boot sector viruses such as the *Italian,* a DOS 'FORMAT' is sufficient, while for master boot sector viruses such as *New Zealand* and *Joshi,* a low-level format should be performed. Data files should then be restored from the backups and the executables restored from the manufacturers' original disks.

One must not forget that **multi-partite viruses infect executables and the bootstrap sector**, all of which need replacing with clean copies.

Disinfection software (as oposed to Virus removal software, see Chapter 7: Anti-virus Software) is unreliable and should normally be avoided.

In the process of eliminating the virus, do not forget to preserve a copy, on a clearly marked disk, for detailed analysis.

6.5.2 CLEANING FLOPPY DISKS

To clear infected floppy disks, switch the PC off and bootstrap it from a write-protected system floppy disk. Back up any valuable data (not executables) from the infected floppy disk using the COPY command (**not** DISKCOPY). The disk can then be reformatted, e.g.

```
FORMAT A:
```

6.5.3 REINFECTION

Reinfection often occurs after the 'cleanup' has been completed, sometimes minutes after completion: all that is needed is one overlooked floppy disk. Although thoroughness will reduce the likelihood of reinfection, one should anticipate this possibility.

6.5.4 RECOVERY FROM VIRUS SIDE-EFFECTS

Recovery from virus side-effects depends on the virus. In the case of innocuous viruses such as *Cascade,* recovery from side-effects is not necessary, while in the case of a virus such *as Michelangelo*, recovery will involve the restoration of a complete hard disk from the most recent backups.

The most important thing when recovering from virus side-effects is the existence of **sound backups**. Original executables should be kept on write-protected disks, so that any infected programs can easily be replaced by the original clean versions.

Sometimes it is possible to recover data from disks damaged by a virus. This is a rather specialist task performed by commercial data recovery agencies and can be very expensive.

6.5.3 OTHER POINTS

There are a few other things worth bearing in mind during recovery from a virus attack:

- Discover and close the loopholes which allowed the virus to enter the organisation.

- Inform any possible recipients of the infected disks outside the organisation that they may be affected by the virus.

- Consider the implications to the organisation of the bad publicity.

- In the UK, inform the *Computer Crime Unit* of *New Scotland Yard* in London about the attack (Tel 071 230 1177, Fax 071 831 8845).

7

ANTI-VIRUS SOFTWARE

I have too dearly bought, with price of mangled mind, thy worthless ware.

Sir Philip Sidney, 'Desire'

The exponential growth of the virus threat has been closely followed by a similar exponential growth of anti-virus software. PC users are faced with a bewildering choice when trying to pick the package which will be most effective against something they have never seen, and do not particularly wish to see. How do they test it? What should they use and why? How much can they rely on evaluations in general-purpose computer journals?

Virus non-specific	Virus-specific
Checksumming software	Scanning software
Monitoring software	Monitoring software
Integrity shells	'Inoculation' software
Virus removal software	Disinfection software

Fig. 7.1 - Anti-virus software types

7.1 ANTI-VIRUS SOFTWARE TYPES

The many anti-virus software packages on the market can be divided into two categories: **Virus non-specific** and **Virus-specific.** Each category can, in turn, be divided into four sub-categories, as shown in Fig. 7.1.

7.1.1 SCANNING SOFTWARE (VIRUS-SPECIFIC)

Description: A virus-scanning program searches for known viruses. When a new virus appears in the wild, it is analysed, and its characteristics recorded; this is normally a 16- to 24-byte pattern extracted from the virus. The scanning program will examine all executables on a disk, including the operating system and the bootstrap sector(s), and compare their contents with its library of known virus characteristics.

    The program SEARCH in Appendix B is an example of a virus-specific scanning program, though the listing does not include the necessary patterns, which are in Appendix G: Known IBM-PC Viruses.

    Virus scanners are currently the most widely used type of anti-virus software.

Advantages: The main advantage of scanners is that they can be used for virus-checking of potentially infected media. **Scanning software is especially useful for checking incoming floppy disks for the presence of known viruses.**

    Scanners identify a virus by name, rather than just informing the user that something is amiss.

Disadvantages: Scanning software can only discover viruses that it 'knows' about. It has to be updated continually, as new viruses appear, which is the main problem with this type of software.

7.1.2 CHECKSUMMING SOFTWARE (VIRUS NON-SPECIFIC)

Description: Checksumming software relies on the detection of change to any executable on the system through the calculation of initial 'clean' checksums, followed by periodic recalculations in order to verify that the checksums have not changed. If a virus attacks an executable, it will have to change one or more bits, which will result in a completely different checksum (provided a strong checksumming algorithm is used).

    Checksumming is often referred to as 'fingerprinting'. The program FINGER in Appendix C is an example of virus non-specific software which produces cryptographic checksums.

The method of performing the checksumming process (the checksumming algorithm) is very important. Three general approaches are possible: **simple checksums**, **cyclic redundancy checks** (CRCs) and **cryptographic checksums**. The results of the checksumming algorithm must not be easily reproducible (lest a virus should do this on infection, preventing its detection), which eliminates the first two. **Cryptographic checksums are the only method which this sort of software should use.**

Advantages: The checksumming approach is the only known method which will detect all viruses, present and future, with absolute certainty. This makes it inherently desirable as a **long-term anti-virus strategy** in any organisation.

Disadvantages: This type of software is reactive rather than proactive, in that a virus attack will be detected **after** it happens. However regular use of such software will almost always find a virus before its side effects trigger.

Checksumming software relies on the fact that the executables should be 'clean' (i.e. virus-free) before the initial checksumming is applied. This can be ensured by using virus-specific scanning software to check the system for the presence of any known viruses. The only case in which the checksumming will fail completely to pick up a virus infection on an infected system is if **all** infectable executables are infected when the checksums are calculated. If the system is **partially** infected when checksums are calculated, irregularities will still be discovered when the virus infects the next executable.

7.1.3 MONITORING SOFTWARE (VIRUS-SPECIFIC)

Description: Monitoring software (also called 'on-line' anti-virus software) installs itself as a memory-resident TSR (terminate-stay-resident) program. From then on, it intercepts various interrupts such as Load and Execute, File open etc. (Fig. 7.2). Whenever an application requests access to a file, the file is first examined for virus presence. The application is allowed to use the file only after it has been certified virus-free.

In common with other TSR programs, virus-specific monitoring software should occupy as little conventional memory as possible. A virus description typically takes about 30 bytes, which means that a virus database containing 2000 viruses occupies 60K of memory. This is, of course, unacceptably large to store in conventional memory, so virus-specific monitoring software employs various tricks such as using extended or expanded memory.

Advantages: Virus detection (if it happens) occurs in real time.

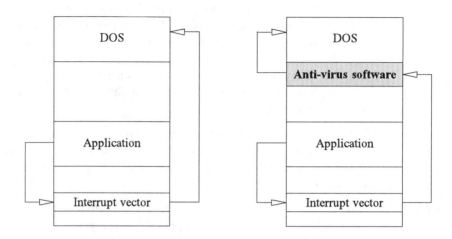

Fig. 7.2 - Interrupt redirection by memory-resident anti-virus software

Disadvantages: System slow-down can be considerable. As a process which is dependent on interrupt interception, this type of program can be subverted. Occupies (often scarce) conventional memory. Compatibility problems with networks, utilities and other resident drivers and programs.

7.1.4 MONITORING SOFTWARE (VIRUS NON-SPECIFIC)

Description: Virus non-specific monitoring software is installed as a TSR program. It intercepts and monitors various interrupts, trying to detect 'virus activity'. 'Virus activity' is a set of actions that are commonly found in viruses such as writing to a boot sector, opening executable files for writing etc.

Advantages: Virus detection (if it happens) occurs in real time.

Disadvantages: There is no fixed 'set of rules' regarding what a virus should or should not do. As a result, false alarms can result from legitimate program activity which is misinterpreted by the anti-virus software (this in turn usually leads to users ignoring all warnings!). Conversely, any virus which does not comply with the monitoring program's concept of virus activity will be ignored. The monitoring activity also degrades system performance and can be incompatible with network software, certain application programs and so on.

The greatest drawback of memory-resident products, however, is that intelligent viruses such as *4K* and *The number of the Beast* can bypass or disable them. The mechanism used by anti-virus software for intercepting disk reads and writes, i.e. to change the DOS interrupt table, is exactly that used by most viruses, and can be easily disabled. There are viruses which were designed to bypass specific monitoring software (eg. *8 Tunes* which bypasses *Flusho*t).

7.1.5 'INOCULATION' SOFTWARE (VIRUS-SPECIFIC)

Description: 'Inoculation' software attempts to label disks or executables in such a way that a particular virus will not infect them.

Advantages: None

Disadvantages: 'Inoculation' software introduces a virus signature into objects it wants to protect, leading the virus to believe that the object is already infected. Apart from the fact that such 'protection' can only be done against one, or at most a few viruses, it is not a long term solution and can introduce a false sense of security as well as false virus alarms when scanning software is run. Some viruses such as *Jerusalem* cannot be 'inoculated' against.

This sort of software should not be used.

7.1.6 INTEGRITY SHELLS (VIRUS NON-SPECIFIC)

Description: The idea behind integrity shells is that a layer is added above the DOS command level, so that the shell 'filters-through' any request to execute a program. Before executing the program, the anti-virus part of the shell will perform on-line checksumming of the executable and compare it with the precomputed value. If the values do not agree, execution of the program will not be permitted.

Advantages: An appealing concept which is more useful under operating systems such as Unix, VMS or OS/2, where inter-process separation is well defined through memory ownership and privileged instruction support in hardware and where the execution of a 'dangerous' instruction (in operating system terms), will cause the offending process to be suspended.

Disadvantages: Integrity shells are impossible to implement in a secure way under DOS which does not distinguish between privileged and non-privileged instructions and any program can do anything, including bypassing the shell and rendering its protection useless.

7.1.7 DISINFECTION SOFTWARE (VIRUS-SPECIFIC)

Description: Disinfection software attempts to remove viruses from infected disks and infected programs in such a way as to restore the infected item to its previous state.

Advantages: This is an intuitive approach which can be used in clearing large-scale virus infections or the restoration of executables where masters are not available.

Disadvantages: Disinfection is not something to be recommended, as it is not a straight-forward operation in the majority of cases. Mistakes are possible, if not probable, since the differentiation between an already known virus and a mutation is extremely difficult. Eliminating just one byte too much in a program can have catastrophic consequences. It is much easier to replace the infected programs with manufacturers' originals.

7.1.8 VIRUS REMOVAL SOFTWARE (VIRUS NON-SPECIFIC)

Description: The simplest forms of virus removal software are the DOS DEL, SYS and FORMAT commands, as well as the low-level formatting procedure for hard disks. The DEL command deletes infected programs and the FORMAT command re-initialises infected floppy disks and DOS partitions of hard disks. The SYS command replaces DOS boot sectors and the operating system files. The low-level format completely re-initialises hard disks.

Virus scanning software often provides automatic file deletion and boot sector immobilisation. This enables a reliable, quick and automatic removal of infected files and immobilisation of infected disks. Once infected items have been removed, they can be replaced with manufacturers' originals.

Advantages: This is a fundamentally sound technique which should always be used in preference to disinfection.

Disadvantages: Can be time-consuming, especially when a lot of executable files are infected.

7.2 TESTING ANTI-VIRUS PRODUCTS

It is strongly recommended that only tested anti-virus products are used. The testing should be done for **usability** as well as **security**.

The user should test products for their usability, whereas the security aspect of testing is a rather specialist task which cannot be done by the average user. Most users have never encountered, nor have any desire to introduce highly infectious and harmful viruses into their system. They do not wish to risk their valuable data just in order to ascertain the effectiveness of anti-virus software. The testing of anti-virus software against viruses should be done in a controlled environment, by experts.

When comparing the effectiveness of virus-specific anti-virus software, users should always compare the tests on more than one virus collection. It is quite common that one product gets the best marks in one test, only to come last in a different test. This is almost always due to the use of different virus collections, although it can also be due to out-of-date products being compared with up-to-date ones, or to the reviewer's incompetence.

PC journals often carry comparative tests of PC software and hardware. When testing anti-virus software, each product is usually tested against an exhaustive virus collection **supplied by an anti-virus software manufacturer**. Needless to say, the objectivity of such reviews is often poor, for two reasons: Firstly, it would be surprising if that manufacturer's product did not score 100% against a collection of viruses with which the manufacturer is clearly familiar. Secondly, the collection will almost always contain thousands of viruses, most of which are of academic interest only. Testing against a large selection of viruses should not necessarily be the main aim of comparative reviews, since testing against **a well chosen sample of viruses found in the wild** can reveal much more (see Section 4.1: The Numbers Game).

The testing for usability should be done by the purchaser on his own typical hardware and software configuration.

7.3 FALSE POSITIVES AND FALSE NEGATIVES

There are two possible pitfalls when using virus-detection software: either the software detects a virus when there is no virus, or the software does not detect a virus when there is one. These are known respectively as false positive and false negative events.

Both false positives and false negatives can occur in all types of virus-detection software under certain conditions.

7.3.1 VIRUS-SCANNING SOFTWARE

There is a very small but finite chance that patterns or virus identification algorithms used by a virus scanner will match the contents of some uninfected and innocuous executable. Data in executable images is not completely random, and certain sequences of instructions used in a virus can occur in a perfectly legitimate program. Patterns from viruses are normally chosen so as to be unlikely to occur in a legitimate program, but this is often difficult, especially if viruses are written in a high-level language.

False negatives are a much more serious problem and can result from a particular virus characteristic not being included in the scanner used, or a characteristic of a virus being included incorrectly. It is of paramount importance to update virus-scanning software regularly, as well as to ensure that the software producer has appropriate access to the latest virus code and a good virus-analysis capability.

Executables infected before compression and delivered in compressed form can also cause false negatives. Compression changes the appearance of any virus that may be attached to them in such a way that virus scanners cannot recognise the virus code. If static compression is used (*PKZIP, ARC* etc.) the executables should be decompressed before scanning. Dynamically compressed files (*PKLITE, LZEXE* etc) are difficult to scan unless the scanner can decompress files while scanning; this is becoming more difficult with the increasing number of compression products and algorithms. Alternatively, a dynamically compressed file can be run on a dirty PC and examined for infectious behaviour, such as changing of other executables or boot sectors. If a dynamically compressed file does carry a virus, any sacrificial executables on the dirty PC which become infected will be scannable in a normal way.

Note that dynamically compressed files can be infected before compression or after compression. If they are infected **before** compression, a scanner is not likely to pick up the infection. If they are infected **after** compression, the infection should be detected.

False negatives can also happen if an anti-virus scanner is used incorrectly. For example, if the PC is bootstrapped from a disk already infected with the *4K* virus, the scanner will not detect it.

7.3.2 CHECKSUMMING SOFTWARE

False positives are a frequent occurence when using checksumming software. The reason for the alarm in most cases is not a virus attack, but a legitimate change in the machine configuration which has not been followed by a recalculation of checksums. This can be partly avoided by fingerprinting only those particular areas of the PC which rarely change but are executed often (operating system, utilities, editors, compilers etc). If a virus infects the PC, it will sooner or later also infect one of the commonly used utilities, which will be picked up by the checksumming software. Some executables introduce legitimate changes in their own contents, e.g. WIN.COM in Windows 3.1.

False negatives are much rarer when using checksumming software than virus scanning software, and are almost always due to incorrect use of the software. If fingerprints are checked while the system is already infected with a stealth virus such as *Joshi* or *4K,* the infection will not be detected.

Using a simple checksumming algorithm is an open invitation to virus writers to produce a virus which could engineer the changes in such a way that infected executables would appear clean. Cryptographic fingerprints combat this particular threat by making the task of engineering the changes intrinsically infeasible to accomplish in a realistic time span.

7.3.3 VIRUS NON-SPECIFIC MONITORING SOFTWARE

Virus non-specific monitoring software resides in memory and reports suspicious activities such as another process attempting to install itself in memory, writing to a boot sector and so on.

False positives often occur when using this type of software, as some of the 'suspicious' activities trapped originate from legitimate software. Furthermore, when an unsophisticated user is presented with a flashing message such as

```
Warning! Attempted write to drive 80 cylinder 0 head 0 sector 1
Proceed (Y/N) ?
```

he probably wishes to type in "I don't know" instead of giving a decisive yes/no answer. After seeing similar messages ten or twenty times a day, he is quite likely to ignore them and after a few days of annoyance, deinstall the virus-monitoring software.

False negatives are a much more serious shortcoming of this type of software. There is no virus equivalent of the 10 commandments, and viruses do exploit weaknesses or bugs in the operating system and the anti-virus software. Several tricks have been used in practice. For example, the *Icelandic-2* virus uses an undocumented feature of DOS to obtain the original value of the INT 21H vector and bypass any monitoring program. Another trick used by at least two viruses to infect files which have been protected against being written to by a memory-resident module, is to open the file in Read-Only mode and then modify the internal flag within DOS which changes access rights to Read-Write.

7.3.4 VIRUS-SPECIFIC MONITORING SOFTWARE

Virus-specific monitoring software suffers from false negative problems which are mainly due to the difficulties in keeping it up-to-date. False negatives can also be caused by the relatively easy subversion of the software by new viruses specifically targeted against particular products.

7.4 SUMMARY OF ANTI-VIRUS SOFTWARE

In summary, the recommended long-term approach is to use virus non-specific checksumming software, based on cryptographic checksums. This will allow convenient everyday checking of system integrity, secure against any present or future viruses. In addition, there are situations in which virus-specific scanning software can be useful, provided its limitations are clearly understood.

Monitoring software is not recommended as it cannot be made effective against all viruses and can lull the user into a false sense of security. The same applies to virus-disinfection and 'inoculation' software for similar reasons.

The advantages of the non-memory-resident approach over memory-resident products are considerable. Above all, the operation can be made fully secure through both bootstrapping the computer and running the anti-virus software from a write-protected floppy disk. Furthermore there is no performance degradation or incompatibility with other software in normal operation, and anti-virus checks can be scheduled or integrated into other procedures as required.

Possibly the greatest difficulty in using anti-virus software in a larger organisation is the enforcement of the agreed procedures. Deciding that all incoming floppy disks will be checked for viruses does not necessarily mean that all incoming disks **will** be checked. The enforcement can be helped by using a disk-authorisation product which will prevent unauthorised disks to be used. This functionality is provided by some access control products, and a number of dedicated packages are also available from anti-virus companies (see Appendix D: Anti-virus Software Manufacturers and Distributors).

8

VIRUSES AND NETWORKS

Something is rotten in the state of Denmark.

William Shakespeare, 'Hamlet'

The interchange of executables on non-networked PCs is almost exclusively done by floppy disks and is, as a consequence, relatively slow and physically controllable. PC networks allow high speed sharing of data and executables. This interchange is also much more difficult to control in practice, with hundreds of simultaneous users.

The danger from a large scale virus attack in a non-networked organisation is comparatively limited, if reliable virus-detection software is used. An attack is likely to be limited to a few PCs before it is spotted and disk interchange is stopped. The possibility of a large scale virus attack in a networked organisation is much greater and the chances of successful containment much smaller, if proper network security features are not used.

This chapter concentrates on Novell *NetWare* and is based on a theoretical and practical study of virus behaviour under *NetWare* 3.11 and *NetWare* 286. Although the practical anti-virus measures described are specific to *NetWare* 3.11, much of it also applies to other network operating systems such as *LAN Manager*. It is assumed that the network will be using a dedicated file server.

8.1 PATHOLOGY OF A VIRUS INFECTION ON NETWARE

Due to the excellent emulation of physical DOS disks under *NetWare*, a large proportion of DOS viruses in existence today are able to attack *NetWare* drives.

The main difference between *NetWare* and local workstation drives is that *NetWare* does not allow individual sector addressing either through the normal DOS interrupts 25H and 26H or the BIOS interrupt 13H. This excludes the possibility of pure bootstrap sector viruses infecting the network, but does not, of course, exclude parasitic, multi-partite and companion viruses, all of which can spread freely on a badly protected network.

8.1.1 VIRUS ENTRY INTO THE NETWORK

The point of entry of a virus into a network is invariably the user workstation. In a typical scenario, the user infects his workstation by executing an infected application (parasitic or multi-partite) or bootstrapping from an infected disk (multi-partite viruses). The virus becomes memory resident and will typically try to infect any application which is run, or any drive which is accessed.

NETX and IPX, which are normally kept on the workstation, may already be memory-resident at this stage.

On accessing the network the user will execute LOGIN.EXE stored on the file server, which will open access to the allotted file areas on the file server. If LOGIN.EXE itself or any other executables are unprotected (see Section 8.6: Practical Anti-virus Measures for *NetWare* 3.11 Administrators), they will become infected. Any user executing an infected application will have his workstation infected, which in turn will spread the infection further.

On a typical active network, an infection can spread onto most workstations within minutes. An infected LOGIN.EXE, or any program executed by the system login script, can cause user workstations to become infected whenever a user logs into the network.

8.1.2 PRACTICAL TRIAL - JERUSALEM ON NETWARE 2.12

The above scenario has been demonstrated in practice by infecting a workstation with the *Jerusalem* virus and then executing LOGIN on the fileserver running NetWare 2.12. In this experiment LOGIN.EXE was purposefully left protected only by the Read-Only (R/O) attribute. *Jerusalem* (like most parasitic viruses) sets the R/O attribute to Read/Write (R/W), infects the file and then resets the attribute to R/O. After LOGIN.EXE has been infected, any workstation logging into the network will become infected (Fig 8.1). Any EXE or COM file residing on the file server will likewise become infected whenever executed by the supervisor.

8.2 NETWARE 3.11 SECURITY MECHANISMS

NetWare 3.11 provides four different aspects of network security: the **login procedure**, **trustee rights**, **directory rights** and **file attributes**.

1. The **login procedure** requires all users to identify themselves by a username and a password.

Infected workstation ...

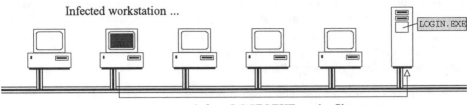

... infects LOGIN.EXE on the file server

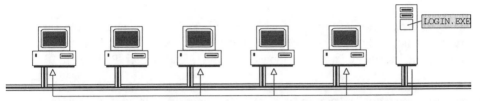

after which every workstation becomes infected as soon as a user logs in

Fig. 8.1 - Large scale network infection through LOGIN.EXE

2. **Trustee rights** are granted to each user by the 'network supervisor' and allow each user various actions such as reading from files, writing to files, creating files etc.

3. **Directory rights** (read, write, open, close, delete, search) are set separately and can be used to limit the access to certain directories such as those containing executables.

4. **File Attributes** (read-only, read-write, share) can be set separately.

Even if a user's PC becomes infected, the infection cannot spread to the file server if the security features are properly implemented.

This security breaks down if the network supervisor's PC becomes infected. Care should be taken when setting network security features, as the appropriate features may not be enabled by default.

8.3 NETWARE 3.11 PRACTICAL EXPERIMENTS

An experimental network consisting of a dedicated file server (on a Compaq 486/25, 310 MByte hard disk, 4MByte RAM) and a workstation (Amstrad PC-ECD, 20 MByte hard disk, 640KByte RAM) was set up with default security parameters.

8.3.1 PARASITIC VIRUSES

It was decided to investigate *NetWare* 3.11's resistance to attack with different levels of protection.

A workstation not logged in was infected with *Jerusalem* (memory-resident, parasitic virus). IPX was executed (and infected) and NET3 was executed (and infected). From then on, no COM or EXE file became infected when run; this applied to files held on floppy, hard or network drives. The interaction between the virus and NET3 appeared to prevent the virus from infecting other executables.

If the sequence was reversed, i.e. if a clean workstation was loaded with IPX and NET3 and then infected, the following error message was produced:

```
Network Error on Server SERVER:Error receiving from network
Abort, Retry?
```

The same experiment was repeated with *Cascade* and *Vacsina*, and in both cases the viruses lost the ability to infect immediately after infecting NET3.COM. Unlike *Jerusalem*, *Cascade* and *Vacsina* did not crash the workstation if loaded after IPX and NET3.

The same trial was then done with *4K* virus. The virus did infect IPX and NET3, did not crash the workstation and proceeded to be infectious in a normal way on floppy and hard disks, but not on the file server.

The same experiment was then performed with the *Eddie 2* virus. A clean workstation was logged into the network and an infected application executed from drive A. This virus successfully infected programs held on all drives, including the file server.

The infectiousness of *Eddie 2* was next tested with various *NetWare* 3.11 file attribute settings. *Eddie 2* is a virus with limited stealth capability. It intercepts DIR's *Find-First* and *Find-Next* calls and displays the original file lengths. In order to establish whether or not a file is infected, a secure bootstrap has to be performed.

8.3.1.1 Default NetWare 3.11 Security

By default the users have full access rights to their home directory (created at the time of user creation) and no write-rights to any subdirectories containing executables. The virus **could** infect files in the user's own directory, irrespective of the setting of file read-only attributes, but could not infect any other files on the server.

8.3.1.2 Rights Set to Read-only

Eddie 2 failed to infect files to which the user did not have 'effective rights' to write, irrespective of whether this right was denied at a directory or file level, or from the 'Inherited Rights' mask.

8.3.1.3 File Attributes Set to Read-only

Eddie 2 succeeded in infecting files which had their file attributes set to read-only. This is the same R/O attribute used by DOS, set by *Eddie 2* (and most other parasitic viruses) to R/W before infection and reset back to R/O after infection.

8.3.1.4 File Attributes Set to Execute-only

NetWare 3.11 allows file attributes to be set to execute-only and such files cannot be read even by the supervisor.

An *Eddie 2*-infected workstation was used to execute an execute-only file as well as a file marked read-only. Only the read-only file was infected.

8.3.1.5 Running Under Supervisor Mode

The supervisor has all rights to all directories and files. A clean workstation was used to log onto the network as the supervisor, and was then infected with *Eddie 2*.

The virus **was able to infect all files** on the file server, **except those marked as 'execute only'**.

8.3.2 BOOT SECTOR VIRUSES

Although boot sector viruses have no means of infecting a network drive (since it does not allow individual sector addressing), the experiment was nevertheless performed.

A workstation was infected with the *New Zealand* virus, which infects the master boot sector on hard disks and the boot sector on floppy disks. The network was accessed (LOGIN followed by running of various applications, followed by LOGOUT).

The workstation was cleared from the infection and the network connection was re-established. The workstation hard disk and its memory, were examined for infection, and as expected, none was found.

8.3.3 MULTI-PARTITE VIRUSES

A clean workstation was used to log into the file server. The workstation was infected with the multi-partite virus *Flip*. Files on the local fixed disk could be infected as usual, but when files on the file server were executed, DOS returned the message

```
EXEC Error
```

In general a multi-partite virus will infect files on a network drive in the same way as a parasitic virus, but in addition the virus will infect the boot sectors of disks attached to any workstation which them becomes infected.

8.4 NETWARE 3.11-SPECIFIC VIRUSES

There are three cases to date of viruses reported to have been written specifically to circumvent *NetWare* security.

8.4.1 FIRST NOVELL 'VIRUS'

In February 1990 there appeared an (unconfirmed) report of a 'Novell' virus which supposedly destroyed the Novell-specific file allocation table. The virus was said to be capable of penetrating a file server from a workstation even if the latter was not logged on to the network. It was suggested that this might be possible by altering the NET$DOS.SYS program, using the *C* libraries released by Novell.

Novell Inc has not encountered this virus, nor has it received any reports of it. There do not seem to have been any further reports about this 'virus' apart from the Editorial in *Virus Bulletin* on February 1990.

8.4.2 JON DAVID'S FALSE ALARM

In July 1990 New York consultant Dr. Jon David released a report about a virus which he claimed to have observed propagating on a Novell LAN. Dr. David said that the virus, a *Jerusalem* mutation, bypassed *NetWare* file server write-protection and deleted write-protected files on the server.

After a heated exchange in the press and the Virus-L bulletin board between Dr. David and Novell (at one point Novell was threatening to sue Dr. David), Novell confirmed that the virus was *Jerusalem*, that it did propagate on unprotected networks, but was denying the allegation that it bypassed *NetWare* security in any way.

Dr. David refused to disassemble the virus himself or release his sample to anybody else for analysis, saying he preferred to observe the virus effects rather than analysing the virus structure.

The universal conclusion seems to be that the virus was a standard copy of *Jerusalem* with no specific ability to subvert *NetWare* security. For more information see the Editorial, *Virus Bulletin*, December 1990.

8.4.3 NETWARE VIRUS FROM THE NETHERLANDS

In April 1991 a virus called *GP1* was received from the Netherlands which contained instructions to subvert *NetWare* security. Interestingly enough, the virus was received in source-code form. It is believed to have been developed in Leiden (the Netherlands) as a result of an unofficial challenge by a civil servant to a student.

8.4.3.1 Virus Structure

The virus is based on the *Jerusalem* virus, with *NetWare*-specific instructions added to a disassembled version of *Jerusalem*. The virus is memory-resident but contains no stealth characteristics. The Novell network handler is accessed via a FAR JMP instead of a FAR CALL; analysis indicated that if the FAR JMP instruction was changed into the FAR CALL instruction, the virus would become fully functional.

The virus is not infective unless it is run on a *NetWare* workstation. It intercepts four different INT 21H services, of which the most interesting is the *NetWare*-specific service E3H. This is checked to see whether the subfunction requesting the service is a user LOGIN procedure. If it is, the LOGIN is executed under control of the virus and the return code is examined. If the LOGIN is successful, the virus sends a copy of the original login request block to socket number 2A9FH. This is suspected to be a broadcast message which could send details to a listening PC.

8.4.3.2 Practical Trials on NetWare 286

The virus was assembled after changing the FAR JMP to FAR CALL instruction. An experimental network consisting of a dedicated file server (on a Compaq 386/s, 80 MByte hard disk) and a workstation (Amstrad PC-ECD, 20MByte hard disk) was set up with default security parameters.

The virus replicated in the same way as *Jerusalem* (when *NetWare* was present), but no other effects could be observed.

The background of this virus continues to be investigated and it does seem that the copy obtained was an unfinished creation.

8.4.3.3 Practical Trials on NetWare 3.11

An experimental network consisting of a dedicated file server (on a Compaq 486/25, 310 MByte hard disk, 4MByte RAM) and a workstation (Amstrad PC-ECD, 20 MByte hard disk, 640KByte RAM) was set up with default security parameters.

The virus was tried under *NetWare* 3.11 where it replicated without problems, unlike the standard *Jerusalem* which refuses to replicate under the same circumstances. After becoming memory-resident the virus infects other files, extending them by 1546 bytes.

There were no other visible side-effects.

8.5 IMPLICATIONS OF STEALTH VIRUSES ON NETWARE 3.11

The main problem of dealing with stealth viruses on any network is the difficulty in establishing a positively 'clean' work environment from which the cleanup can be attempted (see Sections 3.3: Virus Hiding Mechanisms and 8.6.6: Secure Accessing of *NetWare* 3.11).

8.6 PRACTICAL ANTI-VIRUS MEASURES FOR NETWARE 3.11 NETWORK ADMINISTRATORS

8.6.1 DISKLESS WORKSTATIONS

Diskless workstations are PCs in their own right, sometimes equipped with hard disks, but without any floppy disks. The reasoning is that if the user does not have the means of introducing floppy disks into the PC, he will also not have the opportunity of introducing a virus (or stealing data on a floppy).

This no-floppies, no-virus reasoning holds only up to a certain extent. It is quite true that diskless workstations will prevent accidental introduction of viruses onto the network. Malicious introduction of viruses is **not** prevented, as the virus code can be input through the keyboard using the DOS COPY command or DEBUG. The technique is described in

Burger's *Computer Viruses - A High Tech Disease*. Likewise, diskless workstations can still have modem and email connections over which software can be downloaded from BBSs.

Another disadvantage of diskless workstations is that the transfer of legitimate data by users is made much more difficult.

The decision to use diskless workstations in an organisation is a major one. Associated costs and the impact on the efficiency of the organisation should be carefully considered.

8.6.2 REMOTE BOOTSTRAP ROMS

Most network cards can be fitted with a special Read Only Memory (ROM) chip which maps into the PC memory space and when executed on boot-up, reads the operating system and other associated files from the file server instead of from the local disk. Note that the PC will still try to bootstrap from floppy and hard disks first. If none are found, the bootstrapping will be performed remotely.

There are several advantages in using remote bootstrap ROMs. Firstly, the technique diminishes the danger from bootstrap sector virus infection. Secondly, any updates to the operating system used are made much easier, since they can be done on the file server.

The use of remote bootstrap ROMs is recommended for bootstrapping diskless workstations.

8.6.3 ENHANCED ACCESS CONTROL

NetWare 3.11 provides very good access control features and utilities for the administration of users. In addition, a number of access control packages are available which front-end *NetWare* 3.11, providing even more sophisticated access control features and, perhaps, easier administration of users.

8.6.4 ANTI-VIRUS SOFTWARE

It is recommended that **virus-specific** software is installed on a file server for use on workstations; the problems of updating the master copy are minimal. The virus check of the server can be performed overnight, when the server workload is otherwise low. It is recommended that a separate workstation, bootstrapped in a secure way, is used to initiate the task. This workstation can also be used for backing up the network.

It is recommended that **virus non-specific** software be used to fingerprint and check critical areas of the file server regularly. On *NetWare* 3.11 it is recommended that all executables in the \PUBLIC, \SYSTEM and \LOGIN subdirectories are fingerprinted. In addition, each system will have subdirectories containing applications software; these should be fingerprinted as well. Checking of the fingerprints is best done from a separate, securely booted workstation. This should be done before performing backups as well as at a specific time every night.

8.6.5 TWO IDS FOR NETWORK SUPERVISORS

One of the weak points in any multi-user computer system is that one or more users must be given high privileges necessary for system administration. Unfortunately, **these privileges are also assigned to a virus whenever it is in control of a workstation logged in as a network supervisor.** In fact, the *GP1 NetWare*-specific virus seems to exploit exactly that feature by trying to capture the network supervisor password.

One way of reducing the danger from virus penetration via this route is to reduce the time that network supervisors are logged in as network supervisors. They should ideally have two user IDs, one with all privileges and the other with privileges limited to **read** all areas. The use of the former should be limited to system administration functions.

This is extremely important when checking the file server for viruses while logged in as a network supervisor. If a workstation is infected with a 'fast infecting' virus which infects when a file is opened (e.g. *Nomeklatura*, *4K* or *Dark Avenger*), the checking will result in **every executable becoming infected**. The checking of file servers should always be done with the checking worksation logged in as a user with read (but not write) rights to all directories.

8.6.6 SECURE ACCESSING OF NETWARE 3.11

With the advent of stealth viruses, **it is most important to guarantee a clean, virus-free environment on a workstation before running anti-virus software or investigating a virus-infected network.**

To access *NetWare* 3.11 securely, a normal DOS system disk should be prepared, which in addition to a correct version of DOS system files and COMMAND.COM also contains the following *NetWare* 3.11 files:

```
IPX.COM
NETX.EXE
LOGIN.EXE
MAP.EXE
```

This floppy disk should be write-protected.

To access the network, switch the workstation PC off, boot from the floppy disk and then run IPX first, followed by NETX (NET3 with DOS version 3, NET5 with DOS version 5 etc.). Run LOGIN from the floppy disk using the '/S NUL' command line qualifier. This will prevent the execution of both system and user scripts:

```
LOGIN /S NUL <USERNAME>
```

8.6.7 TIGHTENING NETWARE 3.11 SECURITY

NetWare 3.11 allows the setting of file attributes to execute-only. This prevents their modification or reading by any user, including the system supervisor - the only thing that he can do (apart from executing them) is to delete them. Setting the execute-only attributes has mixed blessings. On the one hand it prevents the modification of executables, but on the other hand it makes them unreadable (and unverifiable) by anti-virus software, as well as preventing some software to run.

Note that this attribute will offer protection against viruses **only until somebody writes a virus which targets this attribute.** This is because it is an **attribute** rather than a **right**, and is akin to the Read-Only flag offering protection against some early viruses.

It is recommended that this attribute is not used and that instead 'write rights' are removed from directories containing executable files.

8.6.8 CONCLUSIONS

8.6.8.1 NetWare 3.11 Administration

- Set *NetWare* 3.11 directory and user rights correctly.

- Do not rely on default *NetWare* 3.11 attribute settings.

- Do not use *NetWare* 3.11 'execute only' attributes unless absolutely necessary.

- Use secure bootstrap procedure before running anti-virus software.

8.6.8.2 NetWare 3.11 Virus Infections

- *NetWare* 3.11 seems to cause more memory-resident viruses to malfunction than *NetWare* 2.12.

- Some memory-resident parasitic viruses interact with IPX and NETX losing the ability to infect. Some memory-resident parasitic viruses crash the workstation if IPX and NETX are already loaded when the virus-infected application is run.

- Most parasitic viruses will infect *NetWare* 3.11 files protected with the Read-only attribute.

- Parasitic viruses will not infect *NetWare* 3.11 files when the user's effective rights do not include 'write' rights. The network supervisor has 'write' rights to all directories.

- Parasitic viruses will not infect *NetWare* 3.11 files with the execute-only attribute set, regardless of the user. This, however, is not a foolproof protection against future viruses.

- Pure bootstrap sector viruses will not infect *NetWare* 3.11 drives.

- Multi-partite viruses will infect unprotected *NetWare* 3.11 executables.

- Parasitic and Multi-partite viruses will infect executables regardless of protection levels (execute-only files excepted) if the user is logged in as a supervisor.

8.6.8.3 Other Points

- Consider using diskless workstations.

- Use remote bootstrap ROMs in the workstations.

A

BIBLIOGRAPHY AND OTHER
SOURCES OF INFORMATION

Books and friends should be few but good.

Proverb

A.1 BOOKS ON VIRUSES AND DATA SECURITY

A Pathology of Computer Viruses, Ferbrache, D., *Springer-Verlag,* 1992

A Short Course on Computer Viruses, Cohen, F., *ASP Press,* 1991

Computer Security Reference Book, Jackson, K., Hruska, J., Parker, D., *Butterworth-Heinemann,* 1992

Computer Security Solutions, Hruska, J., Jackson, K., *Blackwells,* 1990

Computer Viruses, Peers, E., Ennis, C., *Deloitte Haskins & Sells*

Computer Viruses, a High Tech Disease, Burger, R., *Abacus,* 1988

Computer Viruses and Data Protection, Burger, R., *Abacus,* 1991

Computer Viruses, What They Are, How They Work, and How to Avoid Them, Mayo, J. L., *Windcrest,* 1989

Data & Computer Security, Dictionary of Standards Concepts and Terms, Longley, D., Shain, M., *Macmillan,* 1987

Data Security Reference Guide 1991/92, *Sophos Ltd.,* 1991

Datapro Reports on Microcomputer Security, *McGraw-Hill,* continuously updated

Dataquest Virus Survey, *NCSA,* 1991

LAN Desktop Guide to Security NetWare Edition, Ed Sawicki, *SAMS,* 1992

PC Viruses, Detection, Analysis and Cure, Solomon, A., *Springer-Verlag,* 1991

Practical Unix Security, Garfinkel, S. and Spafford, G., *O'Reilly & Associates Inc,* 1991

The Complete Computer Virus Handbook, Frost, D., Beale, I., Frost, C., *Price Waterhouse and Pitman,* 1989

The Computer Virus Crisis, Fites, P., Johnston, P., Kratz, M., *Van Nostrand Reinhold,* 1989

The Computer Virus Handbook, Levin, R., *Osborne/McGraw-Hill,* 1990

The Computer Virus Handbook, Highland, H. J., *Elsevier Advanced Technology,* 1990

The Little Black Book of Computer Viruses, Ludwig, M., *American Eagle Publications Inc.,* 1992

Virus Bulletin 1991 International Conference Proceedings, *Virus Bulletin,* 1991

A.2 PERIODICALS ON VIRUSES AND DATA SECURITY *

Computer Fraud and Security Bulletin, *Elsevier Advanced Technology,* 256 Banbury Road, Oxford, OX2 7DH, UK, Tel +44 865 512242, Fax +44 865 310981

Computer Law and Practice, *Tolley Publishing Co Ltd,* Tolley House, 2 Addiscombe Road, Croydon, CR9 5AF, UK, Tel +44 81 686 9141, Fax +44 81 686 3155

The Computer Law and Security Report, *Elsevier Advanced Technology,* 256 Banbury Road, Oxford, OX2 7DH, UK, Tel +44 865 512242, Fax +44 865 310981

Computers & Security, *Elsevier Advanced Technology,* 256 Banbury Road, Oxford, OX2 7DH, UK, Tel +44 865 512242, Fax +44 865 310981

Datenschutz Berater, Prattweg 8, 5024 Pulheim, Germany, Tel +49 2234 82227

Information Security Monitor, *Legal Studies and Services Publishing Ltd,* 9-13 St. Andrew's Street, London, EC4A 3AE, UK, Tel +44 71 936 2016, Fax +44 71 936 2303

Virus Bulletin, *Virus Bulletin Ltd,* 21 The Quadrant, Abingdon Science Park, Abingdon, OX14 3YS, UK, Tel +44 235 559933, Fax +44 235 559935

---

* See Appendix D for notes on telephone numbers

Virus News International, *S&S International Ltd,* Berkley Court, Mill Street, Berkhamsted, HP4 2HB, UK, Tel +44 442 877877, Fax +44 442 877882

A.3 ELECTRONIC BULLETIN BOARDS CARRYING VIRUS-RELATED DISCUSSIONS

BIX is a bulletin board run by Byte magazine in the US. On-line subscription is possible on +1 617 861 9767 (full duplex, 8 bits, no parity, 1 stop bit or 7 bits, even parity, 1 stop bit). Hit the Return key, on *login* prompt enter *bix* and on *Name?* prompt enter *bix.flatfee.* Credit cards are accepted. Packet Switch Network (PSS) address is 310690157800. A number of virus-related conferences are going on; try *law/virus* and *security/critters.*

CIX is a London-based bulletin board which carries regular discussions on a number of security-related topics, including viruses. To register, telephone +44 81 390 1255 (any modem speed up to 14.4 Kbaud). Payment by credit card is accepted.

The author can be contacted via CIX (username *husky*). The source code of all software in this book can be downloaded from CIX: mail *husky* with your username.

Virus-L is an archived moderated bulletin board system which carries virus-related information. It is available from a number of sites including **cert.sei.cmu.edu** (maintained by Ken Van Wyk) and **pdsoft.lancs.ac.uk** (maintained by Steve Jenkins and also available by direct dialup on +44 524 63414). For a complete list of sites see *A Pathology of Computer Viruses* by David Ferbrache.

A.4 VIRUS INFORMATION AVAILABLE ON DISK *

Virus information summary list (VSUM), monthly from Patricia Hoffman, USA, Tel +1 408 988 3733, Fax +1 408 246 3915

PC Virus Index, Brian Clough, UK, Tel +44 273 773959, Fax +44 273 778570

Note: most virus scanning software is supplied with virus information on disk.

A.5 VIRUS TRAINING VIDEOS *

PC's Under Attack, Mediamix, USA, Tel +1 908 277 0058, Fax +1 908 277 0119

The Computer Virus and How to Conrol It, 23 min, James C. Shaeffer & Associates, USA, Tel +1 800 968 9527, Fax +1 313 741 9528

Viruses on Personal Computers training video, 30 min, Sophos Ltd, UK, Tel +44 235 559933, Fax +44 235 559935

---

* See Appendix D for notes on telephone numbers

A.6 OTHER USEFUL BOOKS

80386 Programmer's Reference Manual, *Intel Corporation,* 1986

iAPX 86,88 User's Manual, *Intel Corporation,* 1981

Microsoft Macro Assembler 5.1, *Microsoft,* 1987

Peter Norton Programmer's Guide to IBM PC & PS/2, Norton, P. and Wilton, R., *Micosoft Press,* 1985

Technical Reference for IBM Personal Computer AT, *IBM,* No. 6280070, 1985

Technical Reference for IBM Personal Computer XT, *IBM,* No. 6280089, 1986

The MS-DOS Encyclopedia, Duncan, R., *Microsoft Press,* 1988

B

'SEARCH': VIRUS-SPECIFIC DETECTION PROGRAM

They knew her by the pimple,
the pimple on her nose.

George Robey, 'Song: The Simple Pimple'

This appendix contains the source code for a virus-specific detection program called SEARCH which scans the currently logged-in drive for the hexadecimal virus patterns read in from the file SEARCH.PAT.

Virus patterns have to be updated frequently with the latest virus patterns. Appendix G contains a list of virus hex patterns known in June 1992, which can and should be updated as often as possible. One of the main public sources of virus patterns is the monthly journal *Virus Bulletin*, listed in Appendix A.

Most self-modifying encrypting (i.e. polymorphic) viruses cannot be detected by using fixed search patterns. The only way to detect them is to use an algorithmic description of their characteristics; two possible approaches are 'hard coding' the chosen characteristics in a computer language such as 'C' or using a specialised virus-description interpreted language. Each such virus must be analysed completely before reliable detection is possible.

The SEARCH program is not particularly robust in its error-handling, which had to be sacrificed for brevity. It is also not fast and it does not include any code for the detection of polymorphic viruses; enhancing all these shortcomings should prove a useful exercise for a competent 'C' programmer.

B.1 DESCRIPTION OF 'SEARCH'

The SEARCH program is a virus-specific detection program which scans the currently logged-in drive for the presence of known viruses. The virus patterns are read in from the file SEARCH.PAT, which has to reside on the disk in the current drive.

By default, SEARCH will scan COM, EXE, SYS and OVL files recursively (i.e. from the root directory downward, visiting every subdirectory in turn). In addition to that, it will also scan the DOS bootstrap sector 0, as well as the master bootstrap sector on the first hard disk (logical drive 80H). The user can specify file(s) to be scanned in the command line. For example, if you want to scan all BIN files instead of the default files, enter

```
SEARCH *.BIN
```

You can enter more than one file descriptor in the command line. For example

```
SEARCH SUSPECT.BIN ONEMORE.BIN
```

would search the files SUSPECT.BIN and ONEMORE.BIN for the presence of viruses.

Virus patterns are read in from the file SEARCH.PAT. Any text between a semicolon (;) and the end of the line is ignored. Every pattern has a pattern name of up to 16 characters, followed by up to 16 bytes in hexadecimal. Spaces and TAB characters can be used for clarity. For example

```
Virus_1 3E 6B 78 78 00 90 ; This is a comment
; The above is the pattern for Virus 1
Virus_2 ab39 9823 278f fffe 890f
```

defines two virus patterns: Virus_1 and Virus_2, the first one consisting of 6 bytes and the second one of 10 bytes.

Remember that SEARCH can only detect viruses about which it knows. You should make sure that SEARCH.PAT is kept up to date with the patterns of new and mutated viruses.

B.2 COMPILING 'SEARCH'

The majority of SEARCH's code is written in 'C', but some routines make BIOS and DOS calls and are written in assembly language. The 'C' code can be compiled by most compilers, but it has been tested only using Aztec C (Manx Software Systems Inc.). The assembly language routines assume that they will be called from Aztec C (small memory model) and if you are using a different compiler or a different memory model, you should first make sure that you use the correct calling procedure and preserve the right registers.

Aztec C assumes that AX, BX, CX, and DX registers will not be preserved, whereas BP, SP, SI and DI will. Microsoft C, by way of contrast, assumes that SI, DI, BP, SS and DS will be preserved.

Some compiler libraries contain the BIOS and DOS calling routines directly from C and so all of SEARCH can be written in C.

Note that SEARCH's assembly language routines are also used by the FINGER program presented in Appendix C.

Some compilers (like Aztec) provide a 'make' facility similar to that of Unix. This simplifies the preparation of any software. The makefile for the SEARCH's modules is:

```
searchas.o: searchas.asm
search.o: search.c
SEARCH=search.o searchas.o
search: search.exe
@echo search made
search.exe: $(SEARCH)
ln $(SEARCH) -lc
```

To compile SEARCH, type

```
make search
```

and the computer will do the rest.

B.3 'SEARCH' CODE IN 'C'

The C code for SEARCH should be entered into one file called SEARCH.C. The FINGER program in Appendix C can be used to verify the correctness of the code. The fingerprint for SEARCH.C is 7A23B202 (remember to run FINGER with the -N option):

```
FINGER -N SEARCH.C
```

File SEARCH.C:

```
/*
   This utility will search a system for known viruses
*/

#include "libc.h"
#include "fcntl.h"

#define EOF (-1)

#define FALSE (0)
#define TRUE (!FALSE)

#define NORMAL_EXIT 0
#define ERROR_EXIT (-1)

#define NO_ERROR 0
#define ERROR (-2)

#define BUFSIZE 2048*2   /* of buff[] */
```

```c
#define MAX_BUFF 1024      /* used when fingerprinting absolute sectors */

#define MAX_LINE 128
#define MAXRECURSIVE 128

#define SEARCH_PAT "SEARCH.PAT"
#define MAX_PATTERNS 256
#define MAX_NAME 16
#define MAX_PATTERN_LENGTH 16
struct patt{
   char name[MAX_NAME]; /* name of the virus */
   int bytes_in_pattern; /* how many bytes are in pattern */
   unsigned char pattern[MAX_PATTERN_LENGTH];
} patterns[MAX_PATTERNS];
static int max_patterns=0;
static int pattern_line=0;

struct ms_dos_buff{
   char reserved[21]; /* for MS-DOS use on subsequent find_nexts */
   unsigned char attr; /* attribute found */
   unsigned int time;
   unsigned int date;
   unsigned int size_l; /* low size */
   unsigned int size_h; /* high size */
   char pname[13]; /* packed name */
};

struct{
   int drive;
   unsigned available_clusters;
   unsigned clusters_per_drive;
   unsigned bytes_per_sector;
   unsigned sectors_per_cluster;
} disk_space;

struct dir_list {
   char *dir_path_and_name;
   struct dir_list *next;
} root;

#define OVERLAP (MAX_PATTERN_LENGTH-1)
static unsigned char buff[BUFSIZE+OVERLAP];

static int patterns_discovered=0;
static int err=0;
static long int total_bytes_searched=0l;

void nonrecursive_search_files();
void recursive_search_files();
void invert_pattern();

void do_path();
void complete_search_buff();
void complete_search_file();
void add_dir_to_list();

void search_dos_boot_sector();
void search_master_boot_sector();

unsigned int getdosversion();
unsigned int absread();
unsigned int lowdiskread();

void stradd();

char *malloc();
```

```
main(argc,argv)
int argc;
char *argv[];
{
   register int i;

   if(read_patterns()==ERROR) exit(ERROR_EXIT);
   if(max_patterns) printf("Searching for %d patterns.\n",max_patterns);
   else{
      printf("You must specify patterns in SEARCH.PAT file\n");
      exit(ERROR_EXIT);
   }

   if(argc>1) for(i=1;i<argc;i++){
      if(*argv[i]=='-') switch(*(argv[i]+1)){
      default:
         printf("SEARCH will search the current drive for known viruses.\n");
         printf("Virus patterns have to be specified in SEARCH.PAT.\n\n");
         printf("You can name specific groups of files to be searched in the command
line,\nfor example:\n\n");
         printf("\tSEARCH *.EXE\n");
         exit(ERROR_EXIT);
      } else{
         nonrecursive_search_files(argv[i]);
         continue;
      }
   } else{
      recursive_search_files("\\*.COM");
      recursive_search_files("\\*.EXE");
      recursive_search_files("\\*.SYS");
      recursive_search_files("\\*.OVL");
      search_dos_boot_sector();
      search_master_boot_sector();
   }

   if(err) printf("%d error(s) encountered during searching.\n",err);

   printf("%ld bytes searched.\n",total_bytes_searched);

   if(patterns_discovered) printf("%d virus pattern(s)
discovered.\n",patterns_discovered);
   else printf("No virus patterns discovered.\n");

   exit(NORMAL_EXIT);
}


void nonrecursive_search_files(pattern)
char pattern[];
{
   register int i,j;
   struct ms_dos_buff buf;
   char s[MAXRECURSIVE];

   strcpy(s,pattern);

   for(j=strlen(s)-1;j>=0;j--)
      if(s[j]=='\\') break;

   i=getfirst(pattern,0xffe7,&buf); /* no Dir / Vol */

   for(;i==0;i=getnext()){
      strcpy(s+j+1,buf.pname);
      complete_search_file(s);
   }
}
```

```
void recursive_search_files(pattern)
char pattern[];
{
   char init_path[MAXRECURSIVE],descriptor[MAXRECURSIVE];
   char local_path[MAXRECURSIVE];

   strcpy(init_path,"\\");
   strcpy(descriptor,pattern);
   root.next=NULL;

   do_path(init_path,descriptor);
   while(find_dir(local_path)) do_path(local_path,descriptor);
}


void do_path(path,descriptor)
char path[],descriptor[];
{
   register int i;
   char drive_and_path[MAXRECURSIVE],local_path[MAXRECURSIVE];
   struct ms_dos_buff buf;

   strcpy(drive_and_path,path);
   if(drive_and_path[strlen(drive_and_path)-1]=='\\') stradd(drive_and_path,"*.*");
   else stradd(drive_and_path,"\\*.*");

   i=getfirst(drive_and_path,0xffff,&buf);

   for(;i==0;i=getnext()){ /* collect directories */
      if(buf.attr&0x10){ /* Dir */
         if(!strcmp(buf.pname,".") || !strcmp(buf.pname,"..")) continue;
         strcpy(local_path,path);
         if(local_path[strlen(local_path)-1]!='\\') stradd(local_path,"\\");
         stradd(local_path,buf.pname);
         add_dir_to_list(local_path);
      } /* ignore anything which is not a dir */
   }

   drive_and_path[strlen(drive_and_path)-3]='\0'; /* get rid of *.* */
   if(descriptor[0]=='\\') stradd(drive_and_path,descriptor+1);
   else stradd(drive_and_path,descriptor);

   i=getfirst(drive_and_path,0xffe7,&buf); /* ignore Dir/Vol */

   for(;i==0;i=getnext()){
      strcpy(local_path,path);
      if(local_path[strlen(local_path)-1]!='\\') stradd(local_path,"\\");
      stradd(local_path,buf.pname);
      complete_search_file(local_path);
   }
}


void add_dir_to_list(s)
char s[];
{
   struct dir_list *nextp;

   for(nextp = &root;nextp->next;nextp=nextp->next);
   if(nextp->next=(struct dir_list *) malloc(sizeof(root))){
      nextp=nextp->next;
      if(nextp->dir_path_and_name=malloc((unsigned)(strlen(s)+1))){
         strcpy(nextp->dir_path_and_name,s);
         nextp->next=NULL;
         return;
      } else{
         printf("Too many directories to store in memory\n");
         exit(ERROR_EXIT);
```

```
        }
    } else{
        printf("Too many directories\n");
        exit(ERROR_EXIT);
    }
}


void search_dos_boot_sector()
{
    disk_space.drive=currentdisk()+1; /* get current disk drive */
    bytesfree(&disk_space); /* will get drive parameters */

    printf("Checking DOS boot sector of drive %c:\n",disk_space.drive+'A'-1);

    if(absread(disk_space.drive-1,buff,1,0)){
        printf("Could not read DOS boot sector\n");
        err++;
        return;
    }
    complete_search_buff(0,buff,0,disk_space.bytes_per_sector-1);
}


void search_master_boot_sector()
{
    register int i;
    unsigned int drive,head,cylinder,sector;

    drive=0x80; /* first hard disk */
    head=0;
    cylinder=0;
    sector=1; /* location of the master boot sector */

    printf("Checking master boot sector of disk drive number %02x\n",drive);

    for(i=0;i<MAX_BUFF;i++) buff[i]=0x00;


if(lowdiskread((head<<8)|(drive&0xff),buff,(cylinder<<8)|((cylinder>>2)&0xc0)|(sector&0x3f))){
        printf("Could not read master boot sector\n");
        err++;
        return;
    }

    complete_search_buff(1,buff,0,MAX_BUFF-1);
}


void complete_search_buff(what,buff,from_byte,to_byte)
int what;
unsigned char buff[];
int from_byte,to_byte;
{
    register unsigned int j;
    register int i,k;

    total_bytes_searched+=to_byte-from_byte;

    for(j=from_byte;j<=to_byte;j++){
        for(i=0;i<max_patterns;i++){
            if((patterns[i].pattern)[0]!=buff[j]) continue; /* not in */
            if(patterns[i].bytes_in_pattern>j-from_byte+1) continue; /* out of boundary */

            for(k=1;k<patterns[i].bytes_in_pattern;k++)
                if((patterns[i].pattern)[k]!=buff[j-k]) break;
            if(k<patterns[i].bytes_in_pattern) continue; /* not in */
```

```
        switch(what){
        case 0:
            printf("Virus '%s' found in DOS boot sector starting at the address
%04x\n",patterns[i].name,j-k+1);
            break;
        case 1:
            printf("Virus '%s' found in master boot sector starting at the address
%04x\n",patterns[i].name,j-k+1);
            break;
        }
        patterns_discovered++;
    }
  }
}


void complete_search_file(file)
char file[];
{
    register int k,i;
    static int j,fd,bytes_read,bytes_in_pattern;
    static int tot_bytes;
    static unsigned char *pattern;
    static long int byte_number;

    printf("Checking %s\n",file);

    if((fd=open(file,O_RDONLY))==EOF){
        printf("Could not open file %s\n",file);
        err++;
        return;
    }

    for(byte_number=0l;;){
        switch(bytes_read=read(fd,buff+OVERLAP,BUFSIZE)){

        case 0:      /* EOF */
            break;
        case -1:
            printf("Could not read file %s\n",file);
            err++;
            return;
        default:
            tot_bytes=bytes_read+OVERLAP;
            for(k=OVERLAP;k<tot_bytes;k++){
                for(i=0;i<max_patterns;i++){

                    pattern=patterns[i].pattern;

                    if(pattern[0]!=buff[k]) continue;
                    if(pattern[1]!=buff[k-1]) continue;

                    bytes_in_pattern=patterns[i].bytes_in_pattern;

                    for(j=2;j<bytes_in_pattern;j++)
                       if(pattern[j]!=buff[k-j]) break; /* not there */
                    if(j<bytes_in_pattern) continue; /* not there */

                    if(byte_number==0l && k-OVERLAP+1<bytes_in_pattern) continue;

                    printf("Virus '%s' found in file %s starting at the address
%06lx\n",patterns[i].name,file,byte_number+k-OVERLAP-bytes_in_pattern+1);
                    patterns_discovered++;
                }
            }
            byte_number+=bytes_read;
            total_bytes_searched+=bytes_read;
            for(i=0;i<OVERLAP;i++) buff[i]=buff[i+BUFSIZE]; /* copy down */
```

```
            continue;
        }
        break;
    }
    close(fd);
}


int find_dir(s)   /* returns the directory name in s */
char s[];
{
    struct dir_list *nextp,*nextpp;

    if(root.next == NULL) return FALSE;

    for(nextp = &root;nextp->next;nextp=nextp->next);
    strcpy(s,nextp->dir_path_and_name);

/* free space now */

    free(nextp->dir_path_and_name);

    for(nextpp = &root;(nextpp->next)!=nextp;nextpp=nextpp->next);

    free((char *) (nextpp->next));

    nextpp->next = NULL;
    return TRUE;
}


int read_patterns()
{
    FILE *infp;
    char s[MAX_LINE];

    if((infp=fopen(SEARCH_PAT,"r"))==NULL) return NO_ERROR;

    for(;max_patterns<MAX_PATTERNS;){
        switch(fmaxgets(infp,s,MAX_LINE)){
        case EOF:
            fclose(infp);
            return NO_ERROR;
        case ERROR:
            printf("Pattern string too long:\n%s\n",s);
            return ERROR;
        }
        pattern_line++; /* read from the file */
        if(contains_no_pattern(s)) continue;
        if(convert_to_pattern(&patterns[max_patterns++],s)==ERROR) return ERROR;
    }

    printf("Too many patterns in file %s\n",SEARCH_PAT);
    return ERROR;

}


int convert_to_pattern(pattp,s)
struct patt *pattp;
char s[];
{ /* this will convert the pattern in char s[] into the struct *pattp */

    register int i;
    static int noname=0;

    if(s[0]=='\0'){
        printf("Illegal zero pattern in line %d\n",pattern_line);
```

```
      return ERROR;
   }

   if(s[0]==' ' || s[0]=='\t'){/* pattern has no name */
      sprintf(pattp->name,"Noname %d",noname++);
      i=0;
   } else{  /* get name of the pattern */
      for(i=0;i<MAX_NAME && s[i] && s[i]!=' ' && s[i]!='\t';i++)
         pattp->name[i]=(s[i]=='_'?' ':s[i]);
      if(i==MAX_NAME){
         printf("Name too long in '%s'\n",s);
         return ERROR;
      }
      pattp->name[i]='\0';
   }

   if(convert_string_to_pattern(pattp,s+i)==ERROR) return ERROR;
   return NO_ERROR;
}


int convert_string_to_pattern(pattp,s)
struct patt *pattp;
char s[];
{
   register int i,j,c,sum;

   pattp->bytes_in_pattern=0;

   for(i=j=sum=0;;){

      for(;s[i] && (s[i]==' ' || s[i]=='\t');i++); /* ffnb */
      if(s[i]=='\0' || s[i]==';'){
         if(j==1){
            pattp->pattern[pattp->bytes_in_pattern++]=sum;
         }
         if(pattp->bytes_in_pattern<2){
            printf("Illegal pattern in input line %d, '%s';\nmust have at least 2
bytes.\n",pattern_line,s);
            return ERROR;
         }
         invert_pattern(pattp->bytes_in_pattern,pattp->pattern);
         return NO_ERROR;
      }
      if((c=ishexdigit(s[i]))<0){
         printf("Spurious character %c in '%s'\n",s[i],s);
         return ERROR;
      }
      if(pattp->bytes_in_pattern>MAX_PATTERN_LENGTH){
         printf("Pattern longer than %d bytes in '%s'\n",MAX_PATTERN_LENGTH,s);
         return ERROR;
      }

      switch(j++){
      case 0:      /* first digit */
         sum=c;
         break;
      case 1:
         sum=16*sum+c;
         pattp->pattern[pattp->bytes_in_pattern++]=sum;
         j=0;
         break;
      }
      i++;
   }
}
```

```
void invert_pattern(n,s)
int n;
unsigned char s[];
{
    register int i,j,temp;

    for(i=0,j=n-1;i<n/2;i++,j--){
        temp=s[i];
        s[i]=s[j];
        s[j]=temp;
    }
}


int ishexdigit(c)
int c;
{
    switch(c){
    case '0':   return 0;
    case '1':   return 1;
    case '2':   return 2;
    case '3':   return 3;
    case '4':   return 4;
    case '5':   return 5;
    case '6':   return 6;
    case '7':   return 7;
    case '8':   return 8;
    case '9':   return 9;
    case 'a':   case 'A':   return 10;
    case 'b':   case 'B':   return 11;
    case 'c':   case 'C':   return 12;
    case 'd':   case 'D':   return 13;
    case 'e':   case 'E':   return 14;
    case 'f':   case 'F':   return 15;
    default: return (-1);
    }
}


int fmaxgets(infp,s,max)
FILE *infp;
char s[];
int max;
{
    register int c,i;

    for(i=0;c=agetc(infp);) switch(c){
    case '\n':
        s[i]='\0';
        return i;
    case EOF:
        s[i]='\0';
        return i==0?EOF:i;
    default:
        s[i++]=c;
        if(i<max) break;
        s[max-1]='\0';
        return ERROR;
    }
}


contains_no_pattern(s)
char s[];
{
    register int i;

    if(s[0]==';') return TRUE;
```

```
for(i=0;s[i];i++) switch(s[i]){
case ' ':
case '\t':
  continue;
default:
  return FALSE;
}
return TRUE;
}


void stradd(s1,s2)
char *s1,*s2;
{
  for(;*s1;) s1++;
  for(;*s2;) *s1++ = *s2++;
  *s1='\0';
}
```

B.4 SEARCH CODE IN ASSEMBLY LANGUAGE

The assembly language code for SEARCH should be entered into one file called
SEARCHAS.ASM. The FINGER program in Appendix C can be used to verify the
correctness of the code. The fingerprint for SEARCHAS.ASM is CE60DF5F (remember
to run FINGER with the -N option):

> ### FINGER -N SEARCHAS.ASM

File SEARCHAS.ASM:

```
codeseg segment word public
dataseg segment byte public
assume cs:codeseg,ds:dataseg,es:dataseg,ss:dataseg
dataseg ends

;functions for small model aztec c

              public    getfirst_
getfirst_:    mov       bx,sp
              mov       dx,6[bx]    ; dma block address

; set dma address

              mov       ah,1AH
              int       21H

; get first file

              mov       dx,2[bx]    ; pathname pointer
              mov       cx,4[bx]    ; search attributes
              mov       ah,4EH
              int       21H

              jc        getfer
              mov       ax,0
getfer:       ret


              public    getnext_
getnext_:     mov       ah,4FH      ; Function 4FH
              int       21H
```

```
                jc              getner
                mov             ax,0
getner:         ret

                public bytesfree_
bytesfree_:     mov             bx,sp
                push            bp
                mov             bp,2[bx]    ; pars address

                mov             dx,[bp]     ; drive
                mov             dh,0
                mov             ah,36H      ; Function 36H
                int             21H

                mov             2[bp],bx    ; available clusters
                mov             4[bp],dx    ; clusters per drive
                mov             6[bp],cx    ; bytes per sector
                mov             8[bp],ax    ; sectors per cluster

                pop             bp
                ret

                public absread_
absread_:       mov             bx,sp
                push            bp
                mov             bp,bx       ; a copy

; read now

                mov             ax,2[bp]    ; drive
                mov             bx,4[bp]    ; dma block address
                mov             cx,6[bp]    ; number of sectors
                mov             dx,8[bp]    ; first sector number
                int             25H

                pop             bx          ; pop flags
                jc              rdfer
                mov             ax,0
rdfer:          pop             bp
                ret

                public lowdiskread_
lowdiskread_:   mov             bx,sp
                push            bp
                mov             bp,bx       ; a copy

; read now

                mov             dx,2[bp]    ; head + drive
                mov             bx,4[bp]    ; dma block address
                mov             cx,6[bp]    ; cylinder + sector
                mov             ax,0201H    ; service 2, 1 sector only
                int             13H

                jc              rdler
                mov             ax,0
rdler:          pop             bp
                ret

                public currentdisk_
currentdisk_:   mov             ah,19H
                int             21H
                and             ax,0FFH     ; result in al
                ret

codeseg ends
                end
```

C

'FINGER': VIRUS NON-SPECIFIC DETECTION PROGRAM

Very well, I can wait.

Arnold Schoenberg (when told that his violin concerto required a soloist with six fingers)

This appendix contains the source code for a program called FINGER which produces cryptographic fingerprints for a file or group of files.

By fingerprinting the original executable and then subsequently verifying that the fingerprint has not changed, one can detect a virus attack on the executable.

Although FINGER is quite usable as shown here, an average 'C' programmer can easily modify it to store the fingerprints into a file and check them automatically. The program could be improved further by giving it a facility to fingerprint the DOS and master boot sectors in order to discover boot sector viruses. Likewise, the speed of the DES (Data Encryption Standard) code is not very high and offers plenty of scope for optimisation.

Another function of FINGER is to verify the correctness of the contents of source codes.

C.1 DESCRIPTION OF FINGER

FINGER is a program which produces cryptographic fingerprints for one file or a group of files. The fingerprint is produced using DES (Data Encryption Standard) in the mode described in ANSI standard X9.9.

FINGER can be used to produce fingerprints of binary files (such as COM and EXE files) or text files. When fingerprinting binary files, it is important to fingerprint every single byte, but when fingerprinting text files, certain (non-printable) characters can be skipped, without the meaning of the text changed in any way. For example, when entering the source code in C, one can type the TAB character or 8 blanks, without generally changing the meaning of the code. The only exceptions are quoted strings, where it is important to enter the blanks verbatim. When FINGER is fingerprinting files in the text mode, the -N command line argument can be specified to make it ignore any non-printable or 'white space' characters.

FINGER fingerprints files in binary mode by default. For example

```
FINGER *.EXE
```

will produce fingerprints for all EXE files in the current directory, for example

```
Fingerprint of SEARCH.EXE is f44b8704
Fingerprint of FINGER.EXE is dfbe5335
```

To produce fingerprints of the files used to make FINGER, type

```
FINGER -N FINGER.C DES.C
```

and you should get the following output:

```
Fingerprint of FINGER.C is f08f38fe
Fingerprint of DES.C is 1eecc40f
```

If you do not get that, the files with incorrect fingerprints have not been entered correctly. Note that both fingerprints will be wrong if the tables in DES.C have been entered incorrectly, even if FINGER.C is correct.

C.2 COMPILING 'FINGER'

The majority of FINGER's code is written in 'C', but two routines call DOS and are written in assembly language. The 'C' code can be compiled by most compilers, but it has been tested only using Aztec C. The assembly language routines, which are the same as for SEARCH, assume that they will be called from Aztec C using the small memory model. If you are using a different compiler or a different memory model, make sure that you use the correct calling procedure and preserve any registers required by the compiler. Some compiler libraries contain DOS calling routines directly from C, in which case all of FINGER can be written in C.

Some compilers (like Aztec) provide a 'make' facility similar to that of Unix. This simplifies the preparation of any software. The makefile for FINGER is listed below:

```
des.o: des.c
searchas.o: searchas.asm
finger.o: finger.c
```

```
FINGER=finger.o des.o searchas.o
finger: finger.exe
@echo finger made
finger.exe: $(FINGER)
ln $(FINGER) -lc
```

To compile FINGER, type

```
make finger
```

and the computer will do the rest.

C.3 FINGER CODE IN 'C'

The C code for FINGER is divided into two files called FINGER.C and DES.C. The file FINGER.C contains routines for file scanning, while the file DES.C contains an implementation of the Data Encryption Standard (DES), as defined in ANSI standard X3.92-1981. This is used for producing cryptographic checksums as defined in ANSI standard X9.9. Note that X3.92 does not define the way of numbering of bits in an 8-byte block passed to DES for encryption. This implementation uses the convention that the least significant bit in the first byte is bit 1 referred to by DES, most significant bit in the first byte is bit 8 referred to by DES, least significant bit in the second byte is bit 9 referred to by DES etc.

FINGER also uses some code in assembly language, which is the same as the code used for SEARCH and is contained in the file SEARCH.ASM. You only need to enter that file once.

File FINGER.C:

```
/*
    This program can be used to fingerprint any file
*/

#include "libc.h"

struct ms_dos_buff{
    char reserved[21]; /* for MS-DOS use on subsequent find_nexts */
    unsigned char attr; /* attribute found */
    unsigned int time;
    unsigned int date;
    unsigned int size_l; /* low size */
    unsigned int size_h; /* high size */
    char pname[13]; /* packed name */
};

#define SEARCH_MASK 0x07 /* DOS will return only files, not directories */

#define EOF (-1)
#define PARTEOF (-2)
#define NOTEOF (0)

#define FALSE (0)
#define TRUE (!FALSE)
```

```
void fingerprint(),des_init(),des_encrypt(),explain_command_line_arguments();

static int only_printable=FALSE;

main(argc,argv)
int argc;
char *argv[];
{
   register int i,j;
   static char key[8]={
       0x01,0x23,0x45,0x67,0x89,0xab,0xcd,0xef
   }; /* this should be a uniquely chosen key when calculating your fingerprints */
   struct ms_dos_buff fcb;

   des_init(key);

   if(argc>1) for(i=1;i<argc;i++){
       if(*argv[i]=='-') switch(*(argv[i]+1)){
       case 'N':
       case 'n':
          only_printable=TRUE;
          continue;
       default:
          explain_command_line_arguments();
          break;
       }
   }
   if(argc>1) for(i=1;i<argc;i++){
       if(*argv[i]!='-'){
          switch(j=getfirst(argv[i],SEARCH_MASK,&fcb)){
          case 2:
          case 18:
             printf("No file found corresponding to %s\n",argv[i]);
             continue;
          }

          for(;j==0;j=getnext()) fingerprint(fcb.pname);
          continue;
       }
   }
}


void explain_command_line_arguments()
{
   printf("Command syntax:\n\nFINGER [-n] <file1> <file2> ... <filen>\n\n");
   printf("-n causes only printable characters to be fingerprinted.\n");
   exit(-1);
}


void fingerprint(file)
char file[];
{
   register int i;
   unsigned char buf[8],out[8];
   FILE *infp;

   if((infp=fopen(file,"r"))==NULL){
      printf("Cannot open %s\n",file);
      return;
   }

   printf("Fingerprint of %s is ",file);

   for(i=0;i<8;i++) out[i]=0x00; /* initialise forward buffer */

   for(;;) switch(get_bufferfull(infp,buf)){
```

```
  case EOF:
     fclose(infp);
     printf("%02x%02x%02x%02x\n",out[0],out[1],out[2],out[3]);
     return;

  case PARTEOF:
     for(i=0;i<8;i++) buf[i]=out[i]^buf[i];
     des_encrypt(buf);
     for(i=0;i<8;i++) out[i]=buf[i];
     fclose(infp);
     printf("%02x%02x%02x%02x\n",out[0],out[1],out[2],out[3]);
     return;

  case NOTEOF:
     for(i=0;i<8;i++) buf[i]=out[i]^buf[i];
     des_encrypt(buf);
     for(i=0;i<8;i++) out[i]=buf[i];
  }
}


int get_bufferfull(infp,buf)
FILE *infp;
unsigned char buf[];
{
   register int i,c;

   for(i=0;i<8;i++) switch(c=sp_getc(infp)){
   case EOF:
      if(i==0) return EOF; /* file length%8 == 0 */
      for(;i<8;i++) buf[i]=0x00;
      return PARTEOF; /* file length%8 != 0 */
   default:
      buf[i]=c;
      break;
   }
   return NOTEOF;
}


int sp_getc(infp)
FILE *infp;
{
   register int c;

   if(only_printable){
      for(;should_skip(c=getc(infp)););
      return c;
   } else return getc(infp);
}


int should_skip(c)
int c;
{
   return !(c==EOF || c>' ');
}
```

File DES.C:

```
/*
    This is the implementation of the Data Encryption Standard
*/

static int keyout[17][48];

void des_init(),des_encrypt(),des_decrypt();
static void lshift(),cypher();

void des_init(key) /* Calculation of Keys */
unsigned char *key;
{
    unsigned char c[28],d[28];
    static int pc1[56]={
        57,49,41,33,25,17, 9, 1,58,50,42,34,26,18,
        10, 2,59,51,43,35,27,19,11, 3,60,52,44,36,
        63,55,47,39,31,23,15, 7,62,54,46,38,30,22,
        14, 6,61,53,45,37,29,21,13, 5,28,20,12, 4
    };
    static int pc2[48]={
        14,17,11,24, 1, 5, 3,28,15, 6,21,10,
        23,19,12, 4,26, 8,16, 7,27,20,13, 2,
        41,52,31,37,47,55,30,40,51,45,33,48,
        44,49,39,56,34,53,46,42,50,36,29,32
    };
    static int nls[17]={
        0,1,1,2,2,2,2,2,2,1,2,2,2,2,2,2,1
    };
    static int cd[56],keyb[64];
    static int cnt,n=0;
    register int i,j;

    for(i=0;i<8;i++) /* Read in Key */
        for(j=0;j<8;j++) keyb[n++]=(key[i]>>j&0x01);

    for(i=0;i<56;i++) /* Permuted Choice 1 */
        cd[i]=keyb[pc1[i]-1];
    for(i=0;i<28;i++){
        c[i]=cd[i];
        d[i]=cd[i+28];
    }
    for(cnt=1;cnt<=16;cnt++){
        for(i=0;i<nls[cnt];i++){ /* Left Shifts */
            lshift(c);
            lshift(d);
        }
        for(i=0;i<28;i++){
            cd[i]=c[i];
            cd[i+28]=d[i];
        }
        for(i=0;i<48;i++) /* Permuted Choice 2 */
            keyout[cnt][i]=cd[pc2[i]-1];
    }
}


static void lshift(shft)        /* Left Shift Function */
unsigned char shft[];
{
    register int temp,i;

    temp=shft[0];
    for(i=0;i<27;i++) shft[i]=shft[i+1];
    shft[27]=temp;
}
```

```
static void cypher(r,cnt,fout)
int *r,*fout;
int cnt;
{
   static int expand[48],b[8][6],sout[8],pin[48];
   register int i,j;
   static int n,row,col,scnt;
   static int p[32]={
       16, 7,20,21,29,12,28,17, 1,15,23,26, 5,18,31,10,
        2, 8,24,14,32,27, 3, 9,19,13,30, 6,22,11, 4,25
   };
   static int e[48]={
       32, 1, 2, 3, 4, 5, 4, 5, 6, 7, 8, 9,
        8, 9,10,11,12,13,12,13,14,15,16,17,
       16,17,18,19,20,21,20,21,22,23,24,25,
       24,25,26,27,28,29,28,29,30,31,32, 1
   };
   static int s[8][64]={
   {
       14, 4,13, 1, 2,15,11, 8, 3,10, 6,12, 5, 9, 0, 7,
        0,15, 7, 4,14, 2,13, 1,10, 6,12,11, 9, 5, 3, 8,
        4, 1,14, 8,13, 6, 2,11,15,12, 9, 7, 3,10, 5, 0,
       15,12, 8, 2, 4, 9, 1, 7, 5,11, 3,14,10, 0, 6,13
   },
   {
       15, 1, 8,14, 6,11, 3, 4, 9, 7, 2,13,12, 0, 5,10,
        3,13, 4, 7,15, 2, 8,14,12, 0, 1,10, 6, 9,11, 5,
        0,14, 7,11,10, 4,13, 1, 5, 8,12, 6, 9, 3, 2,15,
       13, 8,10, 1, 3,15, 4, 2,11, 6, 7,12, 0, 5,14, 9
   },
   {
       10, 0, 9,14, 6, 3,15, 5, 1,13,12, 7,11, 4, 2, 8,
       13, 7, 0, 9, 3, 4, 6,10, 2, 8, 5,14,12,11,15, 1,
       13, 6, 4, 9, 8,15, 3, 0,11, 1, 2,12, 5,10,14, 7,
        1,10,13, 0, 6, 9, 8, 7, 4,15,14, 3,11, 5, 2,12
   },
   {
        7,13,14, 3, 0, 6, 9,10, 1, 2, 8, 5,11,12, 4,15,
       13, 8,11, 5, 6,15, 0, 3, 4, 7, 2,12, 1,10,14, 9,
       10, 6, 9, 0,12,11, 7,13,15, 1, 3,14, 5, 2, 8, 4,
        3,15, 0, 6,10, 1,13, 8, 9, 4, 5,11,12, 7, 2,14
   },
   {
        2,12, 4, 1, 7,10,11, 6, 8, 5, 3,15,13, 0,14, 9,
       14,11, 2,12, 4, 7,13, 1, 5, 0,15,10, 3, 9, 8, 6,
        4, 2, 1,11,10,13, 7, 8,15, 9,12, 5, 6, 3, 0,14,
       11, 8,12, 7, 1,14, 2,13, 6,15, 0, 9,10, 4, 5, 3
   },
   {
       12, 1,10,15, 9, 2, 6, 8, 0,13, 3, 4,14, 7, 5,11,
       10,15, 4, 2, 7,12, 9, 5, 6, 1,13,14, 0,11, 3, 8,
        9,14,15, 5, 2, 8,12, 3, 7, 0, 4,10, 1,13,11, 6,
        4, 3, 2,12, 9, 5,15,10,11,14, 1, 7, 6, 0, 8,13
   },
   {
        4,11, 2,14,15, 0, 8,13, 3,12, 9, 7, 5,10, 6, 1,
       13, 0,11, 7, 4, 9, 1,10,14, 3, 5,12, 2,15, 8, 6,
        1, 4,11,13,12, 3, 7,14,10,15, 6, 8, 0, 5, 9, 2,
        6,11,13, 8, 1, 4,10, 7, 9, 5, 0,15,14, 2, 3,12
   },
   {
       13, 2, 8, 4, 6,15,11, 1,10, 9, 3,14, 5, 0,12, 7,
        1,15,13, 8,10, 3, 7, 4,12, 5, 6,11, 0,14, 9, 2,
        7,11, 4, 1, 9,12,14, 2, 0, 6,10,13,15, 3, 5, 8,
        2, 1,14, 7, 4,10, 8,13,15,12, 9, 0, 3, 5, 6,11
   }
   };
```

```
    for(i=0;i<48;i++) expand[i]=r[e[i]-1]; /* Expansion Function */
    for(i=n=0;i<8;i++){ /* XOR Function */
        for(j=0;j<6;j++,n++) b[i][j]=expand[n]^keyout[cnt][n];
    }

/* Selection Functions */

    for(scnt=n=0;scnt<8;scnt++){
        row=(b[scnt][0]<<1)+b[scnt][5];
        col=(b[scnt][1]<<3)+(b[scnt][2]<<2)+(b[scnt][3]<<1)+b[scnt][4];
        sout[scnt]=s[scnt][(row<<4)+col];
        for(i=3;i>=0;i--){
            pin[n]=sout[scnt]>>i;
            sout[scnt]=sout[scnt]-(pin[n++]<<i);
        }
    }
    for(i=0;i<32;i++) fout[i]=pin[p[i]-1]; /* Permutation Function */
}

static int p[64]={
    58,50,42,34,26,18,10, 2,60,52,44,36,28,20,12, 4,
    62,54,46,38,30,22,14, 6,64,56,48,40,32,24,16, 8,
    57,49,41,33,25,17, 9, 1,59,51,43,35,27,19,11, 3,
    61,53,45,37,29,21,13, 5,63,55,47,39,31,23,15, 7
};
static int invp[64]={
    40, 8,48,16,56,24,64,32,39, 7,47,15,55,23,63,31,
    38, 6,46,14,54,22,62,30,37, 5,45,13,53,21,61,29,
    36, 4,44,12,52,20,60,28,35, 3,43,11,51,19,59,27,
    34, 2,42,10,50,18,58,26,33, 1,41, 9,49,17,57,25
};

void des_encrypt(input)
unsigned char *input;
{
    static unsigned char out[64];
    static int inputb[64],lr[64],l[32],r[32];
    static int fn[32];
    static int cnt,n;
    register int i,j;

    for(i=n=0;i<8;i++)
        for(j=0;j<8;j++) inputb[n++]=(input[i]>>j&0x01);

    for(i=0;i<64;i++){ /* Initial Permutation */
        lr[i]=inputb[p[i]-1];
        if(i<32) l[i]=lr[i];
        else r[i-32]=lr[i];
    }
    for(cnt=1;cnt<=16;cnt++){ /* Main Encryption Loop */
        cypher(r,cnt,fn); /* Execute Cypher Function */
        for(i=0;i<32;i++){
            j=r[i];
            r[i]=l[i]^fn[i];
            l[i]=j;
        }
    }
    for(i=0;i<32;i++){
        lr[i]=r[i];
        lr[i+32]=l[i];
    }
    for(i=0;i<64;i++) out[i]=lr[invp[i]-1]; /* Inverse Initial Permutation */

    for(i=1;i<=8;i++)
        for(j=1;j<=8;j++) input[i-1]=(input[i-1]<<1)|out[i*8-j];
}
```

```c
void des_decrypt(input)
/* this function is not used by FINGER, but is reproduced for completeness */
unsigned char *input;
{
   static unsigned char out[64];
   static int inputb[64],lr[64],l[32],r[32];
   static int fn[32];
   static int cnt,rtemp,n;
   register int i,j;

   for(i=n=0;i<8;i++)
      for(j=0;j<8;j++) inputb[n++]=(input[i]>>j&0x01);

   for(i=0;i<64;i++){              /* Initial Permutation */
      lr[i]=inputb[p[i]-1];
      if(i<32) l[i]=lr[i];
      else r[i-32]=lr[i];
   }
   for(cnt=16;cnt>0;cnt--){       /* Main Encryption Loop */
      cypher(r,cnt,fn); /* Execute Cypher Function */
      for(i=0;i<32;i++){
         rtemp=r[i];
         if(l[i]==1 && fn[i]==1) r[i]=0;
         else r[i]=(l[i]||fn[i]);
         l[i]=rtemp;
      }
   }
   for(i=0;i<32;i++){
      lr[i]=r[i];
      lr[i+32]=l[i];
   }
   for(i=0;i<64;i++) out[i]=lr[invp[i]-1]; /* Inverse Initial Permutation */

   for(i=1;i<=8;i++)
      for(j=1;j<=8;j++) input[i-1]=(input[i-1]<<1)|out[i*8-j];
}
```

D

ANTI-VIRUS SOFTWARE MANUFACTURERS

The great Unwashed

Henry Peter Brougham (1778-1868)

NOTES ON TELEPHONE AND FAX NUMBERS

All numbers are shown with the country code preceded by a plus sign (+), followed by the number. If dialling a number from the same country, omit the country code and prefix the area code with 0 (in most countries). For example, to dial the UK number +44 235 559933 from the UK, dial 0235 559933.

When dialling internationally, prefix each number with the international code. For example, to dial the Swiss number +41 1 234 5678 from the UK, dial 010 41 1 234 5678. To dial the above number from France, dial 19 41 1 234 5678.

ASP (Advanced Software Protection), PO Box 81270, Pittsburgh, PA 15217, USA.
Tel +1 412 422 4134, Fax +1 412 422 4135

Bangkok Security Associates, PO Box 5-121, Bangkok 10500, Thailand.
Tel +66 2 251 2574, Fax +66 2 253 6868

Brightwork Development International, 766 Shrewsbury Avenue, Bldg 2, Tinton
Falls, New Jersey 07724, USA. Tel +1 908 530 0440, Fax +1 908 530 0622

BRM Technologies Ltd., 67 Dereh Hahoresh, Ranot, Jerusalem, Israel.
Tel +972 2 861092, Fax +972 2 867503

Carmel Software Engineering, Hamachshev Ltd Hahistradrut Av 20, Haifa, Israel
POB 25055. Tel +972 4 416976, Fax +972 4 416979

Central Point Software, 15220 NW Greenbrier Parkway, Suite 200, Beaverton,
Oregon 97006, USA. Tel +1 503 690 8090, Fax +1 503 690 8083

Certus, 6896 W Snowville Road, Brecksville, Ohio 44141, USA.
Tel +1 216 546 1500, Fax +1 216 546 1450

Clurwin Pty. Ltd., 73 Kensington Road, South Yarra, Victoria 3141, Australia.
Tel +61 3 827 8002, Fax +61 3 826 2514

Commcrypt Inc., 10000 Virginia Manor Road, Suite 300, Beltsville, MA 20705,
USA. Tel +1 301 470 2500, Fax +1 301 470 2507

ComNetco, 2475 Lamington Road, Bedminster, NJ 07921, USA.
Tel +1 201 543 4060, Fax +1 201 781 7935

Cybec Pty. Ltd., PO Box 82, Hampton, Victoria 3188, Australia. Tel +61 3 521 0655,
Fax +61 3 521 0727

Cybersoft, 210 West 12th Avenue, Conshohocken, PA 19428-1464, USA.
Tel +1 215 825 4748, Fax +1 215 825 6785

(DDI) Digital Despatch Inc., 55 Lakeland Shores, Lakeland, MN 55043, USA.
Tel +1 612 436 1000, Fax +1 612 436 2085

EliaShim Microcomputers Ltd., PO Box 8691, Haifa 31086, Israel.
Tel +972 4 516111, Fax +972 4 528613

Enigma Logic Inc., 2151 Salvio Street, Ste. 301, Concord, CA 94520, USA.
Tel +1 510 827 5707, Fax +1 510 827 2593

ESaSS BV, PO Box 1380, 6501 BJ Nijmegen, The Netherlands. Tel +31 80 787881,
Fax +31 80 789186

Fifth Generation Systems Inc., 11200 Industriplex Blvd., Baton Rouge,
LA 70809-4112, USA. Tel +1 504 291 7221, Fax +1 504 291 3268

Frisk Software International, PO Box 7180, 127 Reykjavik, Iceland.
Tel +354 1 694749, Fax +354 1 128801

Hilgraeve Inc., Genesis Centre, 111 Conant Avenue, Suite A, Monroe, Michgan 48161, USA. Tel +1 313 243 0576, Fax +1 313 243 0645

IBM, TJ Watson Research Centre, PO Box 218, Route 134, Yorktown Heights, NY 10598, USA. Tel +1 914 945 3000, Fax +1 914 945 2141

Intel Corp., 5200 N E Elam Young Parkway, Hillsborough, OR 97124, USA. Tel +1 503 629 7354, Fax +1 503 629 7227

IP Technologies, 3710 South Susan, Suite 100, Santa Ana, CA 92704, USA. Tel +1 714 549 4284, Fax +1 714 549 5079

Iris Software & Computers, 6 Hamavo Street, Givataim 53303, Israel. Tel +972 3 571 5319, Fax +972 3 318731

Jerry Fitzgerald and Associates, 506 Barkentine Lane Redwood City, CA 94065-1128, USA. Tel +1 415 591 5676, Fax +1 415 593 9316

Leprechaun Software Pty. Ltd., PO Box 184, Holland Park, Queensland 4121, Australia. Tel +61 7 343 8866, Fax +61 7 343 8733

McAfee Associates, 4423 Cheeney St., Santa Clara, CA 95054, USA. Tel +1 408 988 3832, Fax +1 408 988 9727

Microcom, Software Division, PO Box 51489, Durham, NC 27717, USA. Tel +1 919 490 1277, Fax +1 919 419 8312

Orion Microsystems, PO Box 128, Pierrefords, Quebec H9H 4K8, Canada. Tel +1 514 626 9234

Panda Systems, 801 Wilson Road, Wilmington, DE 19803, USA. Tel +1 302 764 4722, Fax +1 302 764 6186

PC Enhancements Ltd., The Acorn Suite, Greenleaf House, Darkes Lane, Potters Bar, Hertfordshire EN6 1AE, UK. Tel +44 707 59016, Fax +44 707 55523

PC Guardian, 118 Alto Street, San Rafael, CA 94901, USA. Tel +1 415 459 0190, Fax +1 415 459 1162

PC Security Ltd., The Old Courthouse, Trinity Road, Marlow, SL7 3AN, UK. Tel +44 628 890390, Fax +44 628 890116

Ports of Trade, 6 Alcis Street, Newlands, Cape Town 7700, South Africa. Tel +27 21 686 8215, Fax +27 21 685 1807

Prime Factors Inc., 1832 Orchard Street, Eugene, OR 97403, USA. Tel +1 503 345 4334, Fax +1 503 345 6818

Quaid Software Ltd., 45 Charles Street East, 3rd Floor, Toronto, Ontario M4Y 1S2, Canada. Tel +1 416 961 8243, Fax +1 519 942 3532

Remarkable Products, 245 Pegasus Avenue, Northvale, NJ 07647, USA.
Tel +1 201 784 0900, Fax +1 201 767 7463

RG Software Systems, 6900 E. Camelback, Suite 630, Scottsdale, AZ 85251, USA.
Tel +1 602 423 8000, Fax +1 602 423 8389

RSA Data Security Inc., 10 Twin Dolphin Drive, Redwood City, CA 94065, USA.
Tel +1 415 595 8782, Fax +1 415 595 1873

Safetynet Inc., 14 Tower Drive, East Hanover, NJ 07936-3220, USA.
Tel +1 908 851 0188, Fax +1 908 276 6575

SA Software, 28 Denbigh Road, London, W13 8NH, UK. Tel +44 81 998 2351,
Fax +44 81 998 7507

S&S International Ltd., Berkley Court, Mill Street, Berkhampstead, Hertfordshire
HP4 2HB, UK. Tel +44 442 877877, Fax +44 442 877882

Software Concepts Design, PO Box 908, Margaretville, NY 12455, USA.
Tel +1 607 326 4423, Fax +1 607 326 4424

Software Services, Niederwiesstrasse 8, CH-5417 Untersiggenthal, Switzerland.
Tel +41 56 281116, Fax +41 56 281116

Sophco Inc., PO Box 7430, Boulder, CO 80306, USA. Tel +1 303 530 7759,
Fax +1 303 530 7745

Sophos Ltd., 21 The Quadrant, Abingdon Science Park, Abingdon, Oxfordshire,
OX14 3YS, UK. Tel +44 235 559933, Fax +44 235 559935

Symantec Corporation, 10201 Torre Avenue, Cupertino, CA 95014-2132, USA.
Tel +1 408 253 9600, Fax +1 310 829 0247

Total Control, Unit 3, Station Yard, Hungerford, RG17 0DY, UK. Tel +44 488 685299,
Fax +44 488 683288

Trend Micro Devices Inc., 2421 W. 205th Street, Suite D-100, Torrance, CA 90501,
USA. Tel +1 310 782 8190, Fax +1 310 328 5892

V Communications Inc., 4320 Stevens Creek Blvd, Suite 275, San Jose, CA 95129,
USA. Tel +1 408 296 4224, Fax +1 408 296 4441

Visionsoft, Unit M11, Enterprise 5, Five Lane Ends, Idle, Bradford, West Yorkshire
BD10 8BW, UK. Tel +44 274 610503, Fax +44 274 616010

Worldwide Software Inc., 20 Exchange Place, 27th Floor, New York, NY 10005,
USA. Tel +1 212 422 4100, Fax +1 212 422 1953

E

GLOSSARY OF TERMS

He said true things, but called them by wrong names.

Rupert Browning, 'Bishop Blougram's Apology'

Access Control:	The process of ensuring that systems are only accessed by those authorised to do so, and only in a manner for which they have been authorised.
Active Attack:	An attack on a system which either injects false information into the system, or corrupts information already present on the system. See also passive attack.
Algorithm:	An algorithm is a set of rules which specifies a method of carrying out a task (eg. an encryption algorithm).
ANSI:	American National Standards Institute is the organisation which issues standards in the US.
ASCII:	American Standard Code for Information Interchange is the standard system for representing letters and symbols. Each letter or symbol is assigned a unique number between 0 and 127.
Asymmetric Encryption:	Encryption which permits the key used for encryption to be different for the key used for decryption. RSA is the most widely used asymmetric encryption algorithm.
Audit Log:	The same as audit trail.
Audit Trail:	Audit trails provide a date and time stamped record of the usage of a system. They record what a computer was

used for, allowing a security manager to monitor the actions of every user, and can help in establishing an alleged fraud or security violation.

Authentication: The process of assuring that data has come from its claimed source, or of corroborating the claimed identity of a communicating party.

Authorisation: Determining whether a subject is trusted for a given purpose.

Availability: The prevention of unauthorised withholding of information or resources.

Back Door: An undocumented means of bypassing the normal access control procedures of a computer system.

Background Operation: The name applied to a program running in a multitasking environment over which the user has no direct control.

Backup: A copy of computer data that is used to recreate data that has been lost, mislaid, corrupted or erased.

Bad Sectors: During formatting of MS-DOS disks, all sectors are checked for usability. Unusable sectors are labelled as bad and are not used by DOS. The remaining areas can then still be used. Viruses sometimes label good sectors as bad to store their code outside the reach of the users and the operating system.

.BAT: The extension given to 'batch' file names in MS-DOS. A batch file contains a series of MS-DOS commands, which can be executed by using the name of the file as a command. AUTOEXEC.BAT is a special batch file which is executed whenever a PC is switched on, and can be used to configure the PC to a user's requirements.

BBS: Bulletin Board System; a computer with one or more modems attached which can be used remotely via the PSTN. Most bulletin boards act as repositories for downloadable software, and have electronic mail systems.

Bell-LaPadula Model: An access security model couched in terms of subjects and objects. Information shall not flow to a lesser or non-comparable classification.

Biba Model: An integrity model in which there can be no contamination by a less trusted or non-comparable subject or object.

Binary: A number system with base 2. The binary digits (bits) are 0 and 1. Binary arithmetic is used by today's computers since the two digits can be represented with two electrical or magnetic states, for example the presence and absence of a current.

Biometrics: A technique for identifying a person by one of his personal characteristics eg. retina pattern, fingerprint etc.

BIOS: The Basic Input/Output System of MS-DOS which constitutes the lowest level of software which interfaces directly with the hardware of the microcomputer. The BIOS is usually stored in a ROM chip.

Bit: The smallest unit of information. It can only have the value 0 or 1. The word 'bit' is derived from the initial and final letters of the phrase 'Binary Digit'.

Bit Copying: A technique for making a copy of a disk by reading all of the individual bits on each track of the disk, and making a direct copy of each track onto a new disk. A bit copying program has no knowledge of the file structure being used on a disk.

Block Cipher: A cipher which provides encryption and decryption by operating on a specified size of data block, eg. 64 bits.

Boot Protection: Method used to prevent bypassing security measures installed on a hard disk by bootstrapping a microcomputer from a floppy disk.

Boot sector Virus: A type of computer virus which subverts the initial stages of the bootstrapping process. A boot-sector virus attacks either the master bootstrap sector or the DOS bootstrap sector.

Booting-up: A process carried out when a computer is first switched on or reset, where the operating system software is loaded from disk (either hard disk or floppy disk).

Bootstrap Sector: Part of the operating system which is first read into memory from disk when a PC is switched on (booted). The program stored in the bootstrap sector is then executed, which in turn loads the rest of the operating system into memory from the system files on disk.

Bootstrapping: Means the same as Booting-up.

Bug: A small electronic device used for covert eavesdropping. Different types are available to listen to voice conversations, data being transmitted across a network, or telephone lines. A fault in a computer program is also called a bug. The two meanings are entirely separate.

Byte: A set of 8 bits which is the amount of information sufficient to store one character. It is usually the smallest individual unit that can be read from or written to memory.

Cache:

High-speed data storage used to hold data retrieved from a slow device. Using a cache increases the overall performance of a system.

CBC:

Cipher Block Chaining, a mode of use of a block cipher.

CCC:

Chaos Computer Club, an infamous group of German hackers based in Hamburg, Germany.

CCTA:

Central Computer and Telecommunications Agency, the UK Government agency responsible for computer purchases (amongst other duties).

CESG:

Communications-Electronics Security Group, a UK government COMPUSEC agency (CCTA is another).

CFB:

Cipher Feedback, a mode of use of a block cipher.

Checksum:

A value calculated from item(s) of data which can be used by a recipient of the data to verify that the received data has not been altered. Usually 32 or 64 bits long.

Cipher:

Encryption algorithm.

Ciphertext:

A term used to describe text (or data) that has previously been encrypted; see encryption.

CMOS:

Complementary Metal-Oxide Semiconductor is a technology used to manufacture chips which have very low power consumption. CMOS chips are used in battery-backed applications such as the time-of-day clock and for the non-volatile storage of parameters in IBM-ATs.

.COM:

The extension given to a type of executable files in MS-DOS. They are similar to EXE files, but can only contain up to 64K of code and data. In operating systems other than DOS, the extension .COM can have a different significance.

Companion virus:

A virus which 'infects' EXE files by creating a COM file with the same name and containing the virus code. They exploit the PC-DOS property that if two programs with the same name exist, the operating system will execute a COM file in preference to an EXE file.

Compiler:

A computer program which translates programs written in a high-level language that can be readily understood by humans, into low level instructions that can be executed by a computer's CPU.

COMPSEC, COMPUSEC: Often used abbreviations for COMPuter SECurity.

Computer Crime:

This phrase has two meanings: Any crime mediated by a computer; or any crime that attacks a computer system as part of the process of committing the crime. The meaning used in any particular situation is context dependent, and not always clear.

Confidentiality: The process of ensuring that data is not disclosed to those not authorised to see it. Also known as secrecy.

Conventional Memory: The bytes of PC memory addressable by the 8086 instruction set.

Co-processor: Specialised computer hardware used in conjunction with a CPU to perform a specific task very efficiently eg. floating point arithmetic, matrix multiplication.

Copy Protection: A method which makes it difficult (if not impossible) to make copies of a computer program. Copy protection tries to prevent software theft.

CPU: Central Processing Unit, the heart of every PC, the device which takes instructions from memory and executes them. In most PCs, the CPU is a single microprocessor.

CRC: Cyclic Redundancy Check, a mathematical method for verifying the integrity of data. It is a form of checksum, based on the theory of maximum length polynomials. While more secure than a simple checksum, CRCs don't offer true cryptographic security. See cryptographic checksum.

Cryptanalysis: The study of an encryption system, often with the intention of detecting any weakness in the encryption algorithm.

Cryptographic Checksum: A checksum calculated by using a cryptographically based algorithm. It is impossible to 'engineer' changes to data in such a way as to leave a cryptographic checksum unchanged.

Data Protection: A group of techniques used to preserve three desirable aspects of data: Confidentiality, Integrity and Availability. Also a legal term with specific meaning (somewhat different to the above definition).

Deciphering: Means the same as decrypting; see decryption.

Decryption: Decryption is the process of transforming ciphertext back into plaintext. It is the reverse of encryption.

Decryption Key: see key.

DES: Data Encryption Standard, an algorithm for encrypting or decrypting 64 bits of data using a 56 bit key. DES is widely used in the financial world.

Device driver: A program used to 'handle' a hardware device such as a screen, disk, keyboard etc. This allows the operating system to use the device without knowing specifically how the device performs a particular task.

Digital Signature: A means of protecting a message from denial of origination by the sender, usually involving the use of

	asymmetric encryption to produce an encrypted message or a cryptographic checkfunction.
Diskless Node:	See diskless workstation.
Diskless Workstation:	A PC which does not contain a floppy disk drive and is connected to a network.
Dongle:	A hardware security product which must be plugged into a computer system before a particular application program will execute. A dongle aims to prevent illegal copying of a computer program.
DOS:	Disk Operating System. See MS-DOS and PC-DOS.
DOS bootstrap sector:	The bootstrap sector which loads the BIOS and DOS into PC RAM and starts their execution. Common point of attack by boot sector viruses.
Downloading:	A process where data is transferred electronically from a 'host' computer to an intelligent terminal or PC.
EAROM:	Electrically Alterable Read Only Memory, a particular type of EEPROM, in which individual bytes can be altered by electrical pulses.
ECB:	Electronic Codebook, a mode of use of a block cipher.
EEPROM:	Electrically Erasable Programmable Read Only Memory, a non-volatile memory which can be written to and read from many times. It is erased by an electrical pulse. EEPROMs are used for storing data which does not change frequently eg. setup parameters.
Electronic Mail:	Messages exchanged over a computer communications network.
Enciphering:	Means the same as encrypting; see encryption.
Encryption:	A process of disguising information so that it cannot be understood by an unauthorised person.
Encryption Key:	see Key.
EPROM:	Electrically Programmable Read Only Memory, a non-volatile memory which can be programmed (written to) once, and read from many times. Most types of EPROM can be erased by exposure to ultra-violet light. EPROMs are used for storing data which is unlikely to be changed.
.EXE:	The extension given to executable files in MS-DOS. These are similar to .COM files, but can contain more than 64K of code and data.
Exhaustive Key Search:	Finding out which key was actually used by an encryption system by testing all possible keys in turn.
Expanded Memory:	PC memory which conforms to the industry standard specification EMS (Expanded Memory Specification), and enables the CPU to access more than 640K of memory.

Extended Memory:	Memory in PCs which lies above 1 MByte in a 80286 (or above) machine.
FAT:	File Allocation Table, a mnemonic term used by the MS-DOS operating system (and others) to describe the part of a disk which contains information describing the physical location on the disk of the chains of clusters forming the files stored on that disk.
File Compression:	The compacting of a file through the process of recoding its bit structure into a shorter form. File compression must be reversible.
File Encryption:	The transformation of a file's contents (in plain text) into an unintelligible form by means of some form of cryptographic system or manipulation.
File Integrity:	Techniques used to provide 'safe' backup files for recovery purposes in the event that critical files have become contaminated through some accidental or intentional mechanism (eg. computer virus attack).
File Labelling:	The classifying of the sensitivity level of a file either by external (visible outside marking) or internal (magnetic coding of the header label) coding, or by a combination of these two methods.
File Server:	A central data repository for a computer network, which may provide other centralised services such as shared printer control.
Firmware:	Jargon for a computer program stored in a non-volatile memory such as an EPROM or an EEPROM.
Floppy Disks:	Interchangeable magnetic disks which are used to store computer data. Usual formats are 3.5" and 5.25" disks, and capacities of the order of 1 Mbyte.
Hacker:	An individual whose interests, motivated for benign or malicious reasons, concern 'breaking into' computer systems. The word hacker is also used to denote someone who produces prodigious amounts of software. The two meanings are completely distinct, and often confused.
Hard disk:	A hermetically sealed magnetic disk, generally fixed within a computer, which is used to store data. Hard disk capacity is of the order of 10 Mbytes to 1 Gbyte.
Hardware:	Any component of a computer system that has physical form. It is a term used to draw a distinction between the computer itself (hardware), and the programs which are executed on the computer (software).

Hash Function:	A function which maps a set of variable size data into objects of a single size. Widely used for fast searching.
Hashing:	The process of calculating a hash function.
Hexadecimal:	A system of counting using number base 16. The numbers 10 to 15 are represented by the characters 'A' through 'F' respectively. Hexadecimal is often abbreviated to hex. Each hex digit is equivalent to four bits (half a byte) of information.
IC:	Integrated Circuit, an electronic device containing many discrete electronic components such as transistors, resistors and the wire links which interconnect them. ICs are usually made in very large numbers and in miniaturised form, on a common base or substrate of silicon.
ID:	An identification code, username, identification card or an identification token.
Integrity:	A security protection aimed at ensuring that data cannot be deleted, modified, duplicated or forged without detection.
Internet:	One of the largest world-wide networks for the transmission of electronic mail messages.
Interrupt:	A mechanism by which a process can attract the immediate attention of the CPU, usually in order to serve an urgent request from an external device. Interrupt table on 8086 microprocessors occupies the bottom 1K of RAM.
I/O port:	A computer communicates with the outside world through Input/Output (I/O) ports. Examples are the RS-232 serial port and printer ports on a PC.
ISO:	International Organisation for Standardisation, the worldwide federation of international standards bodies.
IV:	Initialisation Variable, a value used to initialise modes of use of certain block ciphers.
K:	Shorthand for a thousand (1000), but in computing it is often used to mean 1024 (2^{10}, approximately 1000). For example, 64K or 64 Kbytes refers to 64*1024 (= 65536) bytes.
Key:	When used in the context of encryption, a series of numbers which are used by an encryption algorithm to transform plaintext data into encrypted (ciphertext) data, and vice versa. Confusingly, key can also refer to a physical token which gives access to a system.
Key Management:	The process of securely generating, transporting, storing and destroying encryption keys.

LAN: Local Area Network, a data communications network covering a limited area (up to several kilometres in radius) with moderate to high data transmission speeds.

Letter Bomb: A logic bomb contained in electronic mail, which will trigger when the mail is read.

Link virus: A virus which subverts directory entries to point to the virus code.

Logic Bomb: A program modification which causes damage when triggered by some condition such as the date, or the presence or absence of data eg. a name.

M: Shorthand for a million (1000000), but in computing it is often used to mean 1048576 (2^{20}, approximately one million). For example, 1M or 1 Mbyte refers to 1048576 bytes.

MAC: Message Authentication Code, a cryptographic checksum for a message. Unlike a digital signature, a MAC requires knowledge of a secret key for verification.

Mainframe: Large computer systems, often occupying purpose-built facilities, used for IT applications requiring extremely fast processing speeds or large quantities of data. Typical processing speeds are of the order of 100 MIPS.

Master bootstrap sector: The first physical sector on the hard disk (sector 1, head 0, track 0) which is loaded and executed when the PC is bootstrapped. It contains the partition table as well as the code to load and execute the bootstrap sector of the 'active' partition. Common point of attack by boot sector viruses.

Menu-driven: Software which presents the user with a fixed 'menu' of command choices, often requiring only a single key or mouse button depression to select the required option.

Message Authentication: The process of calculating and then subsequently verifying a message authentication code.

Message Digest: Same as hash function.

Microprocessor: An integrated circuit which condense the essential elements of a computer's CPU into a single device.

Minicomputer: A fixed, generally multi-user, computer designed for use as a communal information processing system. Typical processing speeds are between 10 and 100 MIPS.

MIPS: Millions of instructions per second.

Mirroring: A technique where data is written to two (or more) disks simultaneously, with the intention of enabling data retrieval even when one of the disks fails.

Modem: A MOdulator/DEModulator is a device which translates digital computer data into a form suitable for transmission over an analogue telecommunications path such as a telephone line, radio channel or satellite link.

Mouse: A data input device which, when moved by hand on the surface of a desk, conveys the direction and amount of movement to a computer. A mouse is commonly equipped with one, two or three press-buttons to actuate commands on the computer.

MS-DOS: The Disk Operating System sold by Microsoft. It is the most common microcomputer system in the world, and operates on the IBM PC. See PC-DOS.

Multi-partite virus: A virus which infects both boot sectors and executable files, thus exhibiting the characteristics of both boot sector viruses and parasitic viruses.

Multitasking: The ability of a computer to divide its processing time amongst several different tasks. Although most computers contain only one CPU, they can switch between operations so quickly that several processes appear to run simultaneously.

Non-volatile Memory: Integrated circuits which retain their content when their normal power source is switched off. The main types are ROM, EPROM, EEPROM and battery backed CMOS RAM.

OFB: Output Feedback, a mode of use of a block cipher.

Off-site Backup: A backup stored at a geographically remote location.

One-way Function: A function that can readily be calculated, but whose inverse is very difficult to calculate.

Operating System: The computer program which performs basic housekeeping functions such as maintaining lists of files, running programs etc. PC operating systems include MS-DOS and OS/2, while minicomputer and mainframe operating systems include Unix, VMS and MVS.

Optical Disk: A storage device using a laser to record and read data from a rotating disk.

OS/2:   An operating system for 80286+ based IBM compatibles. It allows true multitasking.

OSI: Open Systems Interconnection, a set of standards defining the protocols for communication between open (non-proprietary) systems.

.OVL: The extension commonly given to overlay files in MS-DOS. Overlay files are used with large programs which cannot fit into RAM: parts of the program are loaded as

	and when needed. Overlay files can have any extension and not just .OVL.
Parasitic Virus:	A computer virus which attaches itself to another computer program, and is activated when that program is executed. A parasitic virus can append itself to either the beginning or the end of a program, or it can overwrite part of the program.
Partition Table:	A 64-bit table found inside the master bootstrap sector on hard disks which contains information about the starting and ending of up to four partitions on the hard disk. The partition table also contains information on the type of the partion, eg. DOS partition, UNIX partition etc.
Passive Attack:	An attack on a system which extracts information and makes use of it, but never injects false information or corrupts any information (which would be an active attack).
Password:	Sequences of characters which allow users access to a system. Although they are supposed to be unique, experience has shown that most people's choices are highly insecure. Humans tend to choose short words such as names, which are easy to guess.
PC:	Personal Computer, a desktop or portable single-user computer usually comprising a CPU, memory, screen, keyboard, and disk drive(s). PC has become synonymous with IBM compatible computer, even though this definition is not strictly correct.
PC-DOS:	Microcomputer operating system originally used by IBM for its PCs. It is functionally identical to MS-DOS.
Peripheral:	External device connected to a computer. Examples include printers, plotters, disk drives, external modems, and a mouse.
Peripheral Access Control:	Technique to restrict the use of certain computer peripherals to authorised users.
Pest Program:	A collective term for programs with deleterious and generally unanticipated side effects eg. Trojan horses, logic bombs, viruses, and malicious worms.
Plaintext:	Data before it has been enciphered. The opposite of ciphertext.
Polymorphic virus:	Self-modifying encrypting virus.
Port Access Control:	Restricting the use of computer data ports to authorised users only.
Processor:	A unit of hardware that is capable of executing instructions contained in a computer program.

Program: A precise sequence of instructions that specifies what action a computer should perform. 'Software' is often used to describe a computer program.

Proprietary Encryption
Algorithm: An encryption algorithm designed to a proprietary (and usually secret) specification.

PS/2:   A series of computers from IBM designed to replace the PC/XT/AT range. All models, except model 30, support the 'microchannel architecture'. Cards designed for the IBM PC/XT/AT are not compatible with PS/2 machines.

Public Domain: Two totally distinct meanings exist:the area which is outside government security arrangements; or something which is neither subject to copyright nor a trademark.

RAM: Random Access Memory, volatile memory which can be written to, and read from, at high speed. It is normal to load programs from disk into RAM, and then to execute them. The operating system takes care of the allocation of RAM to executing programs.

Reverse-engineering: The process of deducing how something works without having access to the design details.

ROM: Read Only Memory, a form of non-volatile memory in a computer. Data is embedded into a ROM during manufacture. A ROM is usually used to store the startup software which is executed by a PC on power up (see bootstrapping).

RS-232:   The most widely used standard for serial data communication. The speed of communication is measured in baud.

Scrambling: Encryption.

Secret Key: Encryption key that must not be disclosed. If it is revealed, the security offered by the encryption algorithm is compromised. Not all encryption keys have to be kept secret, eg. public keys in asymmetric encryption.

Security: Protection against unwanted behaviour. The most widely used definition of (computer) security is *security = confidentiality + integrity + availability.*

Security Policy: A security policy is the set of rules, principles and practices that determine how security is implemented in an organisation. It must maintain the principles of the organisation's general security policy.

Security Server: A special LAN station which runs software that monitors LAN usage, and controls access independently of the LAN operating system.

Server:	See file server and security server.
Smart Disk:	A device in the shape of a 3.5" floppy disk which contains a microprocessor and memory. It can be read from and written to in a standard floppy disk drive.
Software:	See program.
Spoofing:	Pretending to be someone or something else (eg. entering someone else's password).
Stealth virus:	A virus which hides its presence from the PC user and anti-virus programs, usually by trapping interrupt services.
Stream Cipher:	A cipher which provides encryption and decryption by operating on continuous stream of data, without imposing limits on the length of the data.
Symmetric Algorithm:	An algorithm in which the key used for encryption is identical to the key used for decryption. DES is the best known symmetric encryption algorithm.
.SYS:	The extension given to system file names in MS-DOS. An example is the file CONFIG.SYS which sets up various configuration parameters for the operating system on power-up.
Terminal:	A device which consists of a VDU and keyboard. It allows a user to interact with a computer.
Time Bomb:	A logic bomb set to trigger at a particular time.
Timeout:	A logical access control feature which automatically logs-off users of terminals which do not exhibit signs of activity for a certain duration of time.
Token:	A physical object, sometimes containing sophisticated electronics, which is required to gain access to a system. Some tokens contain a microprocessor, and are called intelligent tokens, or smart cards.
Trapdoor:	A hidden flaw in a system mechanism that can be triggered to circumvent the system's security.
Trojan Horse:	A computer program whose execution would result in undesired side effects, generally unanticipated by the user. The Trojan horse program may otherwise give the appearance of providing normal functionality.
TSR:	Terminate and Stay Resident, a term used to describe an MS-DOS programs which remains in memory after being executed. A TSR can be re-activated either by a specific sequence of keystrokes, or at some specific time, or by some specific signal from an I/O port.
UNIX:	UNIX is a multi-user operating system, developed by AT&T. Several versions of UNIX exist, which do not all achieve compatibility with each other.

Uploading:	The process of transferring data from a remote computer to a central host.
UPS:	Uninterruptible Power Supply, a device which detects mains failure and provides power from an internal battery supply for a limited period.
VDU:	Visual Display Unit, a computer peripheral which displays text and/or graphics on a television screen.
Virus:	Sometimes explicitly referred to as a computer virus, a program which makes copies of itself in such a way as to 'infect' parts of the operating system and/or application programs. See boot-sector virus and parasitic virus.
Virus signature:	An identifier recognised by the virus as meaning 'this item is already infected, do not reinfect'. It can take different forms such as the text 'sURIV' at the beginning of the file, the size of the file divisible by a number or the number of seconds in the date stamp set to 62. Some viruses do not recognise their signatures correctly.
WAN:	Wide Area Network, a set of computers that communicate with each other over long distances.
Workstation:	An ill-defined term used to describe a powerful single user, high performance, minicomputer or microcomputer, which is used by individuals for tasks involving intensive processing, perhaps CAD or simulation.
Worm:	A program that distributes multiple copies of itself within a system or across a distributed system.
Worm Attack:	Interference by a program that is acting beyond normally expected behaviour, perhaps exploiting security vulnerabilities or causing denials of service. See worm.
XOR:	An abbreviation of the logical operation known as Exclusive-or. An exclusive-or function is defined as having the value true when either of the input conditions (but not both) is true.

F

VIRUS HUNTER'S CHECKLIST

It is very strange, and very melancholy, that the paucity of human pleasures should persuade us ever to call hunting one of them.

Samuel Johnson (1709-84), 'Johnsonian Miscellanies'

You have been asked to check all PCs on a site for a possible virus attack. You grab your bag, which contains all the tools necessary to deal with the problem, and head for the site. What should the bag contain?

❑ Software for IBM-PC virus investigation. This will include not only virus-detection software but also software tools for investigating a virus attack and recovering from it:

   ❑ An up-to-date copy of a good, trusted virus scanner. You should not use copies which are more than two months old.

   ❑ One or more supplementary virus scanners by other manufacturers.

   ❑ A disk editing tool. Useful for disk investigations, displaying interrupts and recovering from boot sector virus infections.

   ❑ A cryptographic checksumming package for investigating an attack by a virus unknown to your scanners.

   ❑ Sacrificial 'GOAT' programs which can be infected on purpose in order to observe virus behaviour.

   ❑ Diagnostic software for distinguishing a potential hardware problem from a virus problem. This is usually dependent on the hardware used and may be best obtained on site. Virus-scan and write-protect this software before using it.

- ❑   DEBUG, for the adventurous who wish to disassemble the virus *in situ*.
- ❑   Manuals for all the above software as well as a DOS manual.

❑   Software for Apple Macintosh virus investigation. You will need a completely different set of tools and procedures to check Apple Macintosh PCs, although the same principles apply.

❑   Secure bootstrapping means and procedures.

With the advent of stealth viruses, **it is most important to guarantee a clean, virus-free environment on a workstation, before running anti-virus software or investigating a virus-infected network.**

Bootstrapping stand-alone PCs:

- ❑   Correct version(s) of DOS on write-protected $3\frac{1}{2}$" and $5\frac{1}{4}$" disks. Compaq DOS 3.31 or DOS 5.00 are able to boot machines with hard disks running any current version of DOS. Ensure that DOS disks are write-protected. Switch the PC off, insert a boot disk in drive A and then switch it back on.

Bootstrapping a PC in order to check a network:

- ❑   A DOS system disk which also contains all executables needed to set up the network connection, as well as log onto the network. For example, on Novell NetWare 3.11 you will need a DOS system disk with IPX.COM, NETX.EXE, LOGIN.EXE and MAP.EXE. Perform a secure boot of the PC as described above, then run LOGIN from the floppy disk including the '/S NUL' command line qualifier to prevent the execution of both system and user login scripts:

```
LOGIN /S NUL <USERNAME>
```

❑   Pre-formatted disks ($3\frac{1}{2}$" both densities, $5\frac{1}{4}$" both densities) for preserving any virus samples and general use. You can encounter a variety of floppy drives on a site and you should **not** use high density disks in low density drives (or vice-versa) as the information will not be recorded reliably.

❑   Write-protect tabs. Write-protecting a disk is a hardware barrier to any writing operations. Write-protect any disks to which you do not wish to write to.

❑   Floppy disk labels, 'Virus infected' labels, 'Disk free from known viruses' labels.

❑   An up-to-date printout of known viruses and their symptoms.

❑   Education materials. You may be required to give a short presentation on virus prevention to PC users on the site. A video is an excellent tool for conveying the message in a short time. Furthermore, as a virus specialist, you must stay in touch with the latest developments in the virus field. Make sure that your subscription to a journal such as *Virus Bulletin* is current.

❑   Date of next visit. It is best to strike while the iron is hot. After you have finished the investigation, make an appointment for your next visit. Be prepared to catch any re-infection at an early stage.

❑   Virus attack reporting forms.

❑   Contact telephone and fax numbers for the technical support for your virus scanners.

G

KNOWN IBM-PC VIRUSES

For in much wisdom is much grief: and he that increaseth knowledge increases sorrow.

Bible: Ecclesiastes

G.1 VIRUS NAMES AND ALIASES

When a researcher investigates a virus he has not seen before, one of his first problems is to establish whether the virus is one already known. Since that can take time, he may decide on a name for the virus before announcing the find. The result of this is that multiple names for the same virus are common, and when a 'new' virus is reported, it is often only a known virus with a new name.

Some researchers, furthermore, feel an irresistible urge to call parasitic viruses by a number, which is their infective length (the increase in the length of the infected executable). This can be very confusing since one virus can have several infective lengths (*Jerusalem* has an infective length of 1813 bytes for COM files and 1808 bytes for EXE files), and completely different viruses can have identical infective lengths (both *Agiplan* and *Zero Bug* have an infective length of 1536 bytes).

There have been a number of attempts at standardising on virus names, for example the Lotus virus numbering standard (*Virus Bulletin*, October 1991), the US National Institute of Standards and Technology (*NCSA Anti-Virus Products Developers Conference Proceedings*, Washington DC, November 1991), a joint NCSA committee (*Virus Bulletin*,

February 1992). So far none have succeeded and it seems that the speed of new developments in the virus field will be likely to defy any such attempts in the future.

If you discover a new virus at some stage in the future, please do not rush to give it a name. First check whether the virus is already known and only if not, christen it with something suitable, which is preferably not its infective length. Names of viruses are related either to virus side-effects (eg. *Cascade*), to strings embedded in the virus (eg. *Suriv*) or to the name chosen by the author and included in the virus (eg. *Nomenklatura* and *Datacrime*). For further guidance refer to *Virus Bulletin*, February 1992 (see Appendix A: Bibliography).

G.2 VIRUS HEX PATTERNS

One common way of testing executable files for viruses is to search for code or data patterns known to occur in these particular viruses. These patterns are normally represented as hexadecimal digits and referred to as 'hex patterns'.

This section contains short descriptions and hexadecimal patterns of viruses seen by June 1992. This list is maintained from various sources, including *Virus Bulletin's* technical editor Fridrik Skulason and is copyright ©*Virus Bulletin*. Information of this kind will invariably be out of date by the time it is published in a book. The reader is urged to treat it only as a sample of what viruses *could* be around and to find up-to-date information in one of the journals or bulletin boards listed in Appendix A.

The hexadecimal (hex) patterns in the table are normally from 10 to 16 bytes long, and there is a small but finite chance that one of these patterns will be found in some uninfected and innocuous executable. Data in executable images is not completely random, and certain sequences of instructions used in a virus can occur in a perfectly legitimate program. The pattern from a virus is normally chosen so as to be unlikely to occur in a legitimate program, **but there is a chance that this may happen**. For more information on extracting virus patterns see Section 5.2: Dissection of a Captured Virus.

If a pattern-checking program, such as SEARCH in Appendix B, reports a pattern match, it means that a virus **may** have been found. If the alarm turns out to be false, it is known as a 'false positive', which is one of the main problems with poorly tested anti-virus software. All patterns shown in this table have been tested for false positives against about 100 MBytes of executables.

Each entry in the table consists of the virus group name in bold, its aliases and the virus type (see Fig. G.1 for type codes). This is followed by a short description (if available) and a 10 to 16 byte hex pattern. An entry in the form '(*VB* Mar 92)' indicates that further information on the virus can be found in the appropriate issue of *Virus Bulletin*.

Type codes:

C = Infects COM files
E = Infects EXE files
D = Infects DOS boot sector (Logical sector 0 on disk)
L = Link virus
M = Infects master boot sector (Track 0, head 0, sector 1 on disk)
N = Not memory-resident after infection
R = Memory-resident after infection
P = Companion virus

Fig. G.1 - Virus type codes

G.3 IBM-PC VIRUSES

8 Tunes - CER: The virus probably originates in Germany and infects COM and EXE files. The length of the virus code is 1971 bytes. When triggered, it will play one of eight different tunes. The virus attempts to deactivate two anti-virus programs: Bombsquad and Flushot+.

```
8 Tunes          33F6 B9DA 03F3 A550 BB23 0353 CB8E D0BC
```

10 past 3 - CR: A 748 byte virus which is awaiting analysis.

```
10 past 3        B840 008E D8A1 1300 B106 D3E0 2D00 088E
```

191 - CN: A very simple virus with no side effects.

```
191              8BD7 B902 00B4 3FCD 2181 3D07 0874 DF33
```

268-Plus - CN: When this virus is run it will infect all COM files in the current directory increasing the first one by 268 bytes, the second by 269 bytes, the third by 270 bytes and so on. The virus is encrypted and is awaiting analysis.

```
268-Plus         8EC1 0650 BE00 0156 31FF B90B 01F3 A4BD
```

200 - CN: This small virus does nothing but replicate. When an infected program is run, it will infect all COM files in the root directory of drive C.

```
200              33D2 B800 42CD 218B CEB4 40CD 212E 8B0E
```

337 - CR: A small, simple virus which does nothing but replicate.

```
377              5FBF 0001 578B CC2B CEF3 A433 F633 FF33
```

432 - C?: Virus awaiting disassembly.

```
432              50CB 8CC8 8ED8 E806 00E8 D900 E904 0106
```

483 - CER: This virus does not work properly, as infected programs will never run. As this could be fixed by a minor correction, a search pattern for the current version is provided.

```
483              0256 5AB9 1800 F614 46E2 FBCD 215E 81BC
```

535A - CN: A mutation of the Vienna virus. Second generation copies do not appear to replicate.

```
535A                ACB9 0080 F2AE B904 00AC AE75 EEE2 FA5E
```

555 - CER: A compact 555 byte virus awaiting analysis. It does not seem to do anything apart from replicating.

```
555                 5B58 072E FF2E 0500 813E 1200 4D5A 7406
```

656 - CN: Triggers on 14th of any month except January or on any day in April. Overwrites first 80 sectors of drive C.

```
656                 ACB9 0070 F2AE B904 00AC AE75 EEE2 FA5E
```

757 - CR: This virus displays a 'Bouncing-Ball' effect on the screen.

```
757                 B907 00FC F3A4 585B 9DB8 0001 5350 CB9C
```

765 - ER: This virus is probably an older version of the '905' virus. Awaiting analysis.

```
765                 53B4 368E 4602 8B76 0A26 8A14 80EA 40CD
```

777 Revenge - CR: After three infected files have been run, the virus displays the text '*** 777 - Revenge Attacker V1.01 ***' and then trashes drives C and D. (*VB* Mar 92)

```
777 Revenge         B8FF FF33 C9CD 2183 F906 7243 B856 0250
```

800 - CR: Infective length is 800 bytes. The virus code is written into a random location in the infected file. Like Number of the Beast, it uses an undocumented DOS function to obtain the original INT 13H address, and instead of intercepting INT 21H, it intercepts INT 2AH, function 82H. The virus is encrypted. (*VB* June 90)

```
800                 B981 0151 AD33 D0E2 FB59 3115 4747 E2FA
```

864 - CN: This virus adds 864 bytes in front of the files it infects. Awaiting analysis.

```
864                 B04D B449 B742 473A 2575 153A 7D01 7510
```

905 - ER: A Bulgarian virus, still awaiting analysis.

```
905                 488E C08E D880 3E00 005A 7415 0306 0300
```

907 - CR: An encrypted 907 byte virus, awaiting analysis.

```
907                 83C7 0353 2EFF B55D 04BB DE03 B97F 0058
```

928 - CER: Virus awaiting disassembly.

```
928                 E9AD 00B8 BBBB CD21 3D69 6974 03E8 3500
```

1024PrScr - CR: This virus increases the length of infected programs by 1024 bytes. The main side-effect is to perform a Print Screen function at different times.

```
1024PrScr           8CC0 488E C026 A103 002D 8000 26A3 0300
```

1028 - CER: Virus is 1028 bytes long. Awaiting analysis.

```
1028                0606 005E 561E 0E33 FF8E DFC5 0684 002E
```

1067 - CR: This virus is closely related to the Ambulance virus, but is still awaiting analysis.

```
1067                018A 5405 8816 0001 B42A CD21 F6C2 0175
```

1077 - CER: This 1077 byte virus infects COM and EXE files, but is unable to infect EXE files larger than 64K.

```
1077                4E01 EACD 21C3 B44F CD21 C351 33C0 3B86
```

1226 - CR: This Bulgarian virus is related to Phoenix, Proud and Evil. As in the case of its relatives, no search pattern is possible.

1260, V2P1 - CN: Virus infects COM files extending them by 1260 bytes. The first 39 bytes contain code used to decrypt the rest of the virus. A variable number of short (irrelevant) instructions are added between the decoding instructions at random in an attempt to prevent virus scanners from using identification strings. An infected file has the seconds field set to 62. No search pattern is possible. (*VB* Mar 90)

1355 - CR?: 1355 byte virus, not yet analysed.

    1355   8B04 8ED8 BE00 00B0 2EB4 803A 0475 1BB0

1575 - CER: The only side-effect of this virus is that a caterpillar (grasshopper?) moves from the top left-hand part of the screen turning text yellow. This display happens if the virus is already memory-resident and an infected program is run and the memory-resident virus has not infected since it became resident and is at least 3 months old. Infected files grow by 1575-1593 bytes. The date and time of last file modification are not saved. (*VB* Oct 91).

    1575   D087 ECBE 3C01 BF00 00B9 1000 FCF2 A4E9

1600 - CER: A 1600 byte Bulgarian virus, reported to be written by the same author as the Nina, Terror and Anti-Pascal viruses. Many infected programs, including COMMAND.COM will fail to execute when infected.

    1600   8B35 8936 0001 8B75 0289 3602 01C7 4514

1876 - CER: This 1876 byte virus is probably of Polish origin. Not yet analysed.

    1876   8EC0 33FF 33C0 B9FF 7FFC F2AE 26F6 05FF

1963A - CER: A Bulgarian virus, which does not increase the size of the files it infects. Awaiting analysis.

    1963A   B820 12BB 0500 CD2F 534B 4B26 881D B816

2100 - CER: This is a Bulgarian virus, related to the Eddie and Eddie-2 viruses and contains extensive segments of code in common with both. The pattern for Eddie-2 can be found within this virus, but they can easily be differentiated on the basis of length. (*VB* Aug 91)

2144 - CER: A 2144 byte Russian virus which may totally disable the hard disk when it activates. A computer with a disabled disk cannot be rebooted from a system floppy disk without disconnecting the hard disk.

3445 - CER: This 3445 byte encrypted virus has not been fully analysed, but infected programs often fail to execute.

    3445   D2BB 1000 F7E3 03C1 83D2 00F7 F359 50B8

4870 Overwriting - EN: A strange overwriting virus which spreads in LZEXE-packed format. It is not possible to select a search pattern from the code portion of the virus.

5120 - CEN: This virus is 5120 bytes long. When an infected program is run, it will search recursively for EXE and COM files to infect. Infected programs will terminate with an 'Access denied' message after 1st June 1992. Parts of the virus seem to have been written in compiled BASIC.

    5120   40B1 04D3 E88C DB03 C305 1000 8ED8 8C06

5792 - EN: Similar to the RNA2 and Halloween viruses and written in some high-level language (C or Pascal), this virus adds 5792 bytes in front of infected files.

```
5792              8DBE 00FF 1657 8DBE 5CE8 1657 B8A0 1650
```

7808 - CNR: A clumsy virus with an infectious length of 7808 bytes written in a high level language. Infection occurs both by directory search and on load and execute. Awaiting analysis.

```
7808              31C0 A354 04C7 06E6 4201 00EB 04FF 06E6
```

16850 - PN: This large (16850 byte) companion virus seems to be written in Turbo Pascal. Because of the high chance of false positives, it is recommended that search patterns should not be used to detect it. To get rid of the virus, simply remove all hidden 16850 byte COM files corresponding to EXE files in the same directory.

4K, 4096, Frodo, IDF, Israeli Defence Forces - CER: Infective length is 4096 bytes. The virus may occasionally cause damage to files, as it manipulates the number of available clusters, which results in crosslinked files. If the virus is resident in memory, it disguises itself from detection by pattern-searching or checksumming programs. Infected systems hang on 22nd September. (*VB* May 90, Nov 90)

```
4K                E808 0BE8 D00A E89A 0AE8 F60A E8B4 0A53
```

Ada - CR: A 2600 byte virus, reported to have originated in Argentina. Not fully analysed.

```
Ada               4802 0074 0F80 FC41 741B 80FC 1374 163D
```

Advent - CEN: An old 2764 byte mutation of Syslock, which is detected by the Syslock pattern. This virus activates in December and plays a Christmas tune.

Agiplan - CR: Infective length is 1536. The virus attaches itself to the beginning of COM files. Agiplan has only occurred on one site and may be extinct.

```
Agiplan           E9CC 0390 9090 9090 9C50 31C0 2E38 26DA
```

AIDS - CN: Not to be confused with the AIDS Trojan, this virus overwrites COM files and is about 12K long. When an infected program is executed, the virus displays 'Your computer now has AIDS' and halts the system.

```
AIDS              0600 AE42 6E4C 7203 4600 0004 00A0 1000
```

AIDS II - PN: A companion virus, 8064 bytes long, which displays a message when it activates. To locate and remove the virus, search for COM files corresponding to EXE files, but marked 'Hidden' and located in the same subdirectory and delete them.

```
AIDS II           5589 E581 EC02 02BF CA05 0E57 BF3E 011E
```

Aircop - DR: Virus displays the blinking message '.Red State, Germ offensing --Aircop' after infecting every eighth floppy disk. Originated in Taiwan. (*VB* Feb 91).

```
Aircop            32E4 CD16 CD12 33C0 CD13 0E07 BB00 02B9
```

Aircop 2 - DR: Does not infect hard disks. Awaiting analysis.

```
Aircop 2          32E4 CD16 33C0 CD13 0E07 BB00 02B9 0600
```

Akuku - CER: 889 byte virus, probably written by the same author as the Hybrid virus.

```
Akuku             E800 005E 8BD6 81C6 2A01 BF00 01A5 A481
```

Alabama - ER: Infective length is 1560 bytes. May cause execution of wrong files and FAT corruption.

```
Alabama              803D C673 0726 C605 CF4F EBF0 26FF 0603
```

Alabama 2 - ER: Slightly modified version of the original virus, but detected by the Alabama pattern.

Albania - CN: This is a group of 4 viruses, which all contain the word Albania, but they are believed to be written in Bulgaria. The mutations are 429, 506, 575 and 606 bytes long.

```
Albania              83F9 0074 0C80 7CFE 3B74 06AA E803 000E
Albania-429          83F9 0074 0826 807D FE00 7405 41AA E80F
```

Ambulance, RedX - CN: The major effect of this virus is to display a moving ambulance with the sound of a siren. The virus is 796 bytes long.

```
Ambulance            0001 8A07 8805 8B47 0189 4501 FFE7 C3E8
```

Ambulance-B - CN: A 796 byte virus, just like the original, but with a few insignificant modifications.

```
Ambulance-B          0001 8A07 8805 8B47 0189 4501 FFE7 CBE8
```

Amoeba - CER: Virus adds 1392 bytes to the length of the infected files. It does not have any known side-effects.

```
Amoeba               CF9C 502E A107 0140 2EA3 0701 3D00 1072
```

Amstrad - CN: Adds 847 bytes to the front of any COM file in the current directory. The rest contains an advertisment for Amstrad computers. (*VB* June 90). Cancer is a 740 byte long mutation, which infects the same files repeatedly. These viruses are members of the Pixel family.

```
Amstrad              C706 0E01 0000 2E8C 0610 012E FF2E 0E01
```

Amstrad-852 - CN: Almost identical to the original 847 byte version, with only a text string changed.

Amstrad-877 - CN: This mutation is 877 bytes long, and detected by the 'Amstrad' pattern.

Anthrax - MCER: An interesting, multi-partite virus from Bulgaria, which infects the master boot sector, as well as executable files. Infected files usually grow by 1000-1200 bytes.

```
Anthrax              0E1F 832E 1304 02CD 12B1 06D3 E08E C0BF
```

AntiCAD, Plastique - CER: This is a family of 7 viruses from Taiwan, based on the Jerusalem virus, but considerably modified. This group includes a 2900 byte mutation, a 3012 byte mutation and four 4096 byte mutations. Two of these four are known as 'Invader' and one as 'HM2'. The four 4096 byte mutations will also infect the boot sector. The Plastique virus triggers when ACAD.EXE (the AUTOCAD program) is executed. Drives A and B are checked for the presence of a disk which, if found, has head 0 of all tracks overwritten with random data. An 'explosion' routine (speaker noise generated every 4.5 minutes) then commences. The first and second hard disks are overwritten on all heads and tracks. (*VB* Apr 92)

```
AntiCAD (1)          B840 4BCD 213D 7856 7512 B841 4BBF 0001
AntiCAD (2)          C08E D8A1 1304 B106 D3E0 8ED8 33F6 8B44
```

AntiCAD 2576 - CER: A mutation of the AntiCAD series from Taiwan. This 2576 byte mutation is closely related to the 2900 byte mutation.

```
AntiCAD 2576        595B 5807 1F9C 2EFF 1E3B 001E 07B4 49CD
```

AntiCAD/Plastique 3004 - CER: Very closely related to the 3012 byte mutation of Plastique. The virus contains the text string 'COBOL' and is detected by the AntiCAD (1) pattern.

AntiCAD 3088 - CER: The latest member of the AntiCAD/Plastique family. It is 3088 bytes long, and is detected by the same pattern as the 2576 byte version.

Anti-Faggot - ?: Virus sample failed to replicate. Contains destructive code and the text 'Drive Fucked Up by the Anti-Faggot Virus!' plus a few other sentences in broken English. Awaiting analysis.

```
Anti-Faggot         803E DE03 0174 0F80 3EDE 0302 740C 803E
```

Antimon - CN: This 1450 byte virus has also been named Pandaflu, because it is targeted against Flushot and some programs from Panda software.

```
Antimon             83C2 102B D033 C9B8 0042 CD21 BA00 01B9
```

Anti-Pascal (1) - CN: Two Bulgarian viruses 529 and 605 bytes long which add their code in front of infected programs. They are targeted against Turbo-Pascal, and delete .PAS and .BAK files.

```
Anti-Pascal (1)     D1E0 D1E0 80E4 0380 C402 8AC4 8BD8 32FF
```

Anti-Pascal (2) - CN: A second group of Bulgarian viruses written by the author of Anti-Pascal (1) viruses. There are three viruses which belong to this group and their infective lengths are 400, 440 and 480 bytes. They are structurally different from Anti-Pascal (1) since they add their code to the end of infected files. The side-effects are similar since they may delete .PAS, .BAK and .BAT files.

```
Anti-Pascal (2)     21BE 0001 5A58 FFE6 50B4 0E8A D0CD 2158
```

Anto - CN: A small virus, only 129 bytes long, which does nothing other than replicate.

```
Anto                B800 425A 87CF CD21 B440 5A87 CFCD 21B4
```

apilapil - CER: An encrypted virus with an infective length of 1731 bytes. If the date is the first of any month on or after year 1992, it overwrites the first 11 sectors of first 4 heads and first 14 tracks with garbage. It contains the text 'E.U.P.M. 1991'.

```
apilapil            2E8C 0601 008C C88E D8B9 A006 BF03 002E
```

Apocalypse - CER: Slight mutation of the Jerusalem virus. Detected by the Jerusalem-USA pattern.

Apocalypse II - CER: Slight mutation of the Eddie-2000 virus. Detected by the Dark Avenger pattern.

Arab, 834 - CR: Awaiting analysis.

```
Arab                3D00 4B75 368B EC8B 7600 8B7E 028C C98E
```

Arf - CN: A 1000 byte mutation of the Violator virus. Will display 'Arf Arf! Got you!' when it activates. Detected by the 'Violator' pattern.

Armagedon - CR: A 1079 byte virus from Greece, which interferes with the serial port. It will produce control strings for Hayes-compatible modems, dialling number 081-141 (speaking clock in Crete). Virus name is spelt with a single 'd'.

```
Armagedon          018C CBEA 0000 0000 8BC8 8EDB BE00 01BF
```

AT - CR: This is a fairly old group of viruses, but they only work on '286 processors and above. They have no significant effects.

```
AT-144             0042 33C9 CDB4 B440 8D54 FFB1 0389 2CCD
AT-149             33C9 33D2 CD21 B440 8D54 FFB1 0389 2CCD
AT-132             B800 428B CACD E5B4 40B2 2DB1 0389 2CCD
```

Attention - CR: A Russian, 394 byte virus. The virus has some code in common with the 'Best Wishes' virus, which is possibly written by the same author. Infective length is 393 bytes and only files longer than 786 bytes are infected. Disk writing is done by outputting directly to hardware via port 3F2H.

```
Attention          B000 8BDA B501 433A 0775 FB4B 4B81 275F
```

Australian 403 - CR: Destructive, overwriting 403 byte virus which has no side-effects other than destroying the programs it infects.

```
Australian 403     8C06 5B01 8CC8 8ED8 B821 25BA 9401 CD21
```

Azusa - MR: A short boot sector virus, which may damage data on diskettes larger than 360K. When it activates, it will disable COM1: and LPT1:. (*VB* April 91).

```
Azusa              B908 27BA 0001 CD13 72F1 0E07 B801 02BB
```

Backtime - CR: A 528 byte virus which is awaiting analysis.

```
Backtime           2125 CD21 8CC8 8ED8 8EC0 58BB 0001 53C3
```

Bad boy - CR: A 1001 byte virus, which may have been written by the same author as the 'Boys' virus, but is structurally different. Awaiting analysis.

```
Bad boy            0175 0383 C302 5351 8B07 8B4F 108B D830
```

Bandit - EN: This 2653 byte virus is detected by the 'Old Yankee' pattern. Awaiting analysis.

Bebe - CN: A Russian, 1004 byte virus.

```
Bebe               B104 D3EB 240F 3C00 7401 4389 1E0C 00C7
```

Beijing, Bloody! - MR: A primitive 512-byte virus. On 129th boot and every sixth boot thereafter, the virus displays the message 'Bloody! Jun. 4, 1989'. The virus is believed to be a protest against the Tianamen Square massacre. (*VB* Feb 91).

```
Beijing            80FC 0272 0D80 FC04 7308 80FA 8073 03E8
```

Best Wishes - CR: A 1024 byte Russian virus containing the message 'This programm ... With Best Wishes!'. Many programs, including COMMAND.COM will not work properly if infected with this virus.

```
Best Wishes        4C00 268C 1E4E 0007 1FB8 0400 8BF5 81EE
```

Best Wishes-970 - CER: This virus is detected by the search pattern for the Attention virus, but not the pattern for the Best Wishes-1024 virus, which may indicate a common author (or a close relationship). This mutation is generally not able to infect EXE files properly.

Beware, Monday 1st - CN: This 442 byte virus activates on the first day of the month, provided it is Monday, and then overwrites the first track of diskettes in drive A. It contains the text 'BEWARE ME - 0.01, Copr (c) DarkGraveSoft - Moscow 1990'.

    Beware   C3B4 3ECD 21C3 8DB5 8402 57B9 3100 8BFE

Big Joke - CN: A Norwegian virus awaiting full disassembly. Infectious length is 1068 bytes. Contains text: 'At last...... ALIVE !!!!! I guess your computer is infected by the Big Joke Virus. Release 4/4-91 Lucky you, this is the kind version. Be more careful while duplicating in the future. The Big Joke Virus, killer version, will strike harder. The Big Joke rules forever'.

    Big Joke   8BE8 83C5 030E 588E D88E C08D 7643 BF00

Black Monday - CER: This virus was first isolated in Fiji, but may have been written elsewhere. It adds 1055 bytes to infected files. The name is derived from the message 'Black Monday 2/3/90 KV KL MAL'. Infected EXE files cannot be disinfected, as the virus will overwrite a few bytes at the end of the file.

    Black Monday   8B36 0101 81C6 0501 8B04 8B5C 02A3 0001

Black Monday-Borderline - CR: This virus is detected by the Black Monday pattern, but it appears to be an older mutation, as it lacks the ability to infect EXE files. It is also shorter, only 781 bytes.

Black Wizard - EN: A mutation of the 'Old Yankee' virus, and detected by the pattern for that virus. This mutation is 2051 bytes long and plays a different tune than the original virus, but is otherwise similar.

Blinker - CR: A 512 byte mutation of Backtime, and detected by the pattern for that virus. This also applies to a 496 byte mutation which was made available as 'Joker'.

Black Jec - CN: A family of small viruses, which are awaiting analysis. The following mutations are known: Bljec-3 (231), Bljec-4 (247), Bljec-5 (267), Bljec-6 (270), Bljec-7 (287), Bljec-8 (358) and Bljec-9 (369). Four new mutations of this virus have been found, but they are all detected by the original pattern. The differences seem to be caused by the fact that a different assembler has been used to assemble the source code.

    Black Jec   B980 00BE 7FFF BF80 00F3 A4B8 F3A4 A3F9

Black Jec-4B, 6B, 8B - CN: A group of viruses 252, 281 and 363 bytes long and very similar to the mutations Bljec-4,6 and 8. They are functionally identical and detected as Black Jec (Bljec).

Black Jec-Digital F/X - CN: This 440 byte mutation is extremely badly written. It starts with a block of text, which will totally crash on most PCs. However, the virus may work on some '386 machines. Detected with the Black Jec (Bljec) pattern.

Blood - CN: A simple virus from Natal, South Africa. The 418 byte virus does nothing of interest, apart from replicating.

    Blood   1E0E 1FB4 19CD 2150 B202 B40E CD21 B41A

BNB, Beast-N-Black - CN: This 429 byte virus might be re-classified as a Vienna mutation. It contains the text 'Beware the Beast-N-Black'.

    BNB   FC8B F283 C619 BF00 01B9 0300 F3A4 8BF2

Bob - CN: This 718 byte virus seems rather badly written. It overwrites the first 698 bytes of files, storing the overwritten code at the end. The virus activates in January 1993, but its exact effects have not been fully determined.

```
Bob                   81F9 C907 7206 80FE 0175 0145 B200 BE00
```

Boojum - ER: A simple 334 byte virus which does nothing but replicate.

```
Boojum                1E06 06B8 2135 CD21 09DB 7433 2E89 1E18
```

Boys - CN: A 500 byte virus containing the text 'The good and the bad boys'. Awaiting analysis.

```
Boys                  BE01 01AD 0503 0050 8BF0 BF00 01B9 0500
```

Brain, Ashar, Shoe - DR: Consists of a bootstrap sector and 3 clusters (6 sectors) marked as bad in the FAT. The first of these contains the original boot sector. In its original version it only infects 360K floppy disks and occupies 7K of RAM. It creates a label '(c) Brain' on an infected disk. There is a variation which creates a label '(c) ashar'.

```
Brain                 FBA0 067C A209 7C8B 0E07 7C89 0E0A 7CE8
```

Brainy - CR: A 1531 byte virus of Bulgarian origin, which appears to do nothing but replicate. It is rather interesting from a technical point of view, as it may insert itself into the middle of another program, without modifying the program's starting instructions. Brainy uses a simple 'byte-swap' encryption.

```
Brainy                1B90 8BEC 0E1F BC34 00FC AD86 C489 44FE
```

Brunswick, Stoned 16 - MR: Infects first fixed drive and floppy drives A and B. On floppy disks the original boot sector is stored in head 1 cylinder 0 sector 3 and may cause directory corruption. On hard disks the original boot sector is stored in head 0, track 0 sector 16.

```
Brunswick             D4FF E8E7 FF74 252E C606 2901 00B8 0103
```

Bulgarian 123 - CN: A simple 123 byte virus from Bulgaria, which does nothing but replicate. It may infect the same file over and over.

```
Bulgarian 123         B103 8D54 F4B4 40CD 21B4 3ECD 21B4 4FCD
```

Burger - CN: Just like the 405 virus, this primitive 560 byte virus overwrites infected files, which makes it easily detectable. Several mutations with slightly different lengths are known.

```
Burger 1              B447 0401 508A D08D 3646 02CD 2158 B40E
Burger 2              CD21 B43E CD21 2E8B 1E00 E081 FB90 9074
```

Burger 382 - CN: Simple overwriting virus from Taiwan which overwrites part of the program.

```
Burger 382            B417 8D16 5502 CD21 3CFF 7514 B42C CD21
```

Burger 405 - CN: Infects one COM file (on a different disk) each time an infected program is run by overwriting the first 405 bytes. If the length of the file is less than 405 bytes, it will be increased to 405. The virus only infects the current directory and does not recognise previously infected files.

```
Burger 405            26A2 4902 26A2 4B02 26A2 8B02 50B4 19CD
```

Burger-Pirate - CN: This 609 byte overwriting virus is a simple modification of the original Burger virus, with a text message added at the end, which indicates the virus is written in Portugal.

```
Burger-Pirate       B800 002E A371 032E A3F9 022E A2FB 02B4
```

Burghofer - CR: A simple 525 byte virus from Switzerland, which appears to do nothing of interest.

```
Burghofer           B448 CD21 5B48 8EC0 FA26 C706 0100 0000
```

Cadkill - CR: Awaiting analysis. Infectious length is 1163 bytes. A mutation with an infectious length of 2367 bytes exists.

```
Cadkill             E800 005B 5056 B4CB CD21 3C07 7535 81C3
```

Cannabis - DR: A Dutch boot sector virus, which contains the text 'Hey man, I don't wanna work. I'm too stoned right now.' The virus is very badly written and just barely qualifies being classified as a virus.

```
Cannabis            B810 008E D8A1 1303 4848 A313 031F B106
```

Captain Trips - CER: A mutation of Jerusalem, of the same length as the original (1808/1813 bytes), but with numerous minor modifications. Most of them appear intended to invalidate the signature strings used by various scanners.

```
Captain Trips       B842 0150 EAFC 0300 008C C88E D0BC 0007
```

CARA - CR: A 1025 byte virus. Awaiting analysis.

```
CARA                812E 0200 C000 B44A BB00 B0CD 2181 EBC0
```

Carioca - CR: This virus adds 951 bytes to the end of infected programs, but it has not been analysed yet.

```
Carioca             01FC F3A4 B800 0150 C32E 8B1E 0301 81C3
```

Cascade, Fall, Russian, Hailstorm - CR: This encrypted virus attaches itself to the end of COM files, increasing their length by 1701 or 1704 bytes. The encryption key includes the length of the infected program, so infected files of different lengths will look different. After infection it becomes memory-resident and infects every COM file executed, including COMMAND.COM. The original version will produce a 'falling characters' display if the system date is between 1st October and 31st December 1988. The formatting version will format the hard disk on any day between 1st October and 31st December of any year except 1993. Both activations occur a random time after infection with a maximum of 5 minutes. (*VB* Sept 89)

```
Cascade (1)  01     0F8D B74D 01BC 8206 3134 3124 464C 75F8
Cascade (1)  04     0F8D B74D 01BC 8506 3134 3124 464C 75F8
Cascade (1)  Y4     FA8B CDE8 0000 5B81 EB31 012E F687 2A01
Cascade format      0F8D B74D 01BC 8506 3134 3124 464C 77F8
```

Cascade-1621 - CR: This Cascade mutation has the encryption routine changed.

```
Cascade-1621        FAE8 0000 5B81 EB07 0183 BF01 0100 740E
```

Cascade-1661 - CR: A rewritten version of the Cascade virus. It has been modified in several ways, changing the activation date to December of any year other than 1980 and 1990.

```
Cascade-1661        012E F684 9301 0174 0F8D BCB6 01BC 5A06
```

Cascade 1701-F - CR: Very closely related to the 1701-A mutation, but the encryption routine has been changed.

    Cascade 1701-F   012E F687 2A01 0174 0F8D B74D 01BA 8206

Cascade-1701-S - CR: A minor modification of the Cascade virus, with the encryption routine changed, probably to bypass some scanner. Reported to be written in Sweden.

    Cascade 1701-S   FA8B ECE8 0000 5B81 EB31 01F6 872A 0101

Cascade-1706 - CR: This mutation seems to be based on the 1704 byte mutation, but it has been changed and reassembled.

    Cascade-1706   3001 F687 2901 0174 0F8D B74B 01BC 8806

Cascade Y1 - CR: A mutation of Cascade.

    Cascade Y1   FA89 E5E8 0000 5B81 EB31 012E F687 2A01

Cascade YAP - CR: A mutation of Cascade with a slightly modified encryption routine.

    Cascade YAP   0F8D B74D 01BC 8206 3124 3134 464C 75F8

Casino - CR: Virus infects COM files smaller than 62905 bytes and when triggered it destroys the FAT and then offers to play the Jackpot game. If you win, it reconstructs the FAT, while if you lose, the machine hangs. The virus triggers on 15th January, 15th April and 15th August of any year. (*VB* Mar 91)

    Casino   594B 7504 B866 06CF 80FC 1174 0880 FC12

Casper - CN: This virus was written by Mark Washburn and uses the same encryption method as the 1260 virus. The infective length is 1200 bytes. The virus sets the seconds field to 62. The source code for this virus has been widely circulated and it includes a 'manipulation task' (payload) which will format cylinder 0 of the hard disk. No search pattern is possible.

CAZ - CER: 1204 byte virus. Not yet analysed.

    CAZ   8BEC 7207 8366 0AFE EB08 9083 4E0A 01EB

CAZ-1159 - CER: Similar to the 1204 byte version, and detected with the same pattern.

CB 1530 - CER: This 1530 byte virus is detected by the 'Dark Avenger' pattern.

Cemetery - ER: A 1417 byte mutation of the Murphy virus. Detected by the Murphy 2 pattern.

Checksum - CR: Version 1.00 of this Russian virus is 1233 bytes long and version 1.01 is 1232 bytes long, with only minor differences. As the name implies, the virus calculates a checksum for itself, and if changed it will not activate. The virus is designed to replace older versions of itself.

    Checksum   832E 0300 4F83 2E02 004F 0BC9 740B 508C

Chinese Fish - MR?: This boot sector virus has not been fully analysed, because at the moment only a part of the virus code (the boot sector) is available.

    Chinese Fish   7CB9 0B00 FCAC 2680 3D00 7400 268A 058A

Christmas in Japan - CN: A 600 byte virus from Taiwan, which will activate on 25th December, and display the message 'A merry christmas to you'.

    Christmas Japan   32E4 CF8A 1446 80F2 FE74 06B4 06CD 21EB

Christmas Tree, Father Christmas, Choinka - CN: This is a Polish 1881 byte version of the Vienna virus, which only activates from 19th December to the end of the year and displays a 'Merry Christmas' message. Damage to files has been reported, but not confirmed. This virus is also detected by the Vienna (4) string.

```
Christmas Tree    CD21 81FA 130C 7308 81FA 0101 7202 EB0E
```

Christmas Violator - CN: A 5302 byte mutation of the Violator virus.

```
Xmas Violator     11AC B900 80F2 AEB9 0400 ACAE 75ED E2FA
```

Cinderella - CR: The name of this 390 byte virus is derived from the text 'cInDeReL.la' contained within the virus. After a certain number of keystrokes, the virus creates a hidden file, and jumps to a location in ROM, which caused a cold-boot on a test machine.

```
Cinderella        FA0E 1FBE 8A03 BF90 00AD 8905 AD89 4502
```

Close - ER: This 656 byte virus may damage either C:\IO.SYS or C:\IBMBIO.COM, making the hard disk unbootable.

```
Close             FE0F 1F83 2C31 1E8B CE36 FE07 0726 836C
```

Cookie - CER: This 2232 byte virus may display the message 'I want a COOKIE!', and wait for input from the user. It is closely related to the Syslock/Macho/Advent viruses, and is identified by the Syslock string.

Cookie - CEN: This virus is not related to the 'Cookie' mutations of the 'Japanese Christmas' and 'Syslock' families, but it is large and was compiled with one of the Borland compilers. As the name indicates, the virus demands a cookie, but has not been analysed, because of its size. Two mutations are known, 7360 and 7392 bytes long.

```
Cookie-7392       BFD6 3E1E 57BF 4820 1E57 B8E0 1C50 BF5A
Cookie-7360       BFE2 3E1E 57BF 4820 1E57 B8C0 1C50 BF66
```

Copmpl - CER: This is a 1111 (COM) or 1114 (EXE) byte Polish mutation of the Akuku virus. The name is derived from the following text, which can be found inside the virus 'Sorry, I'm copmpletly dead'. The only effect of the virus is to play a tune.

```
Copmpl            80E6 0F8A D680 FA00 7407 80FA 0B76 06B2
```

Copyright - CN: A 1193 byte virus from East Europe, which contains a fake Award BIOS copyright message. Awaiting analysis.

```
Copyright         AB4A 75F2 E2EA 33C0 CD16 B800 06B7 0733
```

Cossiga - EN: This is a family of two viruses, an 883 byte version, which is clearly older and more primitive, and a 1361 byte mutation which contains the string 'FRIENDS OF MAIS and CLAUDIA SAHIFFER'. Not yet analysed.

```
Cossiga           8BC1 83E1 0FBB 1000 2BD9 53F8 8B55 1C03
Friends           5158 83E1 0FBB 1000 2BD9 53F8 8B55 1C03
```

Crazy Eddie - CER: A 2721 byte virus which has not been fully analysed.

```
Crazy Eddie       0653 B803 01CF 813C 4D5A 7404 813C 5A4D
```

Crazy Imp - CR: A 1445 byte virus, which is very stealthy. It was received from Minsk. It uses several tricks to hide from debuggers but has no effects other than replication.

```
Crazy Imp         B413 CD2F 33C0 8ED8 832E 1304 048C C88E
```

Creeper - CR: There seems to be some confusion regarding the 'Creeper' name, as various 'Creeper' viruses have been reported, and their descriptions do not match at all. This one is 475 bytes long, and is found at the beginning of COM files.

```
Creeper            0E0E 071F C3CD 2050 2D00 4B74 2658 3DFF
```

Creeper-252 - CR: Similar to the mutation reported earlier.

```
Creeper-252        C6FE C60E 07CD 2750 2D00 4B74 2558 3DFF
```

Crew, 2480 - CR: This virus only spreads if the year is set to 1988, so it is not a serious threat. It is rather long, 2480 bytes, but has not been analysed yet. This virus first appeared in Finland. Two versions exist.

```
Crew               81C6 0301 01C6 B904 008C C88E C08E D8BF
```

Criminal - CN: Contains an encrypted message in bad English which urges the user to turn himself in for illegal copying. Not fully analysed, but suspected of being destructive.

```
Criminal           C604 E989 4401 C744 03FF 20B4 42B0 008B
```

CSL, Microelephant - CR: A 381 byte virus from Eastern Europe, which contains the text '26.07.91.Pre-released Microelephant by CSL'. This virus does nothing but replicate.

```
CSL                E800 0058 2D04 0051 521E 068B F005 9200
```

CSL-V4 - CR: A 517 byte mutation of the CSL (or Microelephant) virus reported in the December edition and probably written by the same author. Not yet analysed. The CSL-V5 is another new mutation of the same virus, but it is only 457 bytes long.

```
CSL-V4             5152 1E06 8BF0 0590 008B D88C C88E D8BF
CSL-V5             5152 1E06 8BF0 0592 008B D88C C88E D8BF
```

CZ2986 - CER: This Czechoslovak virus reported by Pavel Baudis of ALWIL software is based upon Old Yankee. It infects files on load and execute request and if the NetWare LOGIN.EXE is executed, the virus collects the ID and password information. It maintains a list of the 15 most recent pairs in encrypted form.

```
CZ2986             9074 13EB 3090 BF6F 09E8 3300 AA3C 6F90
```

Dada - ER: A Russian virus which contains the text 'da,da' - Russian for 'yes, yes'. Awaiting analysis.

```
Dada               CB50 8CC0 2603 0603 0040 8EC0 58C3 33C0
```

Damage - CER: Two related viruses 1063 and 1110 bytes long which cause 'Sector not found' errors by reformatting selected areas of disks. Detected by the 'Diamond' pattern.

Danish Tiny-251 - CN: This virus seems to be derived from the 163 byte mutation, but is not particularly interesting.

```
Danish-251         8BFA B903 00CD 2180 3DE9 7407 B44F EBDC
```

Danish Tiny-Brenda: This 256 byte virus is similar to the 251 byte version, but the effects are different - when an infected program is run, it may occasionally display the text '(C) '92, Stingray/VIPER Luv, Brenda'.

```
Danish-Brenda      8BD7 B902 0090 B43F CD21 813D 0708 74DD
```

Danish Tiny-Stigmata - CN: A 1000 byte version, with a considerable part of the virus' body taken up by a greeting to various virus writers and anti-virus developers.

```
Danish-Stigmata    5053 5156 8B9C EB04 81C6 5C01 B98D 0390
```

Dark Avenger, Eddie - CER: The virus infects when a file is opened and closed as well as when it is executed. This means that a virus-scanning program will cause it to infect every program scanned. Infective length is 1800 bytes. It only infects if a program is at least 1775 bytes long and it may overwrite data sectors with garbage. There is a mutation which extends the file by 2000 bytes. (*VB* Feb 90)

```
Dark Avenger       A4A5 8B26 0600 33DB 53FF 64F5 E800 005E
```

Darklord - CER: A mutation of the Terror virus, this 921 byte virus contains the string 'Dark Lord, I summon thee! MANOWAR'. Awaiting further analysis.

```
Darklord           8EC0 488E D88B 1E03 008 3EB6 503C 326A3
```

Darth Vader - CR: A family of small viruses, probably from Bulgaria. Some of the 4 known mutations contain code which will only work on '286 and above. Awaiting analysis.

```
Darth Vader        B820 12CD 2F26 8A1D B816 12CD 2F
```

Datacrime - CN: The virus attaches itself to the end of a COM file, increasing its length by 1168 or 1280 bytes. On execution of an infected program, the virus searches through the full directory structure of drives C, D, A and B for an uninfected COM file which will be infected. Files with 7th letter D will be ignored (including COMMAND.COM). If the date is on or after 13th October of any year, the first 9 tracks of the hard disk will be formatted after displaying the message: 'DATACRIME VIRUS', 'RELEASED: 1 MARCH 1989'. This message is stored in an encrypted form in the virus. (*VB* Aug 89)

```
Datacrime (1)      3601 0183 EE03 8BC6 3D00 0075 03E9 0201
Datacrime (2)      3601 0183 EE03 8BC6 3D00 0075 03E9 FE00
```

Datacrime II - CEN: This encrypted virus attaches itself to the end of a COM or EXE file, increasing their length by 1514 bytes. The virus searches through the full directory structure of drives C, A and B for an uninfected COM or EXE file. It ignores any file if the second letter is B. If the date is on or after 13th October of any year, but not a Monday, a low level format of the first 9 tracks will be done on the hard disk after displaying the message: 'DATACRIME II VIRUS' which is stored in an encrypted form. Datacrime IIB displays the message '* DATACRIME *'. (*VB* Aug 90)

```
Datacrime II       2E8A 072E C605 2232 C2D0 CA2E 8807 432E
Datacrime IIB      2BCB 2E8A 0732 C2D0 CA2E 8807 43E2 F3
```

Datalock - CER: The name of this 920 byte virus is included at the end of infected programs, but its effects are not known yet.

```
Datalock           C31E A12C 0050 8CD8 488E D881 2E03 0080
```

Day/10 - CN: This 674 byte virus was made available to virus researchers under the name of 'Numlock', but that is just the name of the original sample. The effects of the virus have nothing to do with the NumLock key - instead it will overwrite the first 80 sectors on the hard disk if the date of the month is divisible by 10.

```
Day/10             8E06 2C00 B900 10FC 33FF B050 F2AE 7518
```

dBASE - CR: Transposes bytes in dBASE (DBF) files. Creates the hidden file BUGS.DAT in the root directory of drive C and generates errors if the absolute difference between the month of creation of BUGS.DAT and the current month is greater than or equal to 3.

Infective length is 1864 bytes. The destroy version destroys drives D to Z when the trigger point is reached. (*VB* Dec 89)

```
dBASE               50B8 0AFB CD21 3DFB 0A74 02EB 8A56 E800
dBASE destroy       B900 01BA 0000 8EDA 33DB 50CD 2658 403C
```

DBF Blank - CER: This virus waits for a dBASE (DBF) file to be opened and returns a blank record once every 20 disk reads. Only one DBF file is affected at a time. Infective length is 1075 bytes.

```
DBF Blank           F3A4 C38C C02E 0344 1A05 1000 502E FF74
```

December 24th - ER: A mutation of the Icelandic (3) virus. It will infect one out of every 10 EXE files run, which grow by 848-863 bytes. If an infected file is run on December 24th, it will stop any other program from running and display the message 'Gledileg jol' (Merry Christmas in Icelandic).

```
December 24th       C606 7E03 FEB4 5290 CD21 2E8C 0645 0326
```

December 28th, Spanish April - CR?: Awaiting analysis.

```
December 28th       B44A CD21 8BD4 B41A CD21 B42A CD21 32C0
```

Dedicated, Fear - CN: Two viruses which use the Mutation engine. No search pattern is possible.

Deicide - CN: A primitive 666 byte overwriting virus. When it activates, it will wipe out the first 80 sectors on drive C. According to a message inside the virus, it is written by a person named Glenn Benton.

```
Deicide             3C00 7502 FEC0 FEC0 3C03 7516 B002 BB00
```

Delyrium-1638, Move - CER: A virus by Cracker Jack detected by the HIV pattern.

Demolition - CR: A 1585 encrypted virus which contains destructive code, as well as various text messages.

```
Demolition          E800 005B 8D77 178A 04D0 E09C 81C6 0106
```

Demon - CN: A primitive 272 byte overwriting virus, written by the person calling himself 'Cracker Jack'.

```
Demon               02EB 02EB EFB4 2ACD 213C 0274 04B4 4CCD
```

Den Zuk, Search - DR: The majority of the virus is stored in a specially formatted track 40, head 0, sectors 33 to 41. When Ctrl-Alt-Del is pressed, the virus intercepts it and displays 'DEN ZUK' sliding in from the sides of the screen. This does not happen if KEYBUK or KEYB is installed. Den Zuk will remove Brain and Ohio and replace them with copies of itself.

```
Den Zuk (1)         FA8C C88E D88E D0BC 00F0 FBE8 2600 33C0
Den Zuk (2)         FA8C C88E D88E D0BC 00F0 FBB8 787C 50C3
```

Destructor - CER: A 1150 byte Bulgarian virus containing the string 'DESTRUCTOR V4.00 (c) 1990 by ATA'.

```
Destructor          5255 FBCB 3D00 4B74 1980 FC3D 740F 80FC
```

Devil's Dance - CR: A simple virus which infects COM files, adding 951 bytes at the end of infected files. The virus is believed to have originated in Spain or Mexico. It monitors the keyboard and will destroy the FAT after 5000 keystrokes.

```
Devil's Dance       B800 0150 8CC8 8ED8 8EC0 C306 B821 35CD
```

Dewdz - CN: This 601 byte virus adds itself in front of the files it infects. When it activates it will display the text 'Kewl Dewdz!' in the middle of the screen.

    Dewdz   434B 7409 B44F CD21 72BA 4B75 F7B4 2FCD

Diabolik - CER: A 1171 byte mutation of the Murphy virus. Detected by the Murphy 2 pattern.

Diamond, 1024 - CER: A Bulgarian virus, possibly written by the person calling himself 'Dark Avenger'. This virus may be an earlier version of the Dark Avenger virus. No side-effects or activation dates have been found. Diamond-B is a minor mutation.

    Diamond   00B4 40CD 2172 043B C174 01F9 C39C 0EE8

Diamond-1173, David - CER: A modification of the Diamond-B virus, produced by inserting NOP instructions and making other minor changes. Contains errors which will generally cause infected COM files to crash. Detected by the 'Diamond' pattern.

Dir - CR: A 691 byte Bulgarian virus, which only infects files when the DIR command is issued. No other effects have been found.

    Dir   CD26 0E1F 580E 1FBE 0001 56C3 0E0E 1F07

DIR-II - LCER: A new type of 'link' virus from Bulgaria. It is 1024 bytes long and it infects executable files by linking a single cluster containing virus code with the starting cluster of each file in the directory entry. The original cluster number is saved encrypted in the unused part of the directory entry. The virus does not have any side-effects. (*VB* Nov 91)

    DIR-II   BC00 06FF 06EB 0431 C98E D9C5 06C1 0005

DIR-II-1 - LCER: Two new mutations of this virus have appeared. The pattern will detect all three mutations.

    DIR-II-1   26FF 77FE 26C5 1F8B 4015 3D70 0075 1091

Discom - CR: A 2053 byte mutation of the Jerusalem virus. Awaiting analysis.

    Discom   57CD 2172 1F8B F18B FAB8 0242 B9FF FFBA

Diskjeb - CER: A disk-corrupting virus with an infective length of 1435 bytes (COM) and 1419 bytes (EXE). Only infects COM files longer than 1000 bytes and EXE files longer than 1024 bytes. In October, November and December disk writes will be intercepted and corrupted. A possible mutation of the Tenbyte virus.

    Diskjeb   5351 061E 9C8C C88E D8E8 5D00 803E 4903

Diskspoiler, 1308 - CN: A 1308 byte Russian virus, which uses very simple encryption. The virus searches the FAT for free clusters and marks them as bad, slowly eating up the entire disk.

    Diskspoiler   E800 005E 8BFE B90B 0580 750E FF90 47E2

Disk Killer, Ogre - DR: The virus infects floppy and hard disks and if the computer is left on for more than 48 hours, it will encrypt the contents of the bootable disk partition. The infection of a disk occurs by intercepting a disk read - INT 13H function 2. When the virus triggers, it displays the message 'Disk Killer -- Version 1.00 by Ogre Software, 04/01/1989. Warning !! Don't turn off the power or remove the diskette while Disk Killer is Processing!'. A mutation (Disk Killer 2) assembled with a different assembler has been found. (*VB* Jan 90)

```
Disk Killer       2EA1 1304 2D08 002E A313 04B1 06D3 E08E
Disk Killer 2     7423 2E3A 16F4 0175 EE2E 3A36 F501 75E7
```

DM-310 - CR: Probably an older and more primitive version of the DM-400 virus. It does not seem to do anything but replicate.

```
DM-310            F7C1 FEFF 7405 B801 43CD 63C3 E800 005D
```

DM-330 - CR: This encrypted virus contains text stating that it is version 1.05 of the DM virus, but it is considerably different from the earlier versions. Only a partial search string (which includes wildcards) is possible.

DM-400 - CR: This 400 byte virus does not seem to do anything but replicate. It contains the text '(C)1990 DM'.

```
DM-400            80FC 4B74 3380 FC56 7419 FE04 80FC 3D74
```

DM-400 (1.01) - CR: A slightly improved version of the DM-400 virus, with extra encryption. It is also 400 bytes long. The virus corrupts files that fit the *.TP? pattern - overwriting the first 8 bytes.

```
DM-400 1.01       56B9 2401 3024 46E2 FB5E C3E8 0100 CF5D
```

Do-nothing - CR: A badly-written virus from Israel that assumes a 640K system.

```
Do nothing        8CCA 8EDA BA00 988E C2F3 A41E B800 008E
```

Doom2 - CER: This 1252 byte virus is not always able to infect files. The machine hangs immediately after a file is infected.

```
Doom2             803E 0A01 4574 052E 033E 0301 2E30 0547
```

Doom II-B - CER: This mutation of Doom-2 has not been able to replicate under test conditions - infected programs hang or overwrite the FAT and root directory on drive C. Version B uses the same encryption method as the other known mutation.

```
Doom-II-B         803E 0901 4574 052E 033E 0301 2E30 0547
```

Dot Killer - CN: This 944 byte Polish virus will remove all dots (.) from the screen when they are typed. The effect can be disabled by typing a caret '^'. Seconds field is set to 62. Files set to Read-Only will not be infected.

```
Dot Killer        582E A301 0158 2EA2 0001 B800 01FF E0B8
```

Durban, Saturday 14th - CER: Adds 669 bytes to the end of infected files. On any Saturday 14th the first 100 logical sectors of drives C, then B and then A are overwritten.

```
Durban            B911 00A4 E2FD B4DE CD21 80FC DF74 47C6
```

Dutch Tiny-99 - CN: One of the smallest viruses which do not infect by overwriting existing files. It does nothing but replicate.

```
Dutch Tiny-99     93B4 3FCD 2180 3C4D 741D B002 E820 0097
```

Dutch Tiny-124 - CR: Another small virus from the Netherlands, probably written by the same author as the previous one. Rather badly written and crashes on certain types of hardware.

```
Dutch 124         930E 1FB4 3FCD 218B F280 3C4D 741C B002
```

Dutch Tiny-126 - CR: This virus from the Netherlands is an attempt to create the smallest resident virus, but it has no effect other than replicating. Detected by the Dutch 124 pattern.

Dyslexia, Solano - CR: Virus adds 1991 bytes in front of the infected file and 9 bytes at the end. Occasionally transposes two adjacent characters on the screen.

    Dyslexia   B4C0 CD21 3D34 1275 0E2E 8B0E 0301 1E07

Eddie-2, 651 - CER: A non-destructive virus from Bulgaria. It marks infected files with a value of 62 in the seconds field of the timestamp, which makes them immune from infection by Vienna or Zero Bug. Infected files grow by 651 bytes, but this will not be seen if a DIR command is used - the virus intercepts the find-first and find-next functions, returning the correct (uninfected) length. (*VB* June 90)

    Eddie-2   D3E8 408C D103 C18C D949 8EC1 BF02 00BA

Eddie-1801 - CER: A minor mutation of the Dark Avenger virus, one byte longer and detected by the same pattern.

E.D.V. - DR: E.D.V. marks infected disks with 'EV' at the end of the boot sector and stores the original boot sector code in the last sector of the last track on 360K disks, just like the Yale virus. Program crashes and data loss have been reported on infected systems.

    E.D.V.   0C01 5083 EC04 B800 01CF B601 B908 2751

Eliza - CN: This 1193/1194 byte virus works very badly. It damages EXE files, instead of infecting them, and second-generation copies of the virus will normally not work.

    Eliza   FFE0 5E81 C600 01BF 0001 5951 56AC AAE2

EMF - CN: This 404 byte virus conatins the text 'Screaming Fist', but is quite different from the Screamer virus. It may have been written by the same author. Not fully analysed.

    EMF   E810 00B4 408B D583 EA03 B993 01CD 21E8

Enemy - CER: This virus is difficult to detect, as its length is variable, and it uses a self-modifying encryption routine. The virus includes the text 'I am a stranger in a strange land'. No effects have been found.

Enigma - ER: A mutation of the 'Old Yankee' virus, claiming to have been written by the same author as HIV. It is 1624 bytes long, and is detected by the Old Yankee pattern.

Enola - CER: A 1864 byte virus, probably of Russian origin, but not yet analysed.

    Enola   FF74 081F 8ED8 B800 0150 C38C C805 1000

Erasmus - CER: A 1682 byte version of the Murphy virus. Detected by the HIV pattern.

ETC - CN: A 700 byte virus, containing the text 'Virus, (c) ETC'. Awaiting analysis.

    ETC   8B16 0201 83C2 33CD 2172 CD89 D68B 043D

Europe '92 - CR: This 421 byte virus will only activate if the year is set to 1992, when it will display the message 'Europe/92 4EVER!'

    Europe '92   B450 CD21 8CD8 488E D8C6 0600 005A 891E

Europe '92-424 - CR: Three bytes longer than the original mutation, but very similar, and detected with the same pattern.

Even Beeper - EN: This companion virus is highly unusual. It creates a COM file for every EXE file it 'infects'. The COM files are structurally EXE files, written in a high-level-language, but their length is variable, and they have been compressed with LZEXE. As a result it is impractical to use a signature to detect infected files.

Evil - CR: This is a close relative of the Bulgarian Phoenix virus, but is shorter, 1701 bytes instead of 1704. It uses the same encryption method, which makes the extraction of a search pattern impossible.

Evil Empire - MR: Virus infects Master Boot Sector and relocates original boot sector to Sector 6, Head 0, Track 0. Virus displays a text message questioning the United States' involvement in the recent Gulf War. (*VB* May 91)

```
Evil Empire        734C 80FC 0275 4731 C08E D880 3E6C 0416
```

Evil Empire B - MR: An encrypted mutation, probably written by the same author as Evil Empire.

```
Evil Empire B      8CC8 8ED8 8EC0 BF05 00B9 9A01 FC8A 0504
```

F-709 - CR: This 709 byte virus is reported to have originated either in Sweden or in Finland. It has not been fully analysed, but appears to do nothing but replicate.

```
F-709              8BF2 33FF F3A5 068C C633 C08E C026 A184
```

Faggot - ?: Virus sample failed to replicate. A mutation of the Anti-Faggot virus discovered by the same search pattern. Contains text 'Hi Guy! Nice to meet you! I am the little FAGGOT Virus' and some more obscenities.

Fake-VirX - CN: A 233 byte virus from Finland which activates on any Friday the 13th, when it displays the message 'VirX 3/90'.

```
Fake-VirX          408B D5B9 0600 CD21 B801 575A 59CD 21B4
```

Faust, Spyer - CER: Infects on calling the Load-and-Execute function, but does not infect COMMAND.COM. On 13th day of every month the virus displays the message 'Chaos!!! Another Masterpiece of Faust...' and the machine hangs. The virus also writes random garbage to disk. Infective length is 1184 bytes. (*VB* Feb 91)

```
Faust              B87A 0050 06B8 FD00 5026 C706 FD00 F3A4
```

Feist - CER: A 670 byte Russian virus, awaiting analysis.

```
Feist              B10C D3E2 5233 D2B9 1000 F7F1 8BCA 5A03
```

Fellowship - ER: This 1019 byte virus attaches itself to the end of EXE files, damaging them by overwriting the last 10 bytes or so. Other effects are being analysed.

```
Fellowship         BAF5 02E8 3A00 B60A E84A 00BA 1403 E82F
```

FGT - CN: 651 bytes. Not yet analysed.

Fichv 2.0 - CN: Very similar to the more common 903 byte mutation, but is only 896 bytes long.

```
Fichv 2.0          B801 35CD 218C 0629 0189 1E2B 01B8 0335
```

Fichv 2.1 - CN: A 903 byte encrypted virus, which contains the text 'FICHV 2.1 vous a eu'. Awaiting analysis.

```
Fichv              B801 35CD 218C 0602 0189 1E04 01B8 0335
```

Filler - DR: A Hungarian virus with unknown effects.

```
Filler                CD12 BB40 00F7 E32D 0010 8EC0 BA00 00EB
```

Finger - CER: A 1172 byte version of the Murphy virus. Detected by the Murphy-2 pattern.

Fingers 08/15 - CER: A 1322 byte virus which is awaiting analysis.

```
Fingers 08/15         AE26 803D 0075 F847 4747 8BD7 1E2E 8C16
```

Fish 6 - CER: A partial mutation of 4K having an infective length of 3584 bytes. The virus is encrypted and the decryption routine is so short that it is impossible to extract a hex pattern longer than 14 bytes. The virus seems to activate in 1991, but the exact effects are as yet unknown.

```
Fish 6                E800 005B 81EB A90D B958 0D2E 8037
```

Flash - CER: This 688 byte virus is awaiting analysis.

```
Flash                 005E 8BDE 81C3 0F00 B000 FAD5 0A88 07EB
```

Flash-Gyorgy - CER: Like the Brenda and Milana viruses, this mutation of the Flash virus seems to be written by a lovesick virus author. In this case the message is 'I LOVE GYORGY'.

```
Flash-Gyorgy          1E06 0E1F FCE8 0000 5E8B DE83 C30E B000
```

Flip, Omicron - MCER: The primary effect of this 2343 byte virus is to 'flip' the screen by rotating it through 90 degrees on the second day of the month between 10:00 and 10:59. The virus is encrypted and self-modifying. An infected file has the seconds field set to 62. No search pattern is possible for COM/EXE files. Search pattern will be found in the master boot sector. (*VB* Sept 90). Original MBS is stored in the first sector after the end of the partition as recorded in the partition table.

```
Flip (boot)           33DB 33FF 8EC3 2629 0613 04CD 12B1 06D3
```

Forger - EN: A 1000 byte virus which causes subtle corruption - occasionally modifying a byte on the disk.

```
Forger                215A 520E 1F5F 0706 57B8 0000 B980 00F2
```

Form - DR: A boot sector virus from Switzerland infecting hard disks and floppy disks. On the 18th day of every month the virus produces a noise when keys are pressed. The original boot sector is stored in the last physical sector of the hard disk. (*VB* Nov 91)

```
Form                  D3E0 8EC0 33FF B9FF 00FC F3A5 06B8 9A00
```

Formiche - CR: A 6258 byte virus, which uses almost the same encryption method as Cascade.

```
Formiche              0F8D B74C 01BC D217 4631 3431 244C 75F8
```

Freew-692 - CN: When this virus activates (in 1993), it overwrites programs with a trojan, that simply displays the message 'Program terminated normally.' when run. The virus is 692 bytes long.

```
Freew-692             81F9 C907 7206 80FE 0175 0145 B41A BA03
```

Frog's Alley - CR: A 1500 byte virus, which infects program when the DIR command is issued, which makes it highly infectious. The virus activates on the 5th day of any month, overwriting the FAT and root directory.

```
Frog's Alley          0105 0001 26A3 1500 268C 1E13 0026 C706
```

Frogs B - CN: A very minor mutation of the earlier Frogs (Frog's Alley) virus detected by the same pattern.

Fu Manchu - CER: The virus attaches itself to the beginning of a COM file or to the end of an EXE file. Infective length is 2086 bytes (COM) and 2080 (EXE). One in sixteen times on infection a timer is installed, which will trigger a display 'The world will hear from me again' after a random number of half-hours (max. 7.5 hours). The machine then reboots. The same message is also displayed on pressing Ctrl-Alt-Del, but the virus does not survive the reboot. If the date is after 1st August 1989, the virus monitors the keyboard buffer and adds derogatory comments to the names of politicians (Thatcher, Reagan, Botha and Waldheim), overstrikes two four-letter words, and displays 'virus 3/10/88 - latest in the new fun line!' if 'Fu Manchu' is typed. All messages are encrypted. (*VB* July 89)

```
Fu Manchu          FCB4 E1CD 2180 FCE1 7316 80FC 0472 11B4
```

F-word, USSR-417 - CR: A 417 byte virus, probably of Russian origin. The only text inside the virus is the message 'Fuck You'.

```
F-word             C3B4 3FCD 2129 C858 75DD FFE0 B440 EBF3
```

Generic - DR: Awaiting functioning sample for analysis.

```
Generic            31C0 8ED8 A113 042D 0700 A313 04B1 06D3
```

Gergana - CN: A simple 192 byte virus, which does nothing but replicate.

```
Gergana            FFE0 5E81 C600 01BF 0001 B9B6 00F3 A4B8
```

Gergana-222, 300, 450, 512 - CN: Four new mutations of the Gergana virus, which are longer than the original, with improved error handling, and several minor modifications.

```
Gergana-222        BF80 FFB9 3000 F3A4 E9C6 FD5E 81C6 0001
Gergana-300        BF80 FFB9 3000 F3A4 E985 FD5E 81C6 0001
Gergana-450        BF80 FFB9 3000 F3A4 E97E FD5E 81C6 0001
Gergana-512        BA00 FAB4 3FCD 21C3 B900 02B4 40CD 21C3
```

GhostBalls - CN: A strain of Vienna virus. Seconds field changed to 62, as in Vienna. Infective length is 2351 bytes and the virus attaches itself to the end of the file. When run, it will infect other COM files and try to place a modified copy of the Italian virus into the boot sector of drive A. This copy of the Italian runs on 286 machines but is non-infective. Virus contains text 'GhostBalls, Product of Iceland'.

```
GhostBalls         AE75 EDE2 FA5E 0789 BC16 008B FE81 C71F
```

Gliss - CN: A German 'demonstration' virus - very obvious, and does nothing but replicate.

```
Gliss              218B D85F 578B 45FC 0527 00BF 0401 8905
```

Goblin - CER: A 1951 byte mutation of the Murphy virus. Detected by the HIV pattern.

```
Gosia              8BD6 81C2 7001 B001 B900 00B4 43CD 2172
```

Gotcha - CER: Two related viruses from East Europe, 879 and 881 bytes long. They contain the text 'GOTCHA!' at the end, but it is not known when (or if) this text is displayed.

```
Gotcha             9C3D DADA 7428 80FC 3D74 0A3D 006C 7405
```

Gotcha-C - CER: A 906 byte mutation of the Gotcha virus. Awaiting analysis.

```
Gotcha-C           9C3D DADA 7458 5251 5350 5657 1E06 3D00
```

Gotcha-D - CER: The smallest member of the Gotcha family, 627 bytes long.

```
Gotcha-D            9C3D DADA 742E 5251 5350 5657 1E06 80FC
```

Got You - EN: A 3052 byte virus which contains code to overwrite critical portions of the hard disk. Not fully analysed.

```
Got You             6C00 4000 C5AA FFF0 413A 0034 122A 2E2A
```

GP1 - CER: This is a Dutch, Novell NetWare-oriented mutation of the Jerusalem virus. (*VB* June 91)

```
GP1                 B4F7 CD21 80FC F773 1380 FC03 072E 8E16
```

Grapje!! - CEN: Awaiting analysis.

```
Grapje!!            E8F3 01E8 2801 E89C 02E8 E202 730E B90A
```

Gremlin - CER: A 1146 byte 'Diamond' mutation detected by the same pattern.

Grither - CN: A 774 byte mutation of Vienna, which is detected by the Vienna (2) pattern. When it activates, it overwrites part of the hard disk, including the beginning of drive C.

Grune - CR: The name of this virus is derived from an encrypted text message, which refers to the Green party of Switzerland. Infected programs grow by 1241 bytes.

```
Grune               3601 0026 C606 0000 4D5E 5681 C6D5 0483
```

Guppy - CR: A very simple 152 byte virus. It does nothing but replicate, but many programs, including COMMAND.COM will fail to execute if infected.

```
Guppy               521E B802 3DCD 2193 E800 005E 0E1F B43F
```

Hafenstrasse - EN: An 809 byte virus, probably from Germany. Awaiting analysis..

```
Hafenstrasse        F607 FF74 1E8A 170A D274 0743 B402 CD21
```

Hafenstrasse-791 - EN: Very similar to the original version, and detected with the same pattern.

Hafenstrasse-1641 - CEN: Just like the 1689 byte mutation, this virus 'drops' the Ambulance virus. It is detected with the Hafenstrasse-Kilroy pattern.

Hafenstrasse-1689 - EN: This 1689 byte updated version of the Hafenstrasse virus differs considerably from the original. It contains a copy of the Ambulance virus, which it will 'drop', infecting COM files, but the Hafenstrasse virus only infects EXE files. Detected by the pattern for the 809 byte mutation.

Haifa - CER: This virus from Israel uses self-modifying encryption. The length is around 2350 bytes, but variable. No search pattern is possible.(*VB* Jan 92)

Hallochen - CER: A virus which reputedly originated in West Germany. It contains two text strings (ö in Hallochen is character code 148 decimal): 'Hallöchen !!!!!!, Here I'm..', 'Acrivate Level 1..'. The virus will not infect 'old' files. If the value of the month or year fields in the time stamp is different from the current date, the file will not be infected. The virus will only infect files longer than 5000 bytes, increasing their length by 2011 bytes. (*VB* Feb 92)

```
Hallochen           EB8C C903 D98E D3BC DB08 53BB 2E00 53CB
```

Halloween - CEN: Awaiting analysis.

```
Halloween           6F77 6565 6E55 89E5 B8B8 009A 4402 5701
```

Harakiri - CEN: This 5488 byte high level language virus is not expected to become a real threat, as it is much too obvious - it simply overwrites files when infecting.

```
Harakiri            5DC2 0400 052A 2E65 7865 015C 052A 2E63
```

Hary Anto - CR: A 981 byte virus, which has not been analysed yet. Reported 'in the wild' in the UK.

```
Hary Anto           B904 00D3 E8BB 3E01 8907 40B9 0400 D3E0
```

Helloween - CER: Despite the name similarity, this virus is totally unrelated to the Halloween virus. The name of this 1376 byte virus is derived from the string 'HELLOWEEN', which is stored inside it in encrypted form.

```
Helloween           B440 EB02 B43F E815 0072 022B C1C3 33C9
```

Hey You-928 - CER: Unlike the 923 byte sample previously made available, this version is able to replicate without problems. Not yet analysed.

```
Hey You             2181 F9C7 0772 1C80 FE02 7217 80FA 1972
```

Hero - CER: A primitive 506 byte virus, which will not replicate beyond the first generation, as a programming error causes it to corrupt all programs it infects.

```
Hero                C0CF 80FC 4B74 2080 FC25 7516 3C80 7212
```

Hero-394 - ER: Related to the 506 byte Hero virus, but does not damage the files it infects. Awaiting analysis.

```
Hero-394            B98A 0133 C0BF 0002 0305 83C7 02E2 F929
```

HH&H - CR: A 4091 byte encrypted virus, which contains the curious string 'HARD HIT & HEAVY HATE the HUMANS !!'. Not yet analysed.

Hitchcock - CR: A 1247 byte virus. It activates a few minutes after an infected program is run, and starts playing the tune from the Hitchcock TV-series.

```
Hitchcock           2BD0 4A45 03E8 8EC5 4526 8916 0300 2689
```

HIV - CER: This virus is based on Murphy and contains a text message claiming it was written by 'Cracker Jack' in Italy.

```
HIV                 2BC3 1BD1 7204 2906 0600 8BF7 33FF 0E1F
```

Horror - CER: An encrypted, 2319 byte virus.

```
Horror              8BFE 83C7 0AB9 4E04 2E8A 849D 042E 3005
```

Horse, Hacker, Black horse - CER: A family of viruses probably from Bulgaria. Currently 8 different mutations are known, which can be divided into two groups, with a different pattern required for each group. Awaiting analysis. The first group contains Horse-1 (1154), Horse-2 (1158), Horse-2B (1160) and Horse-7 (1152). The second group of Horse viruses contains Horse-3 (1610), Horse-4 (1776), Horse-5 (1576) and Horse-6 (1594).

```
Horse (1)           00A3 0001 8B46 02A3 0201 B800 018C CAEB
Horse (2)           570E 07B9 0800 F3A4 B02E AAB9 0300 F3A4
```

Horse 8 - CER: No search pattern possible, virus awaiting analysis. Infective length is 2248 bytes.

Horse Boot - DR: Infects only floppy disks. Awaiting disassembly.

```
Horse Boot          8F06 727D 8F06 747D 48A3 1304 B106 D3E0
```

Horse Boot 2 - MR: This virus infects the Master boot sector and stores the original on track 0, head 0, sector 7, while on floppy disks it is kept on the track 39, head 1, sector 9.

```
Horse Boot 2      FC29 C08E D8BD 007C FA8E D08B E5FB 5055
```

Hungarian-473 - CR: Closely related to the Hungarian-482 virus, this 372 byte virus activates on June 13th and then overwrites the Master Boot Sector of the hard disk. Detected by the Hungarian-482 pattern.

Hungarian-482 - CR: This 482 byte virus from Hungary activates on November 7th. If an infected program is run on that date it will display the string 'Format ...' and proceed to format the hard disk.

```
Hungarian-482     5603 F7AC 0AC0 740A D0E8 B40E B307 CD10
```

Hybrid - CN: A 1306 byte encrypted mutation of the Vienna virus which marks infected files by setting the seconds field of the time stamp to 62. On any Friday the 13th after 1991 the virus will format the hard disk. It may also overwrite files and cause reboots.

```
Hybrid            81EE 7502 8BFE B9DE 01AC 34DE AA49 75F9
```

Hydra - CN: A group of 9 viruses, which do nothing particularly interesting.

```
Hydra  (01)       B43D B002 BA53 01B0 02CD 218B D806 1FB8
Hydra  (02)       B43D B002 BA53 01CD 218B D806 1FB8 003F
```

Hymn - CER: A Russian, 1865 byte virus related to the 'Eddie' (Dark Avenger) virus, and the 'Murphy' viruses.

```
Hymn              FF64 F500 07E8 0000 5E83 EE4C FC2E 81BC
```

Icelandic, Saratoga - ER: The virus attaches itself at the end of an EXE file and after becoming memory-resident, it will infect only one in ten (one in two for the Icelandic (2) mutation) programs executed. When a program is infected, the disk is examined and if it has more than 20 MBytes, one cluster is marked as bad in the first copy of the FAT. There is a mutation which does not flag clusters. Version (1) will not infect the system unless INT 13H segment is 0700H or F000H, thus avoiding detection by anti-virus programs which hook into this interrupt. Version (3) does not flag clusters and bypasses all interrupt-checking programs.

```
Icelandic (1)     2EC6 0687 020A 9050 5351 5256 1E8B DA43
Icelandic (2)     2EC6 0679 0202 9050 5351 5256 1E8B DA43
Icelandic (3)     2EC6 066F 020A 9050 5351 5256 1E8B DA43
```

Illness - CR: This encrypted 1016 byte virus is probably of Polish origin. It contains the text 'WARNING : USE ONLY ORGINAL PROGRAMS DON^T COPY IT and now .. I AM ILL !!'.

```
Illness           BAF8 0383 EA20 33FF 3E8A 86F3 043E 2883
```

Incom - CN: Awaiting disassembly.

```
Incom             528B FA8B 4D02 8BDF 2BD9 83C3 1783 E92C
```

INT 13 - CR: Overwriting, stealth virus which subverts DOS and BIOS. The virus is 512 bytes long. Only selected COM files are infected during FCB find next function call. (*VB* Mar 91)

```
INT 13            E200 50BF 4C00 5733 ED8E DDC4 1DBF 7402
```

Interceptor-Vienna - CN: This mutation written by Cracker Jack is quite similar to the Monxla-B mutation. The search pattern can also be found in Monxla-B, but the viruses can be distinguished by different lengths.

```
Interceptor        B903 008B D683 C20D CD21 8B54 068B 4C04
```

Internal - EN: Infective length is 1381 bytes. Virus contains the strings 'INTERNAL ERROR 02CH.', 'PLEASE CONTACT YOUR HARDWARE MANUFACTURER IMMEDIATELY !' and 'DO NOT FORGET TO REPORT THE ERROR CODE !'.

```
Internal           1E06 8CC8 8ED8 B840 008E C0FC E858 0480
```

Intruder - EN: This 1319 byte virus seems to delete infected files occasionally, and infected programs sometimes 'hang', but this seems to be due to sloppy programming. Two minor mutations are known, A and B, but both are detected with the same pattern.

```
Intruder           5F32 C0AA B001 0AC0 C35F 32C0 C3BA 0600
```

Iraqui Warrior - CN: A 777 byte mutation of Vienna, where numerous NOP instructions have been added to avoid detection by current scanners.

```
Iraqui Warrior     BF00 0190 B903 00F3 A490 8BF2 B430 90CD
```

Iron Maiden - CN: A 636 byte virus, which contains the text 'IRON MAIDEN' near the end. It has not been fully analysed, but contains destructive code (INT 26H calls).

```
Iron Maiden        2425 CD21 5F0E 1F8B 8557 02A3 0001 8AA5
```

Italian, Pingpong, Turin, Bouncing Ball, Vera Cruz - DR: The virus consists of a boot sector and one cluster marked as bad in the first copy of the FAT. The first sector in the marked cluster contains the rest of the virus while the second contains the original boot sector. It infects all disks which have at least two sectors per cluster and occupies 2K of RAM. It displays a single character 'bouncing ball' if there is a disk access during a one-second interval in any multiple of 30 minutes on the system clock. The original version will hang when run on an 80286 or 80386 machine, but a new version has been reported which runs normally. If a warm boot (Ctrl-Alt-Del) is performed after the machine hangs, an uninfected disk will still become infected. (*VB* Nov 89)

```
Italian-Gen        B106 D3E0 2DC0 078E C0BE 007C 8BFE B900
Italian            32E4 CD1A F6C6 7F75 0AF6 C2F0 7505 52E8
```

Italian 803 - CEN: Extends the length of COMMAND.COM by 805 bytes. Awaiting analysis. Sample would not infect COM files other than COMMAND.COM. Italian 817 mutation, recognised by the same pattern and also known as XDV, overwrites the first 200 sectors on logical drives Z to A on 13th February of any year after 13:00.

```
Italian 803        7502 32C0 3CFF 7502 B001 5051 CD26 83C4
```

Itavir - EN: When the virus activates, it will write random data to all I/O ports causing unpredictable behaviour such as screen flicker, hissing from the loudspeaker etc. Infective length is 3880 bytes.

```
Itavir             83C4 025A 595B 5850 5351 52CD 2672 0D83
```

Itti-191, Itti-99 - CN: A primitive overwriting virus, which displays the text 'EXEC failure' when it has infected a program. The virus will not attempt infection if it determines that FluShot+ is active in memory. A related 99 byte virus also exists, but it does not check for the presence of Flushot+.

```
Itti-99          998B CAB8 0042 CD21 B440 B963 00BA 0001
Itti-191         7415 B44E B927 00BA 8C01 CD21 7215 E81D
```

Jabberwocky - CER: An 812 byte virus, containing the text 'BEWARE THE JABBERWOCK'. Not yet analysed.

```
Jabberwocky      0500 108E C0BE 0000 BF00 00B9 FFFF F3A4
```

Jabberwocky-615 - CR: Detected by the Jabberwocky pattern.

Japanese Christmas-Cookie - CN: This 653 byte mutation of the Japanese Christmas virus has been modified to display the messages 'Give me a Cookie' and 'Cookie'.

```
Jap-Cookie       1B90 32E4 CF50 528A 1446 80F2 FE74 06B4
```

JD - CR: A group of four semi-stealth viruses, 356, 392, 448 and 460 bytes long. In addition there are two shorter mutations, 158 and 276 bytes, with no stealth features. Not fully analysed, but do not appear to do anything but replicate.

```
JD (1)           521E B813 35CD 2106 5304 11CD 2106 53B8
JD (2)           5053 561E 068B F2B4 2FCD 21AC 3774 0383
JD-158           5ABB 4300 8EDB 833D 3D74 08B4 25CD 21B1
```

Jeff - CN: Just like the Klaeren virus, Jeff can not successfully infect files longer than 4096 bytes. The virus is 812 bytes long, (not 814 as originally reported). When it activates it may overwrite sectors on the hard disk.

```
Jeff             B89B FF8E C0B9 3F00 33D2 32E4 8BD9 268A
```

Jerusalem, PLO, Friday the 13th, Israeli - CER: The virus attaches itself to the beginning of a COM file or at the end of an EXE file. When an infected file is executed, the virus becomes memory-resident and will infect any COM or EXE program run, except COMMAND.COM. COM files are infected only once, while EXE files are re-infected every time that they are run. Infective length is 1813 bytes (COM) and 1808 bytes (EXE). The virus finds the end of EXE files from the information in the file header, and if this is less than the actual file length, the virus will overwrite part of the file. After the system has been infected for 30 minutes, row 5 column 5 to row 16 column 16 on the screen are scrolled up two lines, creating a 'black window'. The system then slows down, due to a time-wasting loop installed on each timer interrupt. If the system is infected when the date is set to the 13th of any month which is also a Friday, every program run will be deleted. (*VB* July 89)

Jerusalem mutations matching the following two search patterns:

```
Jerusalem        03F7 2E8B 8D11 00CD 218C C805 1000 8ED0
Jerusalem-USA    FCB4 E0CD 2180 FCE0 7316 80FC 0372 11B4
```

Anarkia: Virus signature is changed from 'sURIV' to 'ANARKIA'. **Anarkia-B**: Minor mutation of Anarkia. **Carfield**: 1508 bytes long. **Frere Jacques**: There are two mutations known as A and B which play the Frere Jacques tune on Fridays. **Groen Links**, GrLkDos: An 1888 byte mutation from The Netherlands. Every 30 minutes it plays the tune 'Stem op Groen Link' or 'Vote Green Left'. **Jerusalem-1600/1605**: A shortened mutation awaiting analysis. **Jerusalem-Nemesis**: A minor mutation of the original virus. **Mendoza**:

A mutation of Anarkia. **Messina**: A very minor mutation. **A-204, Payday, Puerto, Spanish** and **Jerusalem-G**: Mutations.

Jerusalem-1244 - CER: One of the shortest Jerusalem mutations, only 1244 bytes long.

```
Jerusalem-1244    2638 05E0 F906 0E07 1F8B D7B8 004B 83C2
```

Jerusalem-1361 - CER: A stripped-down version of the Jerusalem virus, with all unnecessary code removed. Does not appear to do anything but replicate.

```
Jerusalem-1361    218C C805 1000 8ED0 50B8 2F00 50CB FC06
```

Jerusalem-1735 - CER: A 1730/1735 byte mutation, which seems related to the 1767 mutation. Not fully analysed. Detected by the Jerusalem Mummy pattern.

Jerusalem-1767 - CER: This 1767 byte version contains the text '** INFECTED BY FRIDAY 13th **'. Awaiting analysis.

```
Jerusalem-1767    7F33 C0F2 AF8B D783 C202 B800 4B06 1F0E
```

Jerusalem-2187 - CER: Yet another Jerusalem mutation 2187/2189 bytes long. Detected by the Jerusalem Mummy pattern.

Jerusalem Barcelona - CR?: Unlike most other members of the Jerusalem family, this 1792 byte virus does not seem to infect EXE files. It is of Spanish origin, and seems to be politically motivated. Detected by the Jerusalem Mummy pattern.

Jerusalem-Clipper - CER: A 1408/1413 byte mutation of Jerusalem. It will generally infect EXE files. No COM files were infected during testing, although the original sample was a COM file. Awaiting analysis.

```
Jeru Clipper      B87D 4BCD 213D 5456 7510 072E 8E16 1200
```

Jerusalem-CNDER - CER: A minor mutation of the 1808/1813 byte standard version, with the self-recognition code changed from 'sURIV' to 'CNDER'. Detected with the Jerusalem-USA pattern.

Jerusalem-Einstein - ER: An 878 byte rewritten mutation of the Jerusalem virus, which is not able to infect COM files. Awaiting analysis. (*VB* Jan 92)

```
Einstein          7FF2 AE26 3805 E0F9 8BD7 83C2 0306 1F0E
```

Jerusalem-IRA - CER: What primarily makes this mutation different from the standard one, is the inclusion of a long list of encrypted names, as well as texts like '.. died for Ireland' and '.. is still a political hostage'. Detected by the Jerusalem Mummy pattern.

Jerusalem-Miky - CER: A 2350 byte mutation of the Jerusalem virus, which is reported to have originated in Bolivia.

```
Miky              7F32 C0F2 AE26 3805 E0F9 8BD7 83C2 038C
```

Jerusalem Moctezuma - CER: A 2228 byte polymorphic mutation of the Jerusalem virus, which contains the text 'Moctezuma's Revenge'. Only a short search pattern is possible.

```
Jeru Moctezuma    062E 8F06 0201 1E2E 8F06 0001 0E07 0E1F
```

Jerusalem-Mummy - ER?: This 1489 byte mutation seems only able to infect EXE files. It contains an encrypted text string which claims it was written in the Kaohsiung Senior School. It has not been fully analysed. (*VB* May 92)

```
Jer-Mummy         2638 05E0 F98B D783 C203 B800 4B06 1F0E
```

Jerusalem Nov 30 - CER: This 2000 byte mutation activates on November 30th, instead of Friday the 13th.

```
Jeru Nov 30        2638 05E0 F98B D783 C203 061F 0E07 BB30
```

Jerusalem Sub Zero, Skism11, Skism12 - CER: Three 1808/1813 byte non-remarkable mutations, which are detected by the Captain Trips pattern.

Jerusalem-T13 - CER: An 1807/1812 byte version of the Jerusalem virus. It is detected by the Suriv 3.00 pattern.

Jerusalem-Tobacco - CER: This mutation is almost identical to the AntiCad-2900 mutation, with little more than a few encrypted text strings changed. It is detected with the AntiCad-2576 pattern.

Jerusalem-Triple - CER: A patched minor mutation of the 1808/1813 byte standard version, with the self-recognition code changed and a few code patches. Another sample with the name 'Dragon' appeared, but it seems virtually identical. Detected with the Jerusalem-USA pattern.

Jihuu - CN: A Finnish 621 byte virus, which may display various messages, depending on the current date and time.

```
Jihuu              8BCA 83EF 0489 0D89 4502 B800 4233 C933
```

Jo-Jo - CR: This is a non-encrypted version of Cascade with the encryption code patched out and a few other changes made.

```
Jo-Jo              B800 F08E C0BF 08E0 813D 434F 751B 817D
```

Jocker - CN: An overwriting virus from Poland, written in some high-level language, probably Pascal.

```
Jocker             89E5 81EC 0001 BF00 000E 57BF 401B 1E57
```

Joker-01 - CR: A huge, 29233 byte virus of Polish origin.

```
Joker-01           8CC2 4A8E C28C DA4A 8EDA 5A90 26A1 0300
```

Joshi - MR: This virus from India displays the message 'Type 'Happy Birthday Joshi" on 5th January of every year. Unless the user enters the text verbatim, the computer will hang. The virus traps disk reads and any program trying to discover it while the virus is active in memory, will not locate it. Survives warm boot. (*VB* Dec 90). Original MBS is stored in Head 0, Cylinder 0, Sector 9.

```
Joshi              03F0 03F8 B979 012B C8FC F3A6 7510 8CC0
```

July 13th - ER: This encrypted virus will activate on 13th July, but its exact effects have not yet been determined. It is 1201 bytes long.

```
July 13th          2EA0 1200 3490 BE12 00B9 B104 2E30 0446
```

Justice - CR: A 1242 byte virus which has not been fully analysed. Many computers 'hang' after running an infected program.

```
Justice            509F 83C4 089E 9C83 EC06 58CF 3CFF 7504
```

Kalah - CR: This 390 byte virus is quite harmless - it does not have any effects other than possibly displaying 'VDV 91'.

```
Kalah              B43F CD21 8B0E 0000 2E3B 0E00 0175 0B8B
```

Kamikaze - EN: This overwriting virus from Bulgaria is written in Turbo Pascal, and is fairly large, 4031 bytes. Like other similar viruses it is not a serious threat.

Kamikaze   8AD0 A082 2230 E48B F888 9509 1080 3E82

Karin, Redstar - CN: This German virus adds either 1090 or 1134 bytes to the programs it infects. It is mostly harmless, but will activate on October 23rd when it displays the message 'Karin hat GEBURTSTAG'.

Karin   BB00 0153 F3A4 BE00 F8BF 8000 B980 00F3

Kemerovo - CN: A Russian, 257 byte virus. Some infected programs fail to execute properly, but no other effects are known.

Kemerovo   0400 89C7 B904 00A4 E2FD 89D7 29D3 81EB

Kemerovo-B - CN: Similar to the original Kemerovo virus, but appears to have been assembled with a different assembler. Does nothing of interest.

Kemerovo-B   0400 8BF8 B904 00A4 E2FD 8BFA 2BDA 81EB

Kennedy - CN: A simple COM infecting virus, probably originating from Sweden. When an infected file is run, it will infect a single COM file in the current directory, expanding it by 333 bytes at the end. The virus activates on three dates: 6th June, 18th November and 22nd November and displays the message 'Kennedy er dod - lange leve 'The Dead Kennedys".

Kennedy   E817 0072 04B4 4FEB F38B C505 0301 FFE0

Keyboard Bug - CER: This virus was received from Kiev, but has not yet been fully analysed. Analysis is complicated by the fact that the virus uses multiple layers of encryption, as well as other methods to hide from debuggers. The effects are unknown, but are assumed to be keyboard-related. The length has been reported as 1720, but the actual increase in length is variable.

Keyboard Bug   1E53 2EFF B597 07BB 6E06 B928 0158 2E30

Keydrop - DR: Infects only floppy disks. Awaiting disassembly.

Keydrop   AC0A C075 0832 E4CD 16CD 19EB DBB4 0EB7

Keypress, Turku, Twins - CER: This virus was discovered at the same time in Finland, USSR and Bulgaria, which makes its origin somewhat uncertain. It will infect COM and EXE files, but the length of the virus code is different, 1232 and 1472 bytes, respectively. After being resident for some time the virus will interfere with the keyboard, causing keys to 'repeat'.

Keypress   7405 C707 0100 F9F5 1FC3 F606 1801 0174

Keypress-1228 - CER: Only slightly different from the 1232 byte mutation, but was discovered in Kansas. It is detected by the 'Keypress' pattern.

Keypress-1744 - CER: Not fully analysed, but does not seem to be significantly different from the other mutations.

Keypress-1744   3F02 7405 C707 0200 F9F5 1FC3 F606 1801

Kiev - CR: Infected files grow by 483 bytes, but this increase is not visible when a DIR command is issued.

Kiev   8BD3 81C2 FBFF 8BDF B440 CD21 5B72 0053

Kit - CER: This virus has one serious 'bug' - it will re-infect the same file over and over. It is 2384 bytes long, but has not been fully analysed. Contains the text 'Copyright 1991-1999. KIT VIRUS (version 2.0).'

    Kit   2EC5 1619 00B8 2425 CD21 071F 5F5E 5A59

Klaeren - CER: This 974 byte virus contains a serious error, which prevents it from infecting successfully any file larger than 4096 bytes. This encrypted virus contains the text string 'Klaeren Ha, Ha!' (Klaeren: the name of a professor in the school where the virus was written.)

    Klaeren   5351 E800 005B 81EB AF03 B9A5 0380 37

KO-407, Dodo-Pig, GIP - CR: Closely related to the Ko-408 virus. It contains the text 'GIP'. There is yet another mutation, 408 bytes long, which contains the text 'Birdie Hop!' and is also detected with the same pattern.

    KO-407   B802 4233 C9BA FFFF CD21 508B D033 C9B8

KO-408 - CR: 408 byte virus. Not yet analysed.

    KO-408   5B53 B802 4233 C9BA FFFF CD21 8BD0 33C9

Korea, NJH - DR: A simple boot sector virus with no side-effects. It may cause damage to data, as the original boot sector is always written to sector 11. There are two versions, probably due to two different assemblers being used.

    Korea   C08E D88E D0BC F0FF FBBB 1304 8B07 4848

Kuku - CN: This 448 byte virus may either infect files in an ordinary way, or overwrite them with a small program, which will display the word 'Kuku!' on the screen when it is run.

    Kuku   241F 3C0A 750C B42C CD21 80E6 0775 E3BD

Kylie - CER: A 2272 byte mutation of the Jerusalem virus, which plays a tune when it activates.

    Kylie   E2FE C3E4 6124 FCE6 61C3 5357 4343 8B3E

Lao Duong - ?: A boot sector virus from Thailand awaiting analysis. It reportedly plays a Laotian funeral dirge when it activates.

    Lao Doung   A34C 0006 1FF6 C280 7539 BB00 7EBA 8001

Lazy - CR: A primitive 720 byte virus, which always occupies the same area in memory and may cause system crashes if a large program is run. The major effect of the virus is a slowdown of the computer.

    Lazy   1E84 0026 A186 008E C026 8B07 BB90 5029

LBBCV-Timid - CN: Trivial virus published in the Little Black Book of Computer Viruses by Mark Ludwig. No side effects.

    LBBCV-Timid   2EFC FF09 00BA 2AFF B41A CD21 E83E 0075

LBBCV-Intruder - EN: Trivial virus published in the Little Black Book of Computer Viruses by Mark Ludwig. No side effects.

    LBBCV-Intruder   E867 0375 18E8 6B03 E86E 03E8 2600 7509

LBBCV-Kilroy - DN: Trivial virus published in the Little Black Book of Computer Viruses by Mark Ludwig. No side effects.

    LBBCV-Kilroy   721A 813E FE06 55AA 7512 E8FE 00BA 8001

LBBCV-Stealth - MR: Trivial virus published in the Little Black Book of Computer Viruses by Mark Ludwig. No side effects.

```
LBBCV-Stealth      FB80 FC02 740A 80FC 0374 3C2E FF2E 3070
```

Leech - CR: A 1024 byte virus which has not been analysed yet. It uses self-modifying encryption, which makes the extraction of a usable pattern difficult.

```
Leech              FA1E 078B EC8B E681 C4E4 038C
```

Leech live - CR: Awaiting analysis.

```
Leech live         5E1E FA07 8BEC 8BE6 81C4 E403 8CC8 8CD1
```

Lehigh - CR: The virus only infects COMMAND.COM. It is 555 bytes long and becomes memory-resident when the infected copy is run. If a disk is accessed which contains an uninfected COMMAND.COM, the copy is infected. A count of infection generation is kept inside the virus, and when it reaches 4 (or 10 in a mutated version), the current disk is trashed each time a disk is infected, provided that (a) the current disk is in either the A drive or B drive, (b) the disk just infected is in either the A drive or B drive and (c) the disk just infected is not the current one. The trashing is done by overwriting the first 32 sectors following the boot sector. Infection changes the date and time of COMMAND.COM.

```
Lehigh             8B54 FC8B 44FE 8ED8 B844 25CD 2106 1F33
```

Leningrad, Sov1, Sov2 - CN: Two viruses, 600 and 543 bytes long, first reported in Leningrad (now St. Petersburg), and probably written by the same author. The 600 byte mutation has not been analysed, but the other mutation will activate on any Friday the 13th, and display the message 'That could be a crash, crash, crash!'.

```
Leningrad-1        F3A4 E8D4 01E8 8C01 7303 E8C0 01E8 1900
Leningrad-2        E80D 02E8 9801 3C00 740D E8B4 013C 0074
```

Leprosy - CN: A 666 byte encrypted overwriting virus, similar to Leprosy-B but using a different encryption method.

```
Leprosy            558B EC56 8B76 04EB 0480 2C0A 4680 3C00
```

Leprosy-B - CER: A 666 byte overwriting virus, which is easily detected, as infected programs do not run normally, but instead display a message announcing the virus.

```
Leprosy-B          8A27 3226 0601 8827 4381 FBCB 037E F1C3
```

Leprosy-Busted - CN: A primitive, encrypted, overwriting virus.

```
Leprosy-Busted     8B0E 0B02 51E8 0F00 5BB9 3B02 BA00 01B4
```

Leprosy-C - E?: Awaiting disassembly.

```
Leprosy-C          5633 F6E8 5100 0BC0 740A E818 0046 FE06
```

Leprosy-C2 - CEN: A primitive 666 byte overwriting virus. When run, it displays the message 'Program to big to fit in memory'. This virus is floating around on virus BBSs under the name of 'Durango', but in fact it is just a minor mutation of the Leprosy-C virus.

```
Leprosy-C2         53E8 1000 5B90 B99A 02BA 0001 B440 CD21
```

Leprosy-D - CN: A 370 byte overwriting virus, derived fom one of the earlier mutations. Infected programs must be deleted.

```
Leprosy-D          B43B CD21 4683 FE03 7CE6 EB00 5EC3 8B16
```

Leprosy-Viper - CEN: This 840 byte mutation is similar to the Plague mutation, but it uses a slightly modified encryption algorithm. Just like the C2 mutation it is only found on virus BBSs, and is not a serious threat.

```
Leprosy-Viper       BB3A 018A 2732 2606 0188 2790 9090 4381
```

Leszop - C?: Virus awaiting disassembly.

```
Leszop              1FC7 060C 7C62 008C 060E 7CFB FF2E 0C7C
```

Liberty - CEDR: A multi-partite virus from Indonesia with an infective length of 2857 bytes. When triggered, the virus reformats track 0 on the hard disk. When exhibiting multi-partite behaviour, the virus only infects floppy disk boot sectors. (*VB* Oct 91)

```
Liberty             0174 031F 595B 5053 5152 1E06 1E0E 1FE8
Liberty-1           B931 2833 D2CD 1306 BB5C 0653 CB2E 803E
```

Liberty 1186 - CR: Awaiting analysis. Not connected with the Liberty virus.

```
Liberty 1186        A02E 01CD 2183 FBFF 7431 B403 33DB CD10
```

Liberty-SSSSS - CR: This 1170 virus bears some resemblance to the Liberty virus, but might not be directly related. It is 1170 bytes long, but has not been fully analysed.

```
Liberty-SSSSS       FACD 21FA 0E1F B425 A02E 01BA FFFF 1F1E
```

Little Brother - P: A 299 byte 'companion' virus, which does not seem fully finished.

```
Little Brother      7418 5253 501E 063D 004B 7503 E810 0007
```

Little Pieces - ER: A 1374 byte virus, which has not been fully analysed. It will occasionally clear the screen and display the message: 'One of these days I'm going to cut you into little pieces'.

```
Little Pieces       9DCA 0200 33DB 8EDB C747 4C56 018C 4F4E
```

Locker - CER: A 1642 byte mutation of the Murphy virus, written by Cracker Jack and detected by the HIV pattern. The virus has not been fully analysed yet, but under certain circumstances it will ask the user for a password.

Lozinsky - CR: A Russian, 1023 byte virus, which uses a simple encryption algorithm.

```
Lozinsky            FCBF 2000 03FE B9D0 032E 3005 47E2 FAB8
```

Lozinsky-1018 - CER: Very closely related to the 1023 byte version.

```
Lozinsky-1018       E800 005E 2E8A 44FC BF20 0003 FEB9 CB03
```

LoveChild - CN: Infective length is 488 bytes. Contains strings 'v2 (c) Flu Systems (R)' and 'LoveChild in reward for software sealing.' [sic]. The virus trojanises certain program files which, when trigerred, overwrite sectors 1-16, heads 0-3 on every track of the first hard disk with garbage. (*VB* Feb 91)

```
LoveChild           33C0 8EC0 E800 005E 8BEE BFE0 01FC 2681
LoveChild Trojn     B901 00BA 8003 8BD9 B810 03CD 13FE CE79
```

Lovechild-B3 - MR: This virus is probably written by the author of the Lovechild virus, but it is totally unrelated - very similar to the New Zealand virus.

```
Lovechild-B3        33C0 8EC0 B801 028B DC2E 803E 047D 0074
```

Lucifer - CER: A 1086 byte mutation of the Diamond virus. Detected by the Diamond pattern.

Macedonia - CR: One of the few viruses which carry a political message - 'Macedonia To The Macedonians'. This 400 byte virus has no effects other than displaying this message.

```
Macedonia          7527 E871 002E 8B04 2EA3 0001 2E8B 4402
```

Macho - CEN: Swaps every string 'MicroSoft' with 'MachoSoft' on the hard disk. Searches 20 sectors at a time, storing the last sector searched in IBMNETIO.SYS which is marked hidden and system. After searching the last sector it starts again. This will only happen after 1st January 1985 and if the environment variable VIRUS is not set to OFF. Infective length is 3550 to 3560 bytes. Random directory search for uninfected files. Infects COMMAND.COM. This virus is closely related to Syslock. (*VB* May 91)

```
Macho              5051 56BE 5900 B926 0890 D1E9 8AE1 8AC1
```

Malaga - CERD: One of the relatively rare multi-partite viruses. It is 2610 bytes long, but in addition to infecting files it will also infect DOS boot sectors on diskettes and hard disks.

```
Malaga             2D04 00A3 1304 B106 D3E0 2DC0 078E C08B
```

Maltese Amoeba, Irish, Grain of Sand - CER: A destructive virus which overwrites the first four sectors of tracks 0 to 29 of the hard disk and any diskette in the disk drive, if the date is 1st November or 15th March of any year. A psychedelic screen effect follows. When the machine is powered up, a fragment of a poem (The Auguries of Innocence) by William Blake (1745-1827) appears on the screen and the machine hangs. Infection happens at load-and-execute and file close. The virus employs self-modifying encryption and no search pattern is possible. (*VB* Dec 91)

Mannequin - CER: A 778 byte virus which has only one unusual effect - it intercepts INT 17H (the printer interrupt) and strips the top bit of any character sent to the printer.

```
Mannequin          5251 5350 32C0 1E07 8BFA B941 00FC F2AE
```

Magnitogorsk, 2560 - CER: This virus has not been fully analysed yet, but it contains a greeting to a Mr. Lozinsky, who seems to be the author of an anti-virus program.

```
Magnitogorsk       2E8B 851F 003D FFFF 7413 BE3E 0003 F7B9
```

Manuel - CR: This 957 byte virus contains the text: 'Soy un Manuel Virus de tipo C'. Not fully analysed.

```
Manuel             F9C3 A675 FBF8 C3FC 268A 25AC 3C00 7415
```

Marauder - CN: This virus contains text which indicates it was written by the authors of the Phalcon and Skism viruses. It is polymorphic, and no simple search string is possible from the decryption routine. The virus is 860 bytes long.

```
Marauder           E800 005E 81EE 0E01 E805 00E9 8700
```

Marauder-560 - CN: This seems to be an older and more primitive mutation of the Marauder virus. One significant difference is that the encryption routine is not polymorphic.

```
Marauder-560       0056 5D81 C646 018B FEFC AD33 8619 01AB
```

Mardi Bros - DR: The major effect of the virus is to change the volume label to 'Mardi Bros'. It is believed to be of French origin.

```
Mardi Bros         E08E C0BE 007C 31FF B900 14FC F3A4 06B8
```

MG - CR: A simple, 500 byte Bulgarian virus.

```
MG                        AA1F 1E07 585E 1EBB 0001 53CB 3D04 4B74
```

MG-1A - CR: A minor mutation of the MG virus.

MG-3 - CR: A 500 byte Bulgarian virus, reported to be written by the same author as the MG virus.

```
MG-3                      C43E 0600 B0EA 49F2 AE26 C43D 83EF DFEA
```

MG-4 - CR: A 500 byte virus from Bulgaria, which is closely related to the MG-3 virus, and is detected by the same pattern..

MGTU - CN: A simple, 273 byte Russian virus.

```
MGTU                      03F8 BE00 018B 0589 048B 4502 8944 02B8
```

Michelangelo - MR: A mutation of the New Zealand virus, which will activate on March 6th and overwrite the first 17 sectors on every track of the hard disk, heads 0 to 4. On 360K floppies it will destroy sectors 1 to 9, heads 0 and 1, while on other floppies it will destroy the first 17 sectors of each track. Original MBS is stored in Head 0, Cylinder 0, Sector 7. (*VB* Jan 92)

```
Michelangelo              BE00 7C33 FFFC F3A4 2EFF 2E03 7C33 C08E
```

Micro-128 - CR: This virus from Bulgaria is the smallest memory-resident virus known. It occupies part of the interrupt table and does nothing but replicate.

```
Micro-128                 7501 A5A4 31C0 8EC0 BF03 03B1 7DF3 A4AF
```

Microbes - DR: An Indian virus the effects of which are not fully known, except that booting from an infected disk has been reported to cause some computers to 'hang'.

```
Microbes                  042D 0400 A313 04B1 06D3 E08E C006 C706
```

Migram-1 - ER: A 1219 byte mutation of the Murphy virus. Detected by the Murphy 2 pattern.

Migram-2 - ER: A 1221 byte mutation of the Murphy virus. Detected by the HIV pattern.

Milan Overwriting, BadGuy, Exterminator - CN: A group of primitive, overwriting viruses from Italy. Two mutations are known - BadGuy, which is 265 bytes long and does nothing but replicate and Exterminator which is 451 bytes long. When it activates, it overwrites the beginning of the hard disk, generally destroying the FAT and root directory of drive C.

```
Exterminator              02EB E2B4 2ACD 213C 0174 03EB 2F90 C606
BadGuy                    02EB D9B4 2ACD 213C 0174 11EB 1D90 071F
```

Milana - CER: This 1160 byte virus contains various pieces of code which seem to have been copied from the Dark Avenger virus, so they should probably be classified as belonging to the same family. The name is derived from the string 'I Love Milana', but the effects are not fully known.

```
Milana                    A4A5 1F8B 2606 0033 DB53 FFE0 BA10 00F7
```

Milous, Cadkill - CER: This 1163 byte virus has not been fully analysed yet.

Minimal-30 - CN: This virus is only 30 bytes long. When an infected program is run, it will overwrite the first file in the current directory.

```
Minimal-30                3DBA 9E00 CD21 93B4 408B D68B CECD 21C3
```

Minimal-30-B - CN: This is practically the same virus as the Minimal-30 virus, but it has been assembled with a different assembler, which has produced a slight difference.

```
Minimal-30-B        3DBA 9E00 CD21 93B4 4089 F28B CECD 21C3
```

Minimal-45 - CN: This Bulgarian overwriting virus is only 45 bytes long. When run, it will overwrite all COM files in the current directory with itself.

```
Minimal-45          0001 B92D 00B4 40CD 21B4 3ECD 21B4 4FEB
```

Minimal-46 - CN: A primitive overwriting virus which does nothing but replicate.

```
Minimal-46          D8BA 0001 B12E B440 CD21 B43E CD21 B44F
```

MIR - CER: A 1745 byte mutation of the Dark Avenger virus. The first generation sample contains the text 'M.I.R. *-*-*-* Sign of the time!', but it is corrupted in later generations. Detected by the 'Dark Avenger' pattern.

Mirror - ER: The virus is 924 bytes long, but infected programs may grow by a maximum of 940 bytes. When the virus activates it reverses the contents of the screen, displaying a mirror image of what was there before.

```
Mirror              8A07 2688 0743 E2F8 B821 2506 1FBA DC00
```

Mistake, Typoboot - DR: Exchanges letters for phonetically similar ones (for example 'C' & 'K') while they are being output to the printer. Reportedly written in Israel. A mutation of the Italian virus with about 35% of the code rewritten. The boot sector is almost identical to the Italian virus.

```
Mistake             32E4 CD1A 80FE 0376 0A90 9090 9090 52E8
```

MIX1 - ER: The virus infects only EXE files, attaching itself to the end. When an infected program is run, the virus will copy itself to the top of the free memory. Some programs may overwrite this area, causing the machine to crash. The virus traps printer and asynch interrupts and corrupts traffic by substituting characters. 50 minutes after infection, the virus alters the Num Lock and Caps Lock keyboard settings. 60 minutes after infection, a display similar to the Italian virus (bouncing ball display) will be produced. The virus will infect every tenth program run. Infected files always end in 'MIX1' and the infective length of MIX1 is 1618 to 1633 bytes and MIX1-2 1636 to 1651 bytes. (*VB* Dec 89)

```
MIX1                B800 008E C026 803E 3C03 7775 095F 5E59
MIX1-2              B800 008E C0BE 7103 268B 3E84 0083 C70A
```

MIX2 - CER: This is a 2280 byte Israeli virus based on MIX1 but improved with the addition of encryption and COM file infection.

```
MIX2                EE8C C803 C650 B826 0050 CB55 508C C0E8
```

MLTI - CR: This 830 byte Russian virus contains the following text, which clearly refers to the Dark Avenger virus. 'Eddie die somewhere in time! This programm was written in the city of Prostokwashino (C) 1990 RED DIAVOLYATA Hello! MLTI!'

```
MLTI                5B73 05B8 0001 50C3 83FC E072 F62E C747
```

Mono-1063 - CR: A 1063 byte Polish virus, which deletes files when it activates, provided it is running on a machine with monochrome display.

```
Mono                FDF3 A406 E800 0059 83C1 0651 CB2E 8C4F
```

Monkey - MR: Two viruses based on the New Zealand virus, which store the original boot sector encrypted making disinfection more difficult.

```
Monkey-1           48A3 1304 B106 D3E0 0420 8EC0 C356 8BFB
Monkey-2           48BF 1404 4F89 05B1 06D3 E004 208E C0C3
```

Monxla, Time - CN: A 939 byte mutation of the Vienna virus, which activates on the 13th day of any month and then damages programs, instead of just infecting them.

```
Monxla             8B07 5B8E C0BF 0000 5E56 83C6 1AAC B900
```

Monxla-B - CN: This 535 byte virus is probably an older version of the Monxla virus. It retains code from the Vienna virus which deletes programs instead of infecting them 1 in every 8 times.

```
Monxla-B           8994 1600 B42C CD21 80E6 0775 10B4 40B9
```

Mosquito - ER: A 1024 byte virus awaiting analysis.

```
Mosquito           5650 BE49 002E 8A24 2E32 261E 002E 8824
```

Mosquito-Pisello - ER: 1024 bytes long, just like the original version, but not fully analysed.

```
Mosquito-Piselo    5650 BE51 032E 8A24 2E32 265D 012E 8824
```

Mosquito-Topo - ER: A 1536 byte mutation of the Mosquito virus. Awaiting analysis.

```
Mosquito-Topo      5650 BE68 002E 8A24 2E32 263D 002E 8824
```

MPS-OPC - CN: Three Polish viruses, 469, 640 and 654 bytes long. Not yet analysed.

```
MPS-OPC 1.1        B447 CD21 5E8B FE81 C72D 0232 C0B9 4000
MPS-OPC 3.1/3.2    0ADB 7441 B42C CD21 3ADA 7304 2AD3 EBF8
```

MPS-OPC 4.01 - ER: This virus is probably written by the same author(s) as the other MPS-OPC viruses - a Mr. Marek Pande, according to reports from Poland. Structurally it is very different however, and belongs to a different virus family. Not yet analysed.

```
MPS-OPC 4.01       CD27 A12C 008E D833 FF8B 0547 0BC0 75F9
```

Mshark - CN: The name of this 373 byte virus is derived from the string '(C) Mshark-S v.1.0'. This is a simple virus, with no effects other than possibly causing a reboot.

```
Mshark             0103 D6CD 2132 DB56 81C6 5601 B914 00AC
```

MSTU - CEN: This virus contains the text 'This program was written in MSTU,1990' Not fully analysed, but appears to do nothing of interest. Virus length is 532 bytes.

```
MSTU               BB16 0026 8B07 3DEB 55C3 5E8B C6B1 04D3
```

MSTU-554 - CEN: Closely related to the 532 byte mutation and detected by the same pattern.

Mule - CER: A 4112/4117 byte encrypted mutation of Jerusalem, which was first reported in Australia, but may have originated in Thailand. Not yet analysed. Detected by the Jerusalem 1 pattern.

Multiface, Portugese - CR: This is a 1441 byte virus from Portugal. It is reported to display multiple 'smileys' on the screen. (*VB* May 92)

```
Multiface          8ED8 58C6 075A C747 0100 0089 4703 5B8D
```

Munich - CN: Encrypted 2355 byte virus. Not yet analysed.

Murphy - CER: Two versions exist. One produces a click from the loudspeaker when any DOS functions are called, while the other may produce a bouncing ball effect when the user enters ROM BASIC. The virus will only activate between 10:00 and 11:00 a.m.

```
Murphy 1          1EE8 0000 B859 4BCD 2172 03E9 2801 5E56
Murphy 2          1EE8 0000 B84D 4BCD 2172 03E9 2601 5E56
```

Murphy-3 - CER: A 1284 byte mutation of Murphy detected by the 'HIV' pattern.

Murphy-4 - CER: A 1480 byte mutation of Murphy detected by the 'Murphy 2' pattern.

Murphy-Amilia - CER: This Canadian virus is based on the HIV mutation, and is only slightly modified. It is 1614 bytes long, and detected by the HIV pattern.

Murphy-Bad Taste - CER?: This encrypted virus should be able to infect COM files, but during testing it only infected EXE files, unlike other Murphy mutations. It contains the text 'Bad Taste Ltd. (C) 1991 by Odrowad Trow.....who am I???' This 1188 byte virus is detected by the pattern for Murphy-2, but only in EXE files.

Murphy-Brothers - CER: A 2045 byte mutation of the Murphy virus, which contains the text 'Brothers in arm'. Detected by the HIV pattern. Not yet analysed.

Murphy-Tormentor - CER?: This virus would actually only infect EXE files during testing, but it seems to contain code to infect COM files too. Detected by the HIV pattern.

Murphy-Tormentor-D - ER: This 1040 byte mutation is closely related to the Tormentor mutations. Detected with the HIV pattern.

Music Bug - DR: Contains text strings 'MusicBug v1.06 MacroSoft Corop.' and '-- Made in Taiwan --'. If a machine has been infected for more than 4 months, a random tune of 36 notes may be played (14% probability). (*VB* Nov 91)

```
Music Bug         08FC F3A5 06B8 0002 50CB 5053 5152 2EA3
```

Mutant - CN: Three mutations of this virus are known, of which two, 123 and 127 bytes long, are only able to infect small files correctly. This is 'corrected' in the third mutation, also 127 bytes long. The viruses have no interesting side-effects.

```
Mutant            C98B D1B8 0042 CD21 5972 065A 52B4 40CD
```

Mutation Engine: Not a virus on its own, but provides an easy way of adding self-modifying encrypting behaviour to an existing virus.

```
Mutation Engine   E8BE 0059 5EBF 5905 2BF9 5752 F3A4 595A
```

New BadGuy, Milan Overwriting-208, Crackpot-208 - CN: A 208 byte mutation of the BadGuy virus by Cracker Jack, created by adding NOP instructions at various locations in the code. The only effect other than replication is to display a message on Mondays.

```
New BadGuy        2E8A 1780 F243 90B4 02CD 2190 43FE C990
```

New Zealand, Stoned, Marijuana - MR: The virus consists of a boot sector only. It infects all disks and occupies 2K of RAM. On floppy disks, logical sector 0 is infected, while on hard disks sector 1 head 0 track 0 (Master boot sector) is infected. The original boot sector is stored in track 0 head 1 sector 3 on a floppy disk and track 0 head 0 sector 2 on a hard disk. The boot sector contains two character strings: 'Your PC is now Stoned!' and 'LEGALISE MARIJUANA' but only the former one is displayed, once in eight times, and only if booted from floppy disk. The version (2) stores the original boot sector at track 0 head 0 sector 7 on a hard disk. The second string is not transferred when a hard disk is infected. A mutation displays the message 'Your PC is now Sanded'. A mutation has been reported in Australia which also displays 'LEGALISE MARIJUANA'. (*VB* May 90)

```
New Zealand (1)    0400  B801  020E  07BB  0002  B901  0033  D29C
New Zealand (2)    0400  B801  020E  07BB  0002  33C9  8BD1  419C
```

Nina - CR: Yet another small virus from Bulgaria. This one is 256 bytes long.

```
Nina               03F7  B900  01F3  A458  1EBD  0001  55CB  5858
```

Nines Complement - CR: This 705 byte virus interferes with printer operations, changing numbers 0 to 9, 1 to 8 etc. (*VB* June 92)

```
Nines Complemnt    E800  005B  BE11  0003  F3B9  AA02  89F7  AC30
```

Nines Complement-776, 706 - CR: Two new mutations have appeared, where the initial decryption routine has been modified, in order to bypass scanners detecting the original version.

```
Nines Comp-766     E800  005B  BE0E  0003  F3B9  F402  301C  46E2
Nines Comp-706     E800  005D  BE17  0001  EEB9  A502  89F7  8BDD
```

NKOTB, Cover Girl - CN: A 723 byte overwriting virus, where most of the virus body contains a silly message.

```
NKOTB              BA00  01CD  21B4  3ECD  219F  B908  00D3  C82B
```

No Bock, 440 - CN: When this 440 byte virus activates, it displays the message 'No Bock today error. System Halted' and stops the system.

```
No Bock            A48B  FDC3  B104  D3E0  0AC6  FEC1  D3E0  0AC2
```

NoInt, Stoned III - MR: Boot virus with no payload, infecting floppies in A and B as well as the hard disk. Infects when disk read is attempted, and returns the original boot sector when sector 1 is read. The original boot sector is stored in head 1 cylinder 0 sector 3 on diskettes and head 0 cylinder 0 sector 7 on hard disks.

```
NoInt              0175  2451  B907  00B8  0102  9C2E  FF1E  0C01
```

Nomenklatura - CER: Infective length is 1024 bytes, and only files longer than 1024 bytes are infected. The virus infects on executing a program or opening a file, which means that a virus scanning program will infect all files on the system if the virus is resident in memory. The virus scrambles the FAT on a random basis. (*VB* Dec 90)

```
Nomenklatura       B8AA  4BCD  2173  785E  5606  33C0  8ED8  C41E
```

November 17th, 855 - CER: This virus activates on 17th November, trashing the beginning of the current drive. (*VB* June 92)

```
November 17th      CD21  80FE  0B75  1280  FA11  720D  B419  CD21
```

NTKC, C-23693 - CN: A 23693 byte mutation of Vienna, detected by the 'Vienna (4)' pattern.

Number1 - CN: An old, simple, overwriting, Pascal virus, originally published in the 'Computer Viruses - A High Tech Disease' book by Burger. Infective length depends on the compiler used, but 11980 and 12032 byte examples have been found in the wild.

```
Number1            B800  0050  BFCC  031E  B142  E8E8  FEB8  015C
```

Number1 2 - CN: Mutation of Burger's Pascal Number1 virus

```
Number1 2            B800 0050 BFCA 031E B142 E8E8 FEB8 015C
```

Number of the Beast, 666, V512 - CR: An advanced virus from Bulgaria, only 512 bytes long. The length of the file does not appear to increase since the virus overwrites the first 512 bytes of the programs it infects with itself, storing the original 512 bytes in the unused space of a disk cluster, after the logical end of file. (*VB* May 90, June 90)

```
Number of Beast      5A52 0E07 0E1F 1EB0 5050 B43F CBCD 2172
Number of Bea 1      B800 3DCD 2193 5A52 0E1F 1E07 B102 B43F
Number of Bea E      1607 8BD6 B102 B43F CD21 8AD1 86CD BFFE
Number of Bea F      5A52 0E1F 1E07 06B0 5050 B43F CBCD 2172
```

NV71 - ER?: This virus has been reported elsewhere as '1840', but this name should be avoided, as the virus is only 1827 bytes long. It has also been reported to infect COM files, but this has not been confirmed.

```
NV71                 9CFA FC8C DA83 C210 2E01 1603 0033 C08E
```

Ohio, Hacker - DR: Boot sector virus, which is an older version of Den Zuk and written by the same author.

```
Ohio                 FAFA 8CC8 8ED8 8ED0 BC00 F0FB E845 0073
```

Old Yankee - EN: This is the first of the viruses which play 'Yankee Doodle Dandy'. It only infects EXE files, increasing their length by 1961 bytes. When an infected program is run, it will infect a new file and then play the melody. (*VB* June 90)

```
Old Yankee           03F3 8CC0 8904 0E07 53B8 002F CD21 8BCB
```

Omega - CN: A 440 byte virus, proably from Finland. When it activates it overwrites the beginning of the first two hard disks trashing the partition table.

```
Omega                B05C AA89 7E2E 83EC 15B9 1500 8BFC 8BF5
```

Ontario - CER: A 512 byte encrypted virus. It uses self-modifying encryption, and a full 16-byte search pattern cannot be extracted. The asterisks in the string indicate a byte which may change from one infected file to another.

```
Ontario              8A84 E801 B9E8 01F6
```

Orion - CR: Two simple viruses, probably from Bulgaria. They contain the texts 'Hello,boy! Im a new virus' and 'Orion system !'. The viruses, which are 262 and 365 bytes long contain one error - they cannot properly infect very short files.

```
Orion                AB33 C0AB 1616 1F07 8BC3 CB3D 004B 7406
```

Oropax, Music virus - CR: The length of infected files increases between 2756 & 2806 bytes and their length becomes divisible by 51. 5 minutes after infection, the virus plays three different tunes at 7-minute intervals. Does not infect COMMAND.COM.

```
Oropax               06B8 E033 CD21 3CFF 7423 8CCE 8EC6 8B36
```

Padded - CN: The most unusual feature of this 1589 byte virus is that it is padded with a large block of zero bytes, which serve no apparent purpose.

```
Padded               BA00 00CD 215A 4AB4 40B9 0300 CD21 B802
```

Paris, TCC - CEN: The virus will infect all EXE files in the current directory, when an infected file is run. Length is 4904 bytes.

```
Paris                8CD8 03C3 8ED8 8EC0 8D3E 0301 B000 AAEB
```

Parity - CN: A Bulgarian 441 byte virus which may emulate a memory failure when an infected program is run, displaying the message 'PARITY CHECK 2' and halting the computer.

```
Parity              40B9 B901 BA00 0103 D7CD 21B8 0157 8B8D
```

Path - CN: A 547 byte virus from East Europe, which searches the path for files to infect.

```
Path                B90D 0057 8A07 8805 4347 E2F8 C605 005F
```

Pathhunt - EN: Even though this virus only infects EXE files, they are infected as if they were COM files - the first few bytes are overwritten with a jump to the virus body. Not yet analysed.

```
Pathhunt            03FD 8A0D 2ED2 0F59 43E2 EEEB 1DBB 1A01
```

PC-Flu - CR: This 802 byte virus was made available with the original commented source code from the author. It seems to be intended to bypass three specific anti-virus programs, Flushot, Vstop and Virblock, but this has not been tested. This virus is of Polish origin. (*VB* Jan 92)

```
PC-Flu              501F BB00 0180 3FE9 7537 4380 3F15 7531
```

PC-Flu-2 - CER: An improved 2112 byte mutation of PC-Flu, with several new features, such as self-modifying encryption. No simple search pattern is possible.

PC-Flu mutations - CER: Several mutations of PC-Flu have now appeared. Just like the original virus, no search pattern is possible.

PcVrsDs - CER: A destructive encrypted virus which deletes every file opened and infects every file executed. It does not infect COMMAND.COM. A routine in the virus causes occasional typing errors by incrementing the ASCII value of the character typed by 1. On Monday 23rd of every month, except in 1990, it will format side 0 of the first 32 tracks on the first fixed disk. (*VB* Apr 91)

```
PcVrsDs             33DB BE1C 00B9 4F07 2E8A 9708 002E 0010
```

Peach - CER: Yet another virus targeted against anti-virus programs - in this case Central Point's Anti-Virus. This 887 byte virus contains the text 'No 2 Peach Garden'. (*VB* May 92)

```
Peach               33C9 33D2 E851 FFB4 40B9 1800 8BD7 807D
```

Pentagon - DR: The virus consists of a boot sector and two files. The sample obtained does not work, but it contains the code which would survive a warm boot (Ctrl-Alt-Del). It could only infect 360K floppy disks, and will look for and remove Brain from any disk it infects. It occupies 5K of RAM.

```
Pentagon            8CC8 8ED0 BC00 F08E D8FB BD44 7C81 7606
```

Perfume - CR: The infected program will sometimes ask the user for input and not run unless the answer is 4711 (name of a perfume). In some cases the question is 'Bitte gebe den G-Virus Code ein', but in others the message has been erased. The virus will look for COMMAND.COM and infect it. Infective length is 765 bytes.

```
Perfume             FCBF 0000 F3A4 81EC 0004 06BF BA00 57CB
```

Perfume-731 - CR: A slight mutation of the Perfume virus, only 731 bytes long. This may well be an earlier mutation.

```
Perfume-731         FCBF 0000 F3A4 81EC 0004 06BF BC00 57CB
```

Pest - CER: A 1910 byte mutation of the Murphy virus. Detected by the HIV pattern.

Phalcon, Cloud - CN: A 1117 byte virus, awaiting analysis. It contains a strange text message about a Bob Ross.

```
Phalcon              BE15 0103 3606 018A 24B9 2304 83C6 2D90
```

Phalcon-Ministry - CN: Encrypted, 1168 byte mutation of the Phalcon virus.

```
Phalco-Ministry      BE15 01C3 3606 018A 24B9 5504 81C6 2E00
```

Phantom - CR: A 2201 bytes long virus, which has not yet been fully analysed. The virus contains an encrypted text message stating it was written in Hungary.

```
Phantom              CF8B FA1E 07B0 00B9 5000 FCF2 AE83 EF04
```

Phenome - CER: A minor mutation of the Jerusalem virus 1808 (1813) bytes long, just like the original. Detected by the Jerusalem-USA pattern.

Phoenix, P1 - CR: This Bulgarian virus is 1701 bytes long, but a mutation, 1704 bytes long, has also been reported. Despite the identical lengths, they are not related to the Cascade viruses. These viruses use an advanced encryption method, so that no search pattern is possible.

Phoenix-2000 - CR: This is a polymorphic virus which cannot be detected with a simple search pattern. In addition to infecting COM files, it Trojanizes EXE files - overwriting them with code to trash a part of the hard disk. This Trojan can be detected with a pattern.

```
Phoenix-Trojan    B413 CD2F 06B0 F5E6 6033 C0E6 618E C093
```

Piter - CR: A Russian, 529 byte virus.

```
Piter             8E1E 2C00 33F6 AC0A 0475 FB83 C603 8BD6
```

Pixel - CN: The Pixel viruses are practically identical to the Amstrad virus, although they are shorter: 345 and 299 bytes. No side-effects are noticeable until the 5th generation is reached, at which stage there is a 50 % chance that the following message will appear when an infected program is executed: 'Program sick error: Call doctor or buy PIXEL for cure description'. Several new mutations of the Pixel/Amstrad virus have been discovered, most of which are very similar to previous mutations, and are detectable by the 'Pixel' pattern. (*VB* June 90)

```
Pixel (1)         0E1F 2501 0074 4CBA D801 B409 CD21 CD20
Pixel (2)         BA9E 00B8 023D CD21 8BD8 061F BA2B 01B9
Pixel (3)         0001 0001 2E8C 1E02 018B C32E FF2E 0001
```

Pixel-257, 275, 295, 283 - CN: detected by the 'Pixel (1)' pattern.

Pixel-779, 837, 850, 854 - CN: detected by the 'Amstrad' pattern.

Pixel-892 - CN: detected by the 'Pixel (3)' pattern.

Pixel-897, 899A, 899B, 905 - CN: Four mutations, which are all detected by the Pixel-936 pattern. Contain code to format track 1.

Pixel-936 - CN: A 936 byte mutation of the Pixel/Amstrad virus.

```
Pixel-936         C706 0001 0001 2E8C 1E02 012E FF2E 0001
```

Pixel-Pixie 1.0 - CN: Closely related to the Pixel-936 virus, and detected with the same pattern.

Pixel-Rosen - CN: The smallest member of the Pixel family, only 131 bytes long. Does nothing but replicate.

```
Pixel-Rosen       A433 FF06 57CB 1E07 BE83 01BF 0001 1E57
```

Plague - CR: A simple 591 byte overwriting virus, based on the Leprosy virus.

```
Plague              8A27 3226 0601 8827 4381 FB83 037E F1EB
```

Plaice - CR: 1129 bytes. Not yet analysed. One mutation of this virus exists, which has not yet been named, but the sample circulating in the anti-virus community is named 1720C.COM. This is a variable-length, polymorphic mutation, with a base length of 1701 bytes. It does not work properly on certain types of hardware. No search string is possible for this mutation.

```
Plaice              0001 5033 C033 DB33 C933 D233 F633 FF33
```

Plastique 521 - C?: Virus awaiting disassembly.

```
Plastique 521       0681 002E 8C06 8500 2E8C 0689 008C C005
```

Plovdiv, New Bulgarian 800 - CR: This virus is 800 bytes long, but the increase is hidden while the virus is active. It contains the text '(c) Damage inc.Ver 1.1,Plovdiv,1991', but has not been fully analysed yet.

```
Plovdiv             80E2 1F80 FA1E 7506 2681 6F1D 2003 079D
```

Plovdiv-1.3 - CR: This 1000 byte virus is related to the 800 byte Plovdiv virus. According to a text string inside the virus, it should be named 'Damage', but this name was rejected to avoid confusion with the Diamond/V1024-derived 'Damage' virus. The virus is 'semi-stealth', hiding increases in file length when it is active.

```
Plovdiv 1.3         80E2 1F80 FA1E 7506 2681 6F1D E803 079D
```

Plovdiv 1.3B - CR: 1000 bytes long, but only slightly different from the 1.3 mutation.

```
Plovdiv 1.3B        80E2 1F80 FA1E 7506 2681 6F1D E803 075A
```

Polimer - CN: A 512 byte Hungarian virus, which only displays the following message when an infected program is executed: 'A le' jobb kazetta a Polimer kazetta ! Vegye ezt !'

```
Polimer             8CD8 0500 108E D8B4 40CD 218C D82D 0010
```

Polish 217 - CR: A simple 217 byte virus from Poland, which does nothing but replicate. Polish 217-A is a minor mutation, probably changed to bypass some scanner.

```
Polish 217          D201 BF00 01B9 0300 F3A4 5EB4 4EBA C901
```

Polish Color - CN: A simple 376 byte Polish virus, which does nothing but replicate.

```
Polish Color        56B9 0400 81C6 6D01 8CD8 8EC0 BF00 01F3
```

Polish Minimal-45 - CN: This is a Polish attempt to create the world's smallest virus. As it overwrites the files it infects, they cannot be disinfected.

```
Polish-45           023D CD21 8BD8 B440 BA00 01B1 2DCD 21B4
```

Polish Pixel - CN: Two Pixel mutations from Poland, which contain crude self-modifying code. They are 457 and 550 bytes long, and detected by the Pixel (1) pattern.

Possessed - CER: A 2438 byte virus (a 2446 byte mutation has been reported) which contains the text 'POSSESSED! Bwa! ha! ha! ha! ha! Author JonJon Gumba of AdU'. The virus is reported to delete files occasionally, after it has been resident for a while.

```
Possessed           8BF2 83C6 028B DE80 3C5C 7506 8BDE 43EB
```

Possessed-B - CER: A 2446 byte mutation of the Possessed virus, and detected by the pattern for that virus.

Possessed-2443 - CER: This mutation is very similar to the other two known mutations, which are 2438 and 2446 bytes long, and detected with the same pattern as the original virus.

Pregnant - CR: A 1199 byte encrypted virus, related to the 1024PrScr virus. It activates on Fridays, between 10 PM and 11 PM, making all infected files appear to be named PREGNANT.!!! if the DIR command is used. As the decryption routine is very short, only a 16 byte search pattern containing a wildcard is possible. The virus hides the increase in file length.

Pretoria, June 16th - CN: Overwrites the first 879 bytes of infected files with a copy of itself and stores the original 879 bytes at the end of the file. When an infected program is executed, the virus searches the entire current drive for COM files to infect. On 16th June the execution of an infected file will cause all entries in the root directory to be changed to 'ZAPPED'. The virus is encrypted.

```
        Pretoria          AC34 A5AA 4B75 F9C3 A11F 0150 A11D 01A3
```

PrintScreen - DR: Occasionally performs a Print Screen (PrtSc) operation.

```
        Printscreen       FA33 C08E D0BC 00F0 1E16 1FA1 1304 2D02
```

Protecto - C?: Virus awaiting disassembly.

```
        Protecto          8BD6 83C2 4AB8 003D CD21 7303 EB39 908B
```

Proud - CR: This 1302 byte virus is a member of a Bulgarian family of 4 viruses, which also includes 1226, Evil and Phoenix. As they all use the same encryption method, no search pattern is possible. (*VB* Dec 90)

Prudents - EN: Infective length is 1205 bytes and the virus will destroy the last 32 bytes of any infected file. Activates during the first four days of May of every year, turning every write operation into a verify operation, which results in the loss of data.

```
        Prudents          0E07 BE4F 04B9 2300 5651 E87E 0359 5EE8
```

Ps!ko - CER: A 1803 byte mutation of the Dark Avenger virus, and detected by the same pattern as the original.

PSQR - CER: A mutation of Jerusalem with the signature changed to 'PSQR'. The infective length is 1715 (COM) and 1720 bytes (EXE).

```
        PSQR              FCB8 0FFF CD21 3D01 0174 3B06 B8F1 35CD
```

QMU-1513 - CR: This virus has not been analysed yet, but it appears to contain an entire boot sector.

```
        QMU-1513          5053 8BDA B000 4338 0775 FBB8 4F4D 3947
```

Quiet - CR: 2048 bytes long. Not yet analysed.

```
        Quiet             A12C 008E C0BB FFFF 4326 803F 0075 F926
```

Rage - CR: Encrypted virus which overwrites sectors 0 through 225 of hard drives C to Z on the 13th of every month. Issues an 'are you there' call to test if VIREXPC.COM is in memory and if present, restores control to the host program. (*VB* Oct 91)

```
        Rage              B9FD 018A 2451 8AC8 D2C4 5988 24FE C046
```

Rape - CR: Two viruses with the same primary effect of overwriting the first 256 sectors of each drive. The shorter is 500 bytes long, but the longer one, which is 747 bytes long has limited 'stealth-like' abilities: no increase in file length is visible if the DIR command is given while the virus is active in memory.

Rape   B980 00AC 3C61 7206 3C7A 7702 2C20 8844

Rat - ER: This Bulgarian virus infects EXE files in a very unusual way by locating itself in the unused area between the header and the start of the program, preventing the increase in the file size. Most EXE files are immune to the infection by this virus.

Rat   FCB8 2B35 CD21 8CDD 0E1F 012E 6A0A BE10

Raub - C?: Virus awaiting disassembly.

Raub   A3DC 03E8 9FFB 8CC8 8EC0 E804 FBBA 3F01

Raubkopi - CR: This virus adds 2219 bytes in front of COM files, but much of that is occupied by a text message in German, directed against pirated software. The virus contains code to format the boot sector of the hard disk, but that code contains an error.

Raubkopi   0500 013D 0002 7204 25FF 0142 B104 D3E8

Revenge Attacker - CR: This virus produces a strange effect on some machines, as directories may appear corrupted, containing multiple copies of the same file. The major effect of this virus is the destruction of all files on the disk. It is 1127 bytes long, and reported to have originated in the Philippines.

Revenge Attacker 7510 4080 3F00 750A 4080 3F00 7504 F8E9

RNA - CEN: Like many other large viruses, this one is written in some high-level language, and adds itself in front of the files it infects. Version 1 is 7296 bytes long, and version 2 is 7408 bytes long.

RNA (1)   1E57 C43E F601 0657 B800 2050 BFFF 011E
RNA (2)   1E57 C43E 0C02 0657 B8F0 1C50 BF19 021E

Diamond-Rock Steady - CER: This 666 byte mutation has been modified considerably. A number of 'garbage' instructions have been added, probably to bypass some scanner. The major effect has been changed - the virus now attempts to format the hard disk on the 13th of any month.

Rock Steady   BF00 0150 5857 5058 AB50 58A4 95C3 EB1C

Russian Mirror - CR: This vicious virus from Russia trashes disks. Infective length is 482 bytes.

Russian Mirror   E89D FF80 FC4B 7403 E9C4 002E FE0E 6400

Rybka - CER: This is a mutation of one of the Vacsina (TP-series) viruses. It may infect the same file over and over, increasing its size by 1344 bytes each time. Detected by the Vacsina pattern.

Saddam - CR: This virus extends the file length by 917 to 924 bytes. Displays the following string (which is stored encrypted) 'HEY SADAM LEAVE QUEIT BEFORE I COME' after 8 requests for INT 21H. Resides in the area of memory not labelled as used, so large programs will overwrite it.

Saddam   BB00 0153 5052 1E1E B800 008E D8A1 1304

Sadist - EN: This 1434 byte virus does not seem to do anything but replicate.

Sadist   2EC6 045C B908 0046 4526 8A46 002E 8804

SBC - CER: A polymorphic 1024 byte virus, with full stealth abilities hiding file size increases as well as file changes when active. This virus is not just a laboratory virus - it is spreading in Canada and the US. No search pattern is possible.

Scion, Doomsday One, Null Set - CN: Naming this virus is slightly difficult - it has been named 'Null Set', but this name is far from being obvious. The author named it 'Doomsday One', but the name 'Scion' is recommended, derived from the text 'A scion to none' which it contains. It is 733 bytes long, and has not been fully analysed, but contains potentially destructive code (INT 26H calls). The virus is encrypted, and as the decryption routine is very short, only a partial search string is possible.

Scott's Valley - CER: This virus is closely related to the Australian Slow virus, using an almost identical encryption method. It is somewhat longer, 2126 bytes.

```
Scott's Valley    E800 005E 8BDE 9090 81C6 3200 B912 082E
```

Screamer - CER: A 711 byte virus, which contains the text 'Screaming Fist'. Not yet analysed.

```
Screamer          89D7 B02E B9FF 00F2 AEE3 2889 FE26 AD25
```

Screamer II, Screaming Fist II - CER: Probably written by the same person as wrote the Screamer (Screaming Fist) virus, but more 'advanced'. The virus is now 838 bytes long and includes limited polymorphic ability, but can nevertheless be detected with a string containing wildcards.

Semtex - CR: Infects every COM file opened or executed. Awaiting analysis.

```
Semtex            8B3E 8400 268B 1686 008E C226 813D 9C50
```

Sentinel - CER: This virus is written in Turbo Pascal and is 4625 bytes long.

```
Sentinel          FCAD 2EA3 0001 AC2E A202 0189 EC5D B800
```

Sentinel 3 - CER: Infection length is 5173 bytes, but the virus hides the increase by intercepting find-first / find-next function calls. Written in Turbo-Pascal in Bulgaria. Discovered by Sentinel-5 pattern.

Sentinel 5 - CER: Infection length is 5402 bytes, but the virus hides the increase by intercepting find-first / find-next function calls. Written in Turbo-Pascal in Bulgaria.

```
Sentinel-5        B803 12CD 2F1E 0731 C989 CF49 D1E9 B82E
```

September 18th - CEN: This virus activates on September 18th, after 7:00 AM, overwriting the hard disk. Two mutations are known, 789 and 801 bytes long, but the virus adds 1-16 extra bytes to programs before infecting them. These viruses may be related to the StarDot virus. Detected by the Italian 803 pattern.

Seventh son - CN: A 332 byte virus which contains the text 'Seventh son of a seventh son'. It seems to do nothing but replicate.

```
Seventh son       1F5A B824 25CD 215A B801 33CD 210E 0E1F
```

Seventh Son 350, **Seventh Son 284** - CN: Two slightly modified versions of the 332 byte virus which are 350 and 284 bytes long.

```
Seventh son 350   73F3 1F5A B824 25CD 215A B801 33CD 210E
Seventh son 284   56A5 A55E B800 33CD 2152 9940 50CD 21B8
```

Sex revolution - MR: Two versions are known and they both contain the text 'EXPORT OF THE SEX REVOLUTION'. The virus is a mutation of the New Zealand virus and is detected by the New Zealand (2) pattern.

Shadowbyte - CN: A 723 byte virus which is awaiting analysis.

```
Shadowbyte            8B54 0183 C203 B442 CD21 89F2 83C2 03B9
```

Shadowbyte-2 - CR: A 635 byte mutation of the Shadowbyte virus. When it activates it will format the beginning of the first hard disk in the system.

```
Shadowbyte-2          B405 B280 B600 B500 B002 CD13 B405 B200
```

Shake - CR: A primitive 476 byte virus which reinfects previously infected files. Infected programs sometimes reboot when executed. Occasionally, infected programs display the text 'Shake well before use !' when executed.

```
Shake                 B803 42CD 213D 3412 7503 EB48 90B4 4ABB
```

Shaker - CR: A mutation of Backtime, just like Blinker, and probably written by the same author. Produces a 'shaky' screen when an infected program is run. Detected by the Backtime pattern.

SHHS - CN: A 585 byte overwriting virus. Extremely unlikely to spread, but contains code to trash the hard disk.

```
SHHS                  01C3 BB3E 01A0 0601 0AC0 740B 3007 4302
```

Shirley - ER: A 4096 byte virus, probably from Germany, which contains several long text messages, including the string 'IWANTSHIRLEY'. Awaiting analysis.

```
Shirley               B887 4BCD 213D 6366 7566 2EA1 0E0E 8CDB
```

Shirley-Vivaldi - ER: This is a mutation of the Shirley virus, with the same infective length as the original, 4096 bytes. As it is rather long, and does not seem interesting at all, it has not yet been analysed. Detected by the Shirley pattern.

Simulation - CN: This is a variable length, self-modifying encrypted virus, which adds around 1300 bytes to the files it infects. When it activates it displays a message announcing the infection or a message which is normally associated with a different virus, such as April 1st (Suriv 1), Frodo, Datacrime or Devil's Dance. No search pattern is possible.

Sistor - CER: Two viruses from the USSR. The 2225 byte mutation triggers after 16:00, displaying a familiar bouncing-ball/falling letters effect. The later mutation has been improved somewhat - it is not as obvious, and includes code to bypass interrupt monitoring programs.

```
Sistor-2225           5BFA 891E 7000 8C06 7200 FB33 C08E D8B8
Sistor-2380           5B33 C089 1E70 008C 0672 0033 C08E D8B8
```

Skism - CER: A 1808/1813 byte minor mutation of Jerusalem. Detected by the Jerusalem-USA pattern.

Slow - CER: This encrypted virus is a 1716 byte long mutation of the Jerusalem virus. It originates from Australia and its side-effect is reported to be a slow-down of the infected PC. No other side-effects are known, as the virus is awaiting analysis.

```
Slow                  E800 005E 8BDE 9090 81C6 1B00 B990 062E
```

Smack, Patricia - CER: A mutation of the HIV virus, containing a message for Patricia Hoffman. Two mutations are known, 1835 and 1841 bytes, both probably written by the same person, who calls himself 'Cracker Jack'. Both mutations can be detected by the HIV pattern.

Smallv-115 - CN: A very small virus from Bulgaria. Does nothing of interest.

```
Smallv-115        B802 3DCD 218B D8B9 0300 8BD5 B43F CD21
```

Smiley - CN: A 1983 byte virus which contains code to trash the hard disk. Not yet fully analysed.

```
Smiley            BB05 018B C881 E10F 00D1 E8D1 E8D1 E8D1
```

Socha - CR: This 753 byte virus has not been fully analysed yet, but it contains code which will only be activated if the year is set to 1981.

```
Socha             C0BF F5FF 268B 0547 4726 3305 4747 2633
```

Something - CR: A 658 byte virus, which attaches itself in front of COM files. It has not been fully analysed, but appears destructive, containing code to delete files.

```
Something         8BD8 B9FF FF1E 5233 D22E 8E1E 8303 B43F
```

South African, Friday the 13th, Miami, Munich, Virus-B - CN: Infective length is 419 bytes, but some reports suggest mutations with an infective length between 415 and 544 bytes. Does not infect files with Read-Only flag set. Virus-B is a non-destructive mutation containing South African 2 pattern. COMMAND.COM is not infected. Every file run on a Friday 13th will be deleted.

```
S African 1       1E8B ECC7 4610 0001 E800 0058 2DD7 00B1
S African 2       1E8B ECC7 4610 0001 E800 0058 2D63 00B1
```

South African 408 - CN: A 408 byte version of the South African virus, partially rewritten to foil scanners, but with no new effects.

```
S African 408     1E8B ECC7 4610 0001 E800 0058 2D5A 0090
```

South African 416 - CN: Yet another minor mutation. The following search pattern can be used to detect all known mutations of this virus.

```
S African 416     FF36 0301 FF36 0501 B43F B903 00BA 0301
```

South African 623 - CN: This mutation of the South African Friday the 13th virus was discovered in New Zealand. It will activate on any Friday the 13th, just like the original, and is detected by the same pattern.

Spanish Telecom - MCER: This encrypted virus contains a message by 'Grupo Holokausto' demanding 'lower telephone tariffs, more services'. It proclaims to be an 'Anti-CTNE' virus where CTNE is 'Compania Telefonica Nacional Espana'. A message in English states that the virus was programmed in Barcelona, Spain. The master boot sector part of the virus counts the number of times the PC is rebooted and triggers after 400 boots, overwriting all data on the first two fixed disks. This is a stealth virus: boot sector is substituted and the length of infected files subtracted. Original MBS is stored in Head 0, Cylinder 0, Sector 7. (*VB* Jan 91)

```
Spanish Head 1    8B1D B200 83FB 0074 18BF 5500 B2
Spanish Head 2    83ED 09BE 2001 03F5 FCB6
Spanish Trojan    BB00 7C33 C0FA 8ED0 8BE3 FB8E D8A1 1304
```

Spanish Telecom 2 - MCER: A mutation of the Spanish Telecom virus. The virus is self-encrypting and modifying. No search pattern is possible.

Spanz - CN: A 639 byte virus. All infected files end with 'INFECTED! * SPANZ *'. Virus searches the current directory followed by path for the first uninfected COM file. If the copy of the virus is more than 6 months old, the virus changes the volume label of the current disk to 'INFECTED!' if the test is performed in the first second of any minute. (*VB* Feb 92)

```
      Spanz              8D9C 7D03 0683 BC76 0300 7415 8B84 7403
```

Sparse - CR: This virus is 3840 bytes long, but most of it contains zero byes. It has no interesting side-effects.

```
      Sparse             FF0F CD21 50B4 3DB0 02CD 2189 C3B4 42B9
```

Squawk - CER: An 852 byte virus from Asia is easy to discover, as an infected machine will produce a high-pitch sound.

```
      Squawk             4B8E DBA1 0100 0306 0300 3B06 1200 722F
```

Squeaker - CER: A 1091 byte virus awaiting analysis.

```
      Squeaker           80FC 7F75 03B4 80CF 80FC 4B74 052E FF2E
```

Staf - CN: A 2083 byte 'demonstration' virus, which seems to have no harmful effects. The virus contains the following text: Virus Demo Ver.: 1.1 - Handle with care! By STAF (Tel.: (819) 595-0787).

```
      Staf               89D3 33F6 8038 0074 0343 EBF8 C600 245A
```

Stahlplatte - CR: This 750 byte virus is awaiting analysis.

```
      Stahlplatte        0E58 BB00 7F39 D872 03E9 4701 8EC3 BE00
```

Stardot-600 - EN: This virus by be related to the 'September 18th' viruses. It is destructive, and will overwrite the beginning of each logical drive when activated.

```
      Stardot-600        32F6 B908 0033 DB51 B901 00D1 C250 CD26
```

StinkFoot - CN: This virus from South Africa uses instructions which do not exist on 8088/8086 and it will crash on such machines. It adds 259 bytes to the beginning of files, and 995 bytes at the end.

```
      StinkFoot          600E 59BA 0400 B435 B024 CD21 061F 890F
```

Striker 1 - CN: A 461 byte virus, which has not been analysed yet. It contains an error which causes incorrect infection of COM files shorter than 13 bytes.

```
      Striker 1          5A8B 4606 39C2 7403 42EB E840 8946 06A0
```

Stupid-Profesor - CR: Almost identical to the SADAM mutation, but the text string has been changed to 'The Profesor is in town again'. Detected with the SADAM (Saddam) pattern.

Subliminal - CR: This 1496 byte virus is probably an earlier version of the Dyslexia virus. When active, the virus will attempt to flash the message 'LOVE, REMEMBER' on the screen for a fraction of a second, which is too short to be easily noticed.

```
      Subliminal         AE26 3805 E0F9 8BD7 83C2 0306 1F2E C706
```

Sunday - CER: Variation of Jerusalem. Infective length is 1631 bytes (EXE) and 1636 (COM). Activates on Sunday and displays message 'Today is SunDay! Why do you work so hard? All work and no play make you a dull boy.'. There are unconfirmed reports of FAT damage on infected systems.

```
Sunday          FCB4 FFCD 2180 FCFF 7315 80FC 0472 10B4
```

Suomi - CN: A 1008 byte virus from Finland, which uses self-modifying encryption, like the 1260 virus. The virus seems to disinfect previously infected files under certain conditions, but COMMAND.COM seems to remain permanently infected. No harmful side-effects have been reported, but the virus is awaiting disassembly. No search pattern is possible.

Suriv 1.01, April 1st COM - CR: A precursor to Jerusalem infecting only COM files with the virus positioned at the beginning of the file. Infective length is 897 bytes. If the date is 1st April, the virus will display 'APRIL 1ST HA HA HA YOU HAVE A VIRUS' and the machine will lock. If the date is after 1st April 1988, the virus produces the message 'YOU HAVE A VIRUS !!!' but the machine will not lock. The virus is memory resident and will not infect COMMAND.COM. (*VB* Aug 89)

```
Suriv 1.01       0E1F B42A CD21 81F9 C407 721B 81FA 0104
```

Suriv 1-Argentina - CR: This mutation of the April 1st virus was reported in Argentina. It is 1249 bytes long, and may display messages on various dates which are of patriotic significance in Argentina.

```
Suriv 1-Argenti  0E1F B42A CD21 81FA 1905 7415 81FA 1406
```

Suriv 1-Anti-D - CR: This mutation of the Suriv 1 or 'April 1st' virus was discovered in Argentina. It is 945 bytes long and interferes with the 'D' key on the keyboard.

```
Suriv 1-Anti-D   0E1F C606 4801 00B4 2ACD 2181 F9C4 0772
```

Suriv 1-Xuxa - CR: Yet another Suriv 1 mutation from Argentina. It is reported to play music between 5PM and 6PM. Infective length is 1413 bytes.

```
Suriv 1-Xuxa     0E1F B42A CD21 81F9 C407 720D 81FA 0208
```

Suriv 2.01, April 1st EXE - ER: A precursor to Jerusalem infecting only EXE files with the virus positioned at the beginning of the file. Infective length is 1488 bytes. If the date is 1st April, the virus will display 'APRIL 1ST HA HA HA YOU HAVE A VIRUS'. If the year is 1980 (DOS default) or the day is Wednesday after 1st April 1988, the machine will lock one hour after infection. (*VB* Aug 89)

```
Suriv 2.01       81F9 C407 7228 81FA 0104 7222 3C03 751E
```

Suriv 3.00, Israeli - CER: An earlier version of Jerusalem infecting COM and EXE files and displaying the side-effects 30 seconds after infection instead of 30 minutes. Infective length is 1813 bytes (COM) and 1808 bytes (EXE). Program delete does not work. (*VB* Aug 89)

```
Suriv 3.00       03F7 2E8B 8D15 00CD 218C C805 1000 8ED0
```

Surrender, Jews - CER: A 513 byte Russian virus, containing the text 'Jews never surrender!'. Awaiting analysis.

```
Surrender        061F B800 43CC 51B8 0143 33C9 CCB8 023D
```

SVC-1740 - CER: This 1740 byte virus is closely related to the 1689 byte mutation (SVC 4.0), and is detected by the same pattern.

SVC 3.1 - CER: This 1064 byte virus is probably an older version of the SVC virus.

   SVC 3.1   C39D BA90 19CF 5A1F EBBD 33C0 8EC0 26C4

SVC 4.0 - CER: A Russian, 1689 byte virus, containing the following message '(c) 1990 by SVC,Vers. 4.0'. The virus attempts to avoid detection by the use of 'stealth' methods, so any increase in file length is not visible while the virus is active in memory.

   SVC 4.0   7416 80FC 1174 0E80 FC12 7409 9D2E FF2E

SVC 5.0 - CER: An improved version of the earlier SVC viruses, and fully 'stealth'. (*VB* Dec 91)

   SVC 5.0   5606 86E0 35FF FF8E C00E 1F33 FFB9 990B

SVC 6.0 - MCER : A 4644 byte stealth multi-partite virus. The original Master Boot Sector is not stored anywhere. Virus code is copied to Sectors 1 to 11 of Track 0, Head 0. (*VB* Dec 91)

   SVC 6.0   33D2 B484 CD21 5E56 81FA 9019 750A 2E3A

Sverdlov - CER: A Russian, 1962 byte virus, using a simple XOR-encryption.

   Sverdlov   2D00 03FE 2E30 0547 E2FA E800 005E 83EE

Svir - EN: A simple 512 byte virus with no side-effects. Svir means 'music' in Bulgarian.

   Svir   33F6 4626 8B0C E302 EBF8 8BD6 83C2 04E8

SVS - CR: This virus has been reported elsewhere as 'Terminator', but that name should be avoided, as it conflicts with the other Terminator viruses. It is 526 bytes long and activates on December 25th, when it displays the message 'TERMINATOR 1991. Made by SVS-009'.

   SVS   B104 D3EB 83C3 11B4 4ACD 21D3 E34B 4B8B

Swami, Guru, Bhaktivedanta - CER: A 1250 byte 'Murphy' mutation containing the text 'Bhaktivedanta Swami Prabhupada (1896-1977). Detected by the 'HIV' pattern.

Swap - DR: Does not infect until ten minutes after boot. Creates one bad cluster on track 39, sectors 6 & 7 (head unspecified). Uses 2K of RAM. Infects floppy disks only. Does not store the original boot sector anywhere. Virus creates a display similar to Cascade, but is transmitted via boot sector.

   Swap   31C0 CD13 B802 02B9 0627 BA00 01BB 0020

Swedish Disaster - MR: The name is derived from the text inside the virus. The virus is awaiting analysis.

   Swedish   0102 BB00 02B9 0100 2BD2 9C2E FF1E 0800

Swiss-143 - CN: A simple 143 byte virus with no interesting effects.

   Swiss-143   B44F 8BD5 EBBC C646 0000 45C7 4600 0D00

Sylvia - CN: The virus displays messages including 'This program is infected by a HARMLESS Text-Virus V2.1', 'You might get an ANTIVIRUS program.....' when an infected program is executed, but if the above text is tampered with, the (encrypted) messages 'FUCK YOU LAMER !!!!', 'system halted....$' will be displayed. The victim is told to send a 'funny postcard' to a genuine address of a Dutch woman called Sylvia. When an infected program is run, the virus will look for five COM files on drive C and the current drive. COMMAND.COM, IBMBIO.COM and IBMDOS.COM are not infected. The virus adds 1301 bytes to the beginning of the infected files and 31 bytes at the end.

```
Sylvia          CD21 EBFE C3A1 7002 A378 0233 C0A3 9E02
```

Sylvia-2 - CN: This version of the Sylvia virus has been patched to avoid detection, but appears functionally equivalent to the Sylvia virus. It is 1332 bytes long, just as the original, and detected by the 'Sylvia' pattern.

Sylvia B - CR: A rewritten version of the Sylvia virus, but of the same length. Detected by the Sylvia pattern.

Sylvia Hong Kong - CN?: A message 'to help Hong Kong in 1997' is incorporated in this virus. Mutation of Sylvia but sample does not replicate.

```
Sylvia-HK       CD21 EBFE C3A1 8302 A38B 0233 C0A3 B102
```

Syslock - CEN: This encrypted virus attaches itself to the end of a COM or an EXE file. Infective length is 3551 bytes. It infects a program one in four times when executed. Will not infect if the environment contains SYSLOCK=@.

```
Syslock         8AE1 8AC1 3306 1400 3104 4646 E2F2 5E59
```

Tabulero - ER: A 2048 byte virus, which bears some resemblance to the Jerusalem virus, but is not directly derived from it. Not yet analysed.

```
Tabulero        2E8B 4702 2E89 052E 8B47 042E 8945 022E
```

Tack - CN: A simple 449 byte virus, which may display the message 'Hello, I am virus'. The virus appends itself to the end of infected files, and overwrites the first six bytes, but only restores the first five, which may result in unpredictable behaviour of infected files.

```
Tack            5850 0500 01A3 3C02 C706 3E02 FFE0 C606
```

Taiwan - CN: The virus activates on the 8th day of every month and overwrites the FAT and the root directory of drives C and D. Two versions are known with different infection lengths: 708 and 743 bytes.

```
Taiwan          07E4 210C 02E6 21FB B980 0033 F6BB 8000
Taiwan (2)      07E4 210C 02E6 21FB B980 00BE 0000 BB80
```

Taiwan-C - CN: A new 752 byte mutation of the Taiwan virus. The major effect is unchanged - destruction of the FAT and root directory on C: and D:

```
Taiwan-C        0B00 33F6 BB80 008B 0050 4646 E2F9 FE06
```

Taiwan-D - CN: Closely related to Taiwan-C, but only 677 bytes. It can be detected by the same search pattern.

Tenbyte, Valert - CER: This virus was posted by accident to the V-ALERT electronic mail list recently. Adds 1554 bytes to infected files. Activates on 1st September corrupting data written to disk.

```
Tenbyte         1E0E 1F8D 36F7 04BF 0001 B920 00F3 A42E
```

Tequila - EMR: An encrypted, multi-partite, self-modifying virus from Switzerland. Contains encrypted text 'Welcome to T.TEQUILA's latest production', 'Contact T.TEQUILA/P.o.Box 543/6312 St'hausen/Switzerland'. No pattern for infected files is possible, but the boot sector does not change. The original master boot sector is stored in the first sector after the end of the first partition, which is decreased by 6 sectors after infection. Displays a crude Mandelbrot set pattern on screen. (*VB* June 91). Original

MBS is stored in the first sector after the end of the partition as recorded in the partition table.

```
Tequila boot        B82A 0250 B805 028B 0E30 7C41 8B16 327C
```

Terminator 918 - CR: Overwrites original program. Awaiting analysis.

```
Terminator 918      FA8C C88E D8C6 0678 0200 B435 B0FE CD21
```

Terminator 1501 - CR: 1501 byte overwriting virus without any stealth features.

```
Terminator 1501     FAB8 0000 8EC0 BB6C 0426 8B07 0538 00A3
```

Terror - CER: This Bulgarian virus has not been analysed yet.

```
Terror              2E8C 1E41 0550 B859 ECCD 213B E875 3E0E
```

Testvirus B - CN: This 1000 byte virus is clearly written for demonstration purposes, as it asks the user if it should infect all COM files in the current directory or not. It has no harmful side-effects.

```
Testvirus B         018A 1780 FA00 7501 C3CD 2143 E2F3 2EA1
```

Thursday 12th - CER: An encrypted virus from Germany which triggers every Thursday 12th, popping up window with a warning that the next day is Friday 13th. Calls itself VirCheck V1.2 (C)1991. Text includes 'thanks' to various virus researchers. Avoids infecting any files matching patterns 'SCAN', 'CLEAN', 'VIR', 'ARJ', 'FLU', 'COMMAND'.

```
Thursday 12th       BE0F 01B9 5501 E8BD FFBE 6D02 B9D4 01E8
```

Tic - CN: A simple 109 byte virus which does nothing but replicate.

```
Tic                 B44E EB06 B43E CD21 B44F 0E1F CD21 B91E
```

Timeslice, 2330 - CER: A 2330 byte virus, written in the USSR. It does not appear to do anything but replicate, but the infection mechanism is rather unusual, as the virus intercepts INT 28H and therefore infects at irregular intervals.

```
Timeslice           1E8E C64E 8EDE C745 0108 0009 C975 0581
```

Timid - CN: Two mutation of this 'Little Black Book' virus are now known - 305 and 306 bytes long. Both are very obvious, but as the source code is available, they can easily be modified.

```
Timid-306           8B16 FCFF 83C2 00B9 3F00 B44E CD21 0AC0
Timid-305           8B16 FCFF B93F 00B4 4ECD 210A C075 0BE8
```

Tiny - CN: A mutation of the Kennedy virus only 163 bytes long. It has no side-effects other than replication. (*VB* Sept 90)

```
Tiny                408D 94AB 01B9 0200 CD21 B43E CD21 FFE5
```

Tiny DI - CN: Four new mutations of the family which was previously called Mutant. The viruses are 94, 101, 108 and 110 bytes long and do nothing but replicate. Only the 110 byte mutation works correctly - the shorter mutations are not able to infect most files correctly, but simply destroy them.

```
Tiny DI (01)        B802 3DCD 218B D806 1F8B D749 B43F CD21
Tiny DI (02)        B802 3DCD 218B D806 1F8B D733 C949 B43F
```

Tiny Family - CR: This is a family of at least 10 Bulgarian viruses, which includes the shortest viruses now known. The viruses are not related to the Danish 'Tiny' virus, but just like it, they do nothing but replicate. The lengths of mutations range from 133 to 198 bytes.

```
Tiny Family (1)    CD32 B43E CD32 071F 5F5A 595B 582E FF2E
Tiny Family (2)    2687 85E0 FEAB E3F7 931E 07C3 3D00 4B75
```

Tiny Family-Ghost - CR: This virus differs from the other members of the Tiny family in two ways. It is fairly long, 330 bytes, and it has one effect other than replicating - it will display the message 'This scan program can't find me I'm a GHOST in your machine!!', if it detects the execution of a virus scanner.

```
Tiny-Ghost         9191 2687 85E0 FEAB E3F7 931E 07C3 3D00
```

Tokyo - EN: A 1258 byte virus, which is reported to have originated in Japan. It has not been fully analysed, but appears to do nothing interesting.

```
Tokyo              B42F CD21 8C06 0600 891E 0400 0E07 8D16
```

Tony - CN: This 200 byte Bulgarian virus will only infect files with a name starting with 'B' on the first day of any month. On the second day it will only infects files with a name beginning in 'C' and so on. The virus uses some curious undocumented features, but does nothing of particular interest.

```
Tony               CC8C C880 C410 8EC0 BE00 0133 FF8B CEF3
```

TPworm - PN: A 'companion' virus written by the author of the Vacsina and Yankee Doodle viruses. The virus has been distributed in the form of 'C' source code. The infective length and hexadecimal patterns, hence, depend on the 'C' compiler used.

TPWorm - EN: This Bulgarian virus was first made available in source form only, but now an executable has appeared as well. It is 12969 bytes long, but because of the unreliability of search patterns for HLL viruses (they would be invalidated if the code was compiled with a new compiler) no pattern can be used.

Traceback, Spanish - CER: This virus attaches itself to the end of a COM or EXE file. Infective length is 3066 bytes. It becomes memory-resident when the first infected program is run and will infect any program run. If the date is 5th December or later, the virus will look for, and infect one COM or EXE file either in the current directory or the first one found, starting with the root directory. If the date is 28th December 1988 or later, the virus produces a display similar to Cascade one hour after infection. If nothing is typed, the screen restores itself after one minute. This display will repeat every hour. Spanish is an earlier version with a reported infective length of 2930 or 3031 bytes. (*VB* Sept 89)

```
Traceback          B419 CD21 89B4 5101 8184 5101 8408 8C8C
Spanish            E829 06E8 E005 B419 CD21 8884 E300 E8CE
```

Traceback-3029 - CER: This is the first new member of the Traceback family to appear. Not fully analysed, but does not appear to be significantly different from the other known mutations.

```
Traceback-3029     B419 CD21 89B4 5101 8184 5101 5F08 8C8C
```

Trackswap - DR: A small Bulgarian master boot sector virus, which is awaiting analysis.

```
Trackswap          FBA1 1304 48A3 1304 B106 D3E0 8EC0 06BD
```

Traveller Virus - CER: A 1220 byte virus which infects COM (including COMMAND.COM) and EXE files. Infection is via Function 4Bh (LOAD AND EXECUTE) and Function 36h (GET FREE SPACE). When a LOAD AND EXECUTE call is issued, a program and one other file in current directory are infected. When GET FREE SPACE request is issued (eg. by the DIR command) one file in current directory is infected. Infection marker is the seconds field set to 62 and COM files will increase in size by 1220 bytes and EXE files by 1237 to 1251 bytes. The message '!!!!!!!-->> Traveller (C) BUPT 1991.4 Don't panic I'm harmless <<--!!!!!!!' flashes bright and dim green on blue background on line 13 of the screen after 23 infections and thereafter every twentieth infection.

```
Traveller          A303 0029 1612 00A1 1200 8EC0 0E1F 8BDE
```

Trilogy - ?: Virus awaiting disassembly.

```
Trilogy            9C55 568C CD83 C50A 8DB6 F6FF 56BE 2601
```

Trivial-30D - CN: Yet another attempt to create the smallest overwriting virus. Does nothing but replicate.

```
Trivial-30D        CD21 BA9E 00B8 013D CD21 938B D6B1 1EB4
```

Trivial-38 - CN: Yet another 'minimalist' virus - does nothing but replicate by overwriting the beginning of other programs.

```
Trivial-38         3DCD 2193 B126 BA00 01B4 40CD 21B4 4FEB
```

Trivial-44 - CN: Yet another non-interesting overwriting virus from Bulgaria.

```
Trivial-44         023D CD21 8BD8 B92C 00BA 0001 B440 CD21
```

Trivial-Hastings - CN: This overwriting virus is 200 bytes long, but most of that code is taken up by a long text message. The virus does nothing but replicate.

```
Hastings           B802 3DBA F001 CD21 720C 8BD8 B440 B9C8
```

Troi - CR: A very simple, 322 byte virus, which does nothing but replicate.

```
Troi               0157 A5A4 C32A C0CF 9C80 FCFC 7504 B0A5
```

Tula-419 - CER: Probably a Russian virus. It is 419 bytes long and will only infect on machines with a colour display.

```
Tula-419           B43F CD21 7225 BEA0 0FAC 3C4D 7505 AC3C
```

Tumen - CR: Two mutations are known of this virus. Version 0.5 is 1663 bytes long and plays a tune when Ctrl-Alt-Del is pressed. Version 2.0 is 1092 bytes long, but has not been fully analysed.

```
Tumen              8CC8 488E D881 2E03 0000 0181 2E12 00
```

Tumen 1.2 - CR: A 1225 byte member of the Tumen family. Detected by the pattern for the other two mutations.

TUQ, RPVS - CN: A simple virus from West Germany without side-effects. Infective length is 453 bytes.

```
TUQ                5653 8CC8 8ED8 BE01 012E 8B04 0503 0157
```

Turbo 448 - CR: A 448 byte Hungarian virus which will infect COM files when they are opened, for example by a virus scanner, but not when they are executed. The virus contains the text 'Udv minden nagytudasunak! Turbo @'.

```
Turbo 448          890E 0201 8CD8 8EC0 5958 BB00 01FF E3A1
```

Turbo Kukac - CR: A 512 byte virus, which resembles the Turbo 448 virus, but is somewhat longer, 512 bytes. COMMAND.COM will crash, if infected with this virus.

```
Turbo Kukac        FFE3 8CD8 488E D8A1 0300 2D41 00A3 0300
```

TV-730 - ER: A 730 byte virus, which has also been named Ontario-730, but this name was rejected because the virus does not seem related to another virus named 'Ontario'. Not fully analysed, but contains code to trash the hard disk.

```
TV-730             BF00 01B8 6E4B CD21 3D54 5675 0AC7 05EB
```

Twin - ERP: Companion virus with no payload. Likely to crash where an infected file is larger than about 64K.

```
Twin               B810 FFCD 213C 0775 07E8 2500 B44C CD21
```

Typo, Typo COM, Fumble - CR: Infects all COM files in the current directory on odd days of every month. If typing fast, substitutes keys with the ones adjacent on the keyboard. Infective length is 867 bytes. (*VB* Apr 90)

```
Typo               5351 521E 0656 0E1F E800 005E 83EE 24FF
```

USSR-311 - CN: A 311 byte virus, which does not seem to do anything else apart from replicating.

```
USSR-311           8BF2 83C6 0203 C12D 0300 0500 0189 04B4
```

USSR-492 - CR: A Bulgarian virus which has not been analysed. The only available sample seems to be corrupted.

```
USSR-492           2E8B 1E01 0183 C303 B104 D3EB 8CD8 03C3
```

USSR-516, Leapfrog - CR: This 516 byte Russian virus is the first virus which does not modify the beginning of the programs it infects, but places the jump to the virus code inside the host program.

```
USSR-516           431E 53C5 1F46 5F07 8B07 3DFF FF75 F283
```

USSR-600 - CR: An encrypted, 600 byte Russian virus.

```
USSR-600           BE10 01B9 3200 8A24 80F4 DD88 2446 E2F6
```

USSR-696 - CN: A 696 byte Russian virus awaiting analysis.

```
USSR-696           3C00 7412 8CC8 B10F D3E0 3D00 8074 07BA
```

USSR-707 - CR: A 707 byte Russian virus awaiting analysis

```
USSR-707           83C3 0F33 C08E C033 F68C C040 3DFF 0F76
```

USSR-711 - CR: A 711 byte Russian virus awaiting analysis.

```
USSR-711           C88E C08E D833 C08B F0BF 0000 BB00 01FF
```

USSR-948 - CER: A Russian, 948 byte virus, which seems partially based on the Yankee virus.

```
USSR-948           5051 56B9 FF00 FC8B F28A 0446 3C00 E0F9
```

USSR-1049 - CER: A 1049 byte Russian virus awaiting analysis.

```
USSR-1049          EB10 8CDA 83C2 102E 0316 2000 522E FF36
```

USSR-1594 - EN: A 1594 byte virus which uses a self-modifying algorithm. No fixed search pattern is possible.

USSR-2144 - CER: A 2144 byte Russian virus, not yet analysed.

```
USSR-2144              1E06 33C0 8ED8 FB2E 8B94 1000 EC34 03EE
```

V-1 - DCR: This virus is one of the first to infect both the boot sector and programs. It is 1253 bytes long and destructive. When activated, it overwrites the disk with garbage.

```
V-1                    8EC0 26A1 1304 4848 503D 0001 7203 2D3E
```

V2P2 - CN: This virus, written by Mark Washburn is closely related to the 1260 virus, but is more complicated. It will, for example, add a random number of 'garbage' bytes to the programs it infects, to make identification more difficult. No search pattern is possible.

V2P6 - CN: This virus is written by the same author as 1260 and V2P2, but is longer and more complicated. It uses several different encryption methods, which makes it impossible to provide a search pattern.

V472 - CR: A 472 byte virus, probably from Eastern Europe, which does nothing but replicate.

```
V472                   01D6 31DB 8EC3 BB84 0026 8B0F 890C 4646
```

Vacsina - CER: Infective length is 1206 to 1221 bytes (COM) and 1338 to 1353 bytes (EXE). After successful infection of a COM file, a bell is sounded. Infects any file loaded via INT 21H function 4BH (load and execute), i.e. COM, EXE, OVL and APP (GEM) files. Checks version number of itself (current is 5) and replaces with newer code. A member of the 'Bulgarian 50' (see Yankee). (*VB* June 90, May 92)

```
Vacsina (1)            8CC8 8ED8 8EC0 8ED0 83C4 02B8 0000 502E
Vacsina (2)            E800 005B 2E89 47FB B800 008E C026 A1C5
```

Vcomm - ER: This virus first increases the length of infected programs so that it becomes a multiple of 512 bytes. Then it adds 637 bytes to the end of the file. The resident part will intercept any disk write and change it into a disk read.

```
Vcomm                  80FC 0375 04B4 02EB 0780 FC0B 7502 B40A
```

VCS 1.0 - CN: A 1077 byte virus which will delete AUTOEXEC.BAT and CONFIG.SYS when it activates. Generated by a German program called 'Virus Construction Set' (VCS) which allows the incorporation of a user-specified message into the virus.

```
VCS 1.0                89FE AC32 C4AA E2FA C35E 81EE 0301 56E8
```

VCS-Manta - CN: A virus generated by the VCS program. Detected by the VCS 1.0 pattern.

VCS-VDV-853 - CN: This virus is detected by the same pattern as the VCS 1.0 virus, but is somewhat different; for example, it is only 853 bytes long. Not yet analysed.

VFSI - CN: A simple 437 byte Bulgarian virus.

```
VFSI                   100E 1FB8 001A BA81 00CD 21BE 0001 FFE6
```

Victor - CEN: A 2442 byte virus from the USSR which is awaiting disassembly. The only known damaging effect is the corruption of the FAT.

```
Victor                 8CC8 8BD8 B104 D3EE 03C6 50B8 D800 50CB
```

Vienna, Austrian, Unesco, DOS62, Lisbon - CN: The virus infects the end of COM files. Infective length is 648 bytes. It looks through the current directory and the directories in the PATH for an uninfected COM file. One file in eight becomes overwritten. Seconds stamp of an infected file is set to 62. A number of mutations, shorter than the original, but functionally equivalent, have been reported in Bulgaria.

```
Vienna (1)        8BF2 83C6 0A90 BF00 01B9
Vienna (2)        FC8B F281 C60A 00BF 0001 B903 00F3 A48B
Vienna (3)        FC89 D683 C60A 90BF 0001 B903 00F3 A489
Vienna (4)        FC8B F283 C60A BF00 01B9 0300 F3A4 8BF2
Vienna (5)        CD21 0E1F B41A BA80 00CD 2158 C3AC 3C3B
Vienna (6)        8E1E 2C00 AC3C 3B74 093C 0074 03AA EBF4
```

Vienna-534B - CN: A member of the W13 group in the Vienna family - closely related to 534A, and detected with the W13 pattern.

Vienna-618 - CN: Detected with the Vienna (1) pattern.

Vienna-621 - CN: This mutation is detected with the Vienna (4) pattern. It is similar to the original virus, but instead of overwriting programs with an instruction that resets the computer, it overwrites them with the instruction JMP C800:0000, which may cause a low-level format of the hard disk on certain machines.

Vienna-622 - CN: A new version of the Vienna virus from Bulgaria. It is detected by the Vienna (4) pattern.

Vienna-625 - CN: A minor mutation of Vienna. Detected by the Vienna (4) pattern.

Vienna-637 - CN: Very similar to the original version, and detected with the Vienna (1) pattern.

Vienna-644 - CN: A 644 byte version of the Vienna virus, which does not infect programs every time it is run.

```
Vienna-644        BF00 01FC A5A5 A58B F252 B42C CD21 5A80
```

Vienna-644B - CN: Very closely related to the original 648 byte mutation, but slightly shorter. Detected with the Vienna (1) pattern.

Vienna-645 - CN: A 645 byte mutation of Vienna, detected by the Vienna (1) pattern.

Vienna-645B - CN: Closely related to the Vienna-645 virus. Detected with the Ghostballs pattern.

Vienna-656 - CN: A non-remarkable 656 byte mutation.

```
Vienna-656        895C 018C 4403 07BA 6000 01F2 B41A CD21
```

Vienna-712 - CN: This mutation seems most closely related to the Dr Q. mutation, and just like it, it uses limited encryption. It is detected with the Vienna (4) and Dr Q. patterns.

Vienna-726 - CN: A 726 byte mutation, detected by the Vienna (4) pattern.

Vienna-733 - CN: An encrypted mutation of Vienna. It activates if an infected program is run on the second day of the month and produces a high-pitch sound.

```
Vienna-733        89D6 81EE F201 89F7 B956 01FC ACFE C0AA
```

Vienna-776 - CN: A 776 byte mutation. Not fully analysed, but appears to do nothing of particular interest. One very similar 757 byte mutation has also been found.

```
Vienna-776        B44E BADD 0003 D6B9 0300 CD21 EB04 B44F
Vienna-757        B44E BA5B 0003 D6B9 0300 CD21 EB04 B44F
```

Vienna-822 - CN: The effects of this mutation have not been fully determined, but seem to involve the boot sector. It is detected by the pattern for GhostBalls.

Vienna-Betaboys - CN: This 679 byte mutation was written in Sweden, or possibly in Finland. It activates in February of any year, trashing the beginning of drives C, D and E.

```
Betaboys              90AC B900 80F2 AEB9 0400 ACAE 75EA E2FA
```

Vienna-Dr. Q - CN: An 1161 byte mutation, which includes encryption of the data area. Not yet analysed.

```
Vienna-Dr. Q          8E06 2C00 BF00 005E 5683 C61A ACB9 0080
```

Vienna-Dr. Q 1028 - CN: Very similar to the 1161 byte version and detected by the same search pattern. 1028 bytes long.

Vienna-Infinity - CN: A 732 byte Vienna mutation, with only one unusual feature: it will not infect files if the PSQR virus is active in memory.

```
Vienna-Infinity   ACB9 0080 F2AE B904 00AC AE75 EDE2 FA5E
```

Vienna-Kuzmitch - CN: An encrypted, variable-length mutation of the Vienna virus, which contains a block of text in Russian. The base length of the virus is 810 bytes. No simple search pattern is possible. Second-generation copies of this virus do not always seem able to replicate.

Vienna-Mob 1a - CN: A 1024 byte Canadian member of the Vienna family. Detected by the Parasite 2 pattern.

Vienna-Parasite - CN: Yet another Vienna mutation of Canadian origin - 1132 bytes long. Version 2B of this virus is presumably written by the same author, but is only 903 bytes long. Detected by the Parasite 2 pattern.

Vienna-Parasite-2 - CN: 901 bytes, closely related to the Parasite and Parasite-2B mutations.

```
Parasite 2            ACB9 0080 F2AE B904 00AC AE75 EDE2 FA5E
```

Vienna-Polish 634 - CN: This modified version is detected by the Vienna (1) pattern.

Vienna-Violator-B2 - CN: This 969 byte mutation is not new, and is not expected to become a serious threat, as it only works properly for a single generation - after that copies seem to be corrupted.

```
Vienna-Viola-B2   90AC B900 80F2 AEB9 0400 ACAE 75ED E2FA
```

Vienna-Viperize - CN: One more non-remarkable Vienna mutation - 934 bytes long.

```
Vienna-Viperize   FC8B F290 83C6 0A90 90BF 0001 90B9 0300
```

Vindicator - CR: A 734 byte virus, which can be found at the beginning of infected files. Probably of Russian origin. Awaiting analysis.

```
Vindicator            FAB8 0010 F6E7 0500 B88E D831 F6B8 2000
```

Violator - CN: This is an unsually long mutation of the Vienna virus. It is 1055 bytes long and it activates on 15th August. The virus is awaiting analysis. (*VB* Apr 91)

```
Violator              BF00 01F3 A48B F2B4 30CD 213C 0075 03E9
```

Violator-B - CN: This 716 byte mutation is detected by the Violator pattern.

Violator-B3 - CN: An 843 byte virus, related to the Violator and Christmas Violator viruses, and probably written by the same authors.

```
Violator-B3           803E D003 0274 0B80 3ED0 0303 7407 C3CD
```

Violator-D - CN: Infectious length is 969 bytes. Awaiting analysis.

```
Violator-D        BF00  01F3  A48B  F2B4  30C6  0656  0401  90E8
```

Violetta - CR: This 3840 byte virus contains some of the least interesting pieces of code of any virus - it shows a remarkable lack of talent. Not fully analysed.

```
Violetta          B425  B0FF  061F  89DA  CD21  0E1F  B425  B021
```

Violetta-1024 - CN: Probably just an earlier mutation of the Violetta virus. This mutation has also been reported as 'Thimble'. Detected by the Violetta pattern.

Virdem - CN: This virus was published in the R. Burger book 'Computer Viruses - A High Tech Disease'. Originally intended as a demonstration virus, but now also found in the wild. Infective length is 1336 bytes. Two versions are known to exist with texts in English and German. (*VB* July 90)

```
Virdem            BE80  008D  3EBF  03B9  2000  F3A4  B800  0026
Virdem-1          BE80  008D  3ED7  03B9  2000  F3A4  B800  0026
Virdem-Gen        434B  7409  B44F  CD21  72AC  4B75  F7B4  2FCD
```

Virdem-792 - CN: A destructive mutation of the Virdem virus, which will overwrite the first 5 sectors on all disks when it activates.

```
Virdem-792        431E  8CC0  8ED8  8BD3  B43B  CD21  1FBE  5203
```

Virdem-824 - CN: A new uninteresting member of the Virdem family. It can be detected by the same pattern found in all the other Virdem mutations.

```
Virdem-family     83C3  1C26  C707  205C  431E  8CC0  8ED8  8BD3
```

Virdem-1542 - CN: A longer mutation of the Virdem virus, but detected by the same pattern as the original.

Virdem-Killer - CN: This mutation is closely related to the original Virdem virus. The length is unchanged at 1336 bytes, although some text strings have been altered. The virus is detected by the Virdem pattern.

Virus 9 - CN: Infects all COM files in current directory and recursively back to root directory. Infected files contain virus code at end of file but no link to the code. The virus will replicate only once. There are no side effects.

```
Virus 9           3ECD  21B4  4FCD  2172  02EB  B0B4  3BBA  7501
```

Virus-90 - CN: The author of this virus is Patrick A. Toulme. He uploaded the virus to a number of Bulletin Boards, stating that the source was available for $20. When an infected program is run it will display the message 'Infected', infect a COM file in drive A and display the message 'Done'. Infective length is 857 bytes.

```
Virus-90          558B  2E01  0181  C503  0133  C033  DBB9  0900
```

Virus-101 - CN: This virus was written by the same author as Virus-90. The virus is encrypted and self-modifying. An infected file has the seconds field set to 62. Will not infect if the first instruction in the file is not a 'JMP NEAR'. Infective length is 2560 bytes, but COMMAND.COM length does not change. Awaiting disassembly.

Virus-B - CN: 'Test virus' which was available as a restricted access file from the Interpath Corporation BBS in the USA. It is a mutation of the South African virus, with the destructive code of the original disabled. The identification pattern is the same as for the South African virus.

Void Poem - CR: A strange virus, with a considerable portion of the 1825 byte virus body containing an encrypted poem. Not yet analysed.

```
Void Poem           0AE0 B9CB 0430 2547 E2FB BAD5 04B8 0125
```

Voronezh - CER: A Russian, 1600 byte virus, which overwrites the first 1600 bytes of the host, and moves the original code to the end, where it is written in encrypted form.

```
Voronezh            3E89 078E C0BF 0001 BE00 015B 5301 DE0E
```

Voronezh-370 - CR: This virus is closely related to the Voronezh and USSR-600 viruses, perhaps their common ancestor. It appears to do nothing but replicate.

```
Voronezh-370        0500 018B F0BF 0001 FC8A 0434 BB88 0546
```

Voronezh-Chemist-650 - CR: A 650 byte member of the Voronezh family, reported to have originated at the Moscow State University. It contains a text string in Russian which translates to 'The Chemist & the Elephant'. The virus activates if an infected program is run at xx:03 o'clock when it displays the message 'Video mode 80x25 not supported.' and switches to 40 column mode if possible.

```
VoronezhChem650     0500 018B F0BF 0001 FC8A 0434 CC88 0546
```

VP - CN: Contains a variable number (1 to 15) of NOPs at the beginning followed by 909 bytes of virus code. When an infected program is run, the virus may attempt to locate, infect and execute another program.

```
VP                  0001 FCBF 0001 B910 00F2 A4B8 0001 FFE0
```

Vriest - CN: This virus adds 1280 bytes in front of the COM files it infects. When it activates it will display 'Something's coming up ...', produce a high-pitched sound for a few seconds, and finally display 'Vriest of g greets Vic ear Moeli~'.

```
Vriest              B489 CD21 3D23 0174 32B8 2135 CD21 8C06
```

VVF 3.4 - CR: This Russian virus only works on some machines, but crashes on certain types of hardware, such as IBM XT. Awaiting disassembly.

```
VVF 3.4             7606 81C3 0001 8BF3 FCF3 A41E BB00 0153
```

Water Detect - CN: A destructive virus 621 bytes long. Displays 'Water detected ...' message on 1st of every month, destroys disk on Friday 13th.

```
Water Detect        B42A CD21 80FA 0175 03E9 A301 81F9 D007
```

W13 - CN: A primitive group of viruses from Poland, based on the Vienna virus. They have no known side-effects and two versions which exist are 534 and 507 bytes long. The 507-byte version has some bugs corrected.

```
W13                 8BD7 2BF9 83C7 0205 0301 03C1 8905 B440
```

W13-C - CN: A minor modification of the 507-byte W13-B mutation. The only modification is that this mutation sets the month field to 12, not 13, which makes all files created in December immune to infection. Detected by the W13 pattern.

W13-361 - CN: A member of the W13 group of Vienna-related viruses. It is detected by the W13 pattern, but does not function properly, as infected programs (second generation) will never run. A 377 byte mutation also exists, and it is able to replicate without problems.

W13-REQ! - CN: This 494 byte member of the W13 group contains the text 'REQ ! Ltd (c) 18:41:22 3-I-1991'. It is of Polish origin, but has not been analysed yet.

```
W13-REQ!            8B4F 1683 E11E 83F9 1E74 EC81 7F1A 00FA
```

Warrier - ?: Awaiting analysis

```
Warrier              B430 CD21 3D03 1E75 09B4 34CD 21BB 6014
```

Warrior - EN: This virus adds 1012 bytes to any files it infects. It contains the following text: '...and justice to all! (US constitution) Dream over ... And the alone warrior is warrior. The powerfull WARRIOR!' Awaiting analysis.

```
Warrior              AC2C 8032 E403 F826 8035 01E2 F3B4 19CD
```

We're here - CN: This 836 byte virus has not been fully analysed yet.

```
We're here           B905 00CD 21BF 8600 B090 B90F 00FC F3AA
```

Westwood - CER: A 1824 byte mutation of the Jerusalem virus.

```
Westwood             4D0F CD21 8CC8 0510 008E D0BC 1007 50B8
```

Whale - CER: The infective length of this virus is 9216 bytes. The virus slows the system down by about 50% and uses dynamic decryption of parts of its code. Much of the code is dedicated to disabling DEBUG. Does not run on 8086-based computers. (*VB* Nov 90)

```
Whale 00             56E8 0200 4569 5A0E 81EA A023 1FB9 D80B
Whale 01             FDE8 0200 0E4F 5A0E 81EA A023 1FB9 D70B
Whale 02             E828 008C CB53 8CDB 1F81 C361 DCE8 1E00
Whale 03             E829 008C CB53 8CDB 1F81 C361 DCE8 1F00
Whale 04             E828 008C CB1E 8EDB 5B81 EB9F 23E8 1E00
Whale 05             E801 00C3 BB61 DC59 01CB 0EB9 C411 1FFE
Whale 06             E801 00C3 59BB 61DC 01CB 0EB9 C310 1FFE
Whale 07             50E8 2A00 81C2 60DC B511 B1C3 87DA E8DF
Whale 08             E82B 0087 D381 C361 DCB9 C311 E8E0 FFF6
Whale 09             0E1F E8F8 FF81 C35D DCB9 C111 8B07 4343
Whale 0A             0E1F E8F7 FF81 EBA3 23B9 C111 8B17 4343
Whale 0B             0EFD 1F58 E82B 0093 B9C3 1183 EB1E 8A17
Whale 0C             5B0E 1FE8 2B00 9383 EB1D B9C3 118A 0728
Whale 0D             00D7 EBF6 5A81 EA9D 23F9 87DA B98A 2CF8
Whale 0E             EBF7 582D 9C23 93B9 2EDE 81F1 ABFD F617
Whale 0F             0EF8 1FE8 2300 B184 81ED A123 8BDD B523
Whale 10             0E1F E823 0081 EAA0 2389 D3B9 2384 86CD
Whale 11             E8F1 FFB9 9F23 29CB 83E9 1AE8 1700 75FB
Whale 12             E8F1 FFB8 9F23 29C3 B91A 0033 C8E8 1600
Whale 13             E907 00FE 0743 E2FB EBE1 E822 00B9 8523
Whale 14             0E1F EB13 E8E7 FFF8 75FA 585B 5955 FF36
Whale 15             0E1F EB15 E8E6 FF75 FB58 5BFB 59FF 3666
Whale 16             E800 00EB 0D8B D058 8BD8 5891 FF16 6625
Whale 17             E82F 00FF 1699 25EB F7B8 0200 81C3 61DD
Whale 18             E82E 0059 FF16 9825 EBF6 B802 0081 C361
Whale 19             E803 0040 33DE 0BF6 FEC7 5B81 EBA1 2383
Whale 1A             E802 0033 DE81 F676 185B 5E81 EB9F 23B9
Whale 1B             E803 00BB 0156 5B81 EB9F 23B9 3489 B985
Whale 1C             E829 0081 EB9F 23B9 8723 49F9 4980 3710
Whale 1D             E801 00F8 5B81 EB9F 23B5 23B1 85E8 1900
Whale 1E             E800 000E 1F5B 81EB 9F23 B985 23FE 0F43
Whale 1F             E800 009C 9D0E 5058 1F26 5B24 0581 EB9F
Whale 20             E800 0095 930E 9395 1FFC 5B16 1781 EB9F
```

Wisconsin, Death to Pascal - CR: This virus adds 815 bytes to the beginning of infected programs, and 10 bytes to their end. Infected programs may display the message 'Death to Pascal' and attempt to delete all .PAS files in the current directory.

```
Wisconsin          8B0E 0601 BE08 018A 0434 FF88 0446 E2F7
```

Witcode - ER: A 966 byte virus awaiting analysis.

```
Witcode            83FB 0473 088C C048 8EC0 83C3 1026 8B77
```

Wolfman - CER: A 2064 byte virus from Taiwan with unknown effects.

```
Wolfman            8EC0 BE04 0026 837C FC00 7404 46EB F6EA
```

Wonder - EN: An overwriting virus, 7424 bytes long, which appears to have been written in Borland C++. Not a serious threat, but not yet analysed.

```
Wonder             83C4 0856 B800 1D50 B801 0050 FF76 04E8
```

Words - CER: A series of 4 Polish viruses, 1069, 1085, 1387 and 1503 bytes long. The two longest mutations use self-modifying encryption, and no simple search pattern is possible. The other mutations can be detected by using a pattern.

```
Words              8066 0EFE 5958 8BC1 5E5D 9DCF 528B D6B4
```

Wordswap-1391, Wordswap-1485 - CER: Just as in the case of the 1387 and 1503 byte mutations, no search pattern is possible for these two mutations.

WWT - CN: Very simple, overwriting viruses, with no side-effects other than replication. Two versions are known: WWT-01, which is 67 bytes long and WWT-02 with a length of 125 bytes.

```
WWT-01             B44E B901 00CD 2173 02EB 1EBA 9E00 B802
WWT-02             B44E B901 00CD 2173 02EB 10E8 0F00 BA80
```

XA1 - CN: The XA1 virus overwrites the first 1539 bytes of infected COM files with a copy of itself and stores the original code at the end of the file. On 1st April the boot sector will be overwritten, causing the computer to 'hang' on the next boot. The virus will also activate on 21st December and stay active until the end of the year. It will then display a Christmas tree and the text: 'Und er lebt doch noch: Der Tannenbaum! Frohe Weihnachten'.

```
XA1 (1)            B02C 8846 FF8B 7E00 884E FE8A 4EFF 000D
XA1 (2)            0EE8 0000 FA8B EC58 32C0 8946 0281 4600
```

Xabaras - CER: An encrypted, overwriting 1972 byte virus written by Cracker Jack. A mutation of the Leprosy virus.

```
Xabaras            908A 2790 9090 9090 9090 3226 0601 9090
```

XPEH - CER: Probably related to the Yankee virus, as it is detected by the Yankee pattern, but modified considerably. It is 4016 bytes long and of Eastern European origin. Not yet analysed.

Yafo - CN: A 328 byte virus, which contains the text 'Maccabi Yafo Alufa !!!'.

```
Yafo               03F5 BF80 00B9 8000 FCF3 A4C3 B802 3DCD
```

Yale, Alameda, Merritt - DR: This virus consists of a boot sector and infects floppies in drive A only. It becomes memory-resident and occupies 1K of RAM. The original boot sector is held in track 39 head 0 sector 8. The machine will hang if the virus is run on an 80286 or 80386 machine. If a warm boot is performed after the machine hangs, an uninfected disk will still become infected. It contains code to format track 39 head 0, but this is not accessed. Survives a warm boot.

```
Yale              BB40 008E DBA1 1300 F7E3 2DE0 078E C00E
```

Yankee - CER: This is a member of the 'Bulgarian 50' group of viruses, which consists of some 50 related versions, all written by the same person. Vacsina viruses belong to the same group. All the viruses in the group will remove infections by older versions, and the size varies from 1200 to 3500 bytes. The Yankee viruses will play the tune 'Yankee Doodle Dandy', either at 5:00 p.m. or when Ctrl-Alt-Del is pressed.

```
Yankee            0000 7402 B603 520E 5143 CFE8 0000 5B81
```

Yankee-1150 and **Yankee-1205** - CER: Two closely related, stripped-down versions of the Yankee virus which do not play any music.

```
Yankee-1150       CB5B 5383 EB44 C32E 80BF 0100 0074 0681
Yankee-1202       CB5B 5383 EB45 C32E 80BF 0100 0074 0681
```

Yankee-1905/1909 - CER: Also known as the '83', this mutation is slightly unusual in that EXE files grow by 1905 bytes, but the virus adds 1909 bytes to COM files. Detected with the Yankee pattern.

Yankee-Login - CER: This 3045 byte mutation of the Yankee Doodle virus has been reported to operate as a password 'snatcher' on a network, and to cause irreversible damage to data. It does not seem to work on certain types of hardware, including XTs with monochrome displays. At least four minor mutations have been reported, but they are virtually identical, and have the same length.

```
Yankee-Login      B440 EB02 B43F E809 0072 023B C1C3 32C0
```

Yaunch, Wench - EN: A 2537 byte virus, which has not been analysed.

```
Yaunch            BE5C 012B DB8A 058A 2032 C488 0547 3BFA
```

Yukon - CN: A simple, 151 byte overwriting virus. Does nothing else apart from displaying the message 'Divide overflow'.

```
Yukon             01CD 218B D8B4 57B0 00CD 2151 52B4 40B9
```

Zeleng - CER: Slightly modified mutation of the Dark Avenger virus. It is 1800 bytes long and detected by the Dark Avenger pattern.

Zero Bug, Palette - CR: Infective length is 1536 bytes and the virus attaches itself to the beginning of COM files. The virus modifies the seconds field of the time stamp to 62 (like Vienna). If the virus is active in memory and the DIR command is issued, the displayed length of infected files will be identical to that before the infection. When the virus activates, a 'smiley' (IBM ASCII character 1) may appear on the screen, and 'eat' all zeros found.

```
Zero Bug          81C9 1F00 CD21 B43E CD21 5A1F 59B4 43B0
```

Zero Hunt, Minnow - CR: A 416 byte overwriting virus, which will only infect a file if it locates a sufficiently large block of zero bytes.

```
Zero Hunt         521E B802 3DCD 2193 B43F 33C9 8ED9 41BA
```

Zherkov-1882 - CER: A 1882 byte version of the Zherkov (formerly Lozinsky) virus. It uses a slightly more sophisticated encryption algorithm than the older mutations, and is able to infect EXE files. The 1958, 2968 and 2970 byte mutations are probably later versions. All the viruses are targeted against the AIDSTEST program, a Russian anti-virus program written by D. Lozinzky, deleting it if it is executed. The virus also attempts to corrupt data on diskettes in a unique way - it sets the byte at location 1AH in the boot sector (Number of sides) to zero - causing the DIR command to produce a 'Division by zero' error. The larger viruses have slightly different effects - the 2968 and 2970 byte mutations display a large sign 'AIDSTEST' if no key is typed for 30 seconds, and then restore the screen on the next keystroke. 2970 mutation is detected by the 1915 pattern.

```
Zherkov-1882        5051 061E E800 005E 2E8A 44F8 3C00 740F
Zherkov-1915        5006 1EE8 0000 5E2E 8A44 F93C 0074 118B
Zherkov-2968        5706 1EE8 0000 5E2E 8A44 F53C 0074 118B
```

ZK-900 - CER: A 900 byte virus, which plays a simple tune at regular intervals after an infected program is run.

```
ZK-900              B44A 8CC1 418E C1CD 2172 49B4 484A 8BDA
```

G.4 TROJAN HORSES

AIDS Information Diskette: Widely distributed disk which is an extortion attempt. Installs multiple hidden directories and files, as well as AIDS.EXE in the main directory and REM$.EXE in a hidden subdirectory ($ is the non-printing character FF Hexadecimal). (*VB* Jan 90)

```
REM$.EXE            4D5A 0C01 1E01 0515 6005 0D03 FFFF 3D21
AIDS.EXE            4D5A 1200 5201 411B E006 780C FFFF 992F
```

Twelve Tricks: A Trojan replacing the DOS bootstrap sector with a dummy version. Damage includes corruption of the FAT and twelve effects which may be mistaken for hardware failure.

```
Twelve tricks       BAB8 DBBE 6402 3194 4201 D1C2 4E79 F733
```

INDEX

Little One! Oh, Little One!
I am searching everywhere!

James Stephens, 'The Snare'